TAL S

THE LOST

FORMICANS

AND OTHER PLAYS

TALES OF
THE LOST
FORMICANS

AND OTHER PLAYS

CONSTANCE CONGDON

THEATRE COMMUNICATIONS GROUP

Tales of the Lost Formicans and Other Plays is published by Theatre Communications Group, Inc., 355 Lexington Ave., New York, NY 10017.

Cover design by Susan Mitchell.

Congdon, Constance.
    Tales of the lost formicans and other plays / Constance Congdon. — 1st ed.
    ISBN 1-55936-084-4
    I. Title
PS3553.048776T34 1994
812'.54—dc20
                                      93-51495
                                          CIP

Book design and composition by The Sarabande Press
First Edition, December 1994

CONTENTS

To my husband, Glenn Johnson

INTRODUCTION

By Tony Kushner

This is an introduction, so allow me the pleasure of introducing you to the plays of Constance Congdon, one of the best playwrights our country, and our language, has produced.

Reexamining these texts, I realize with an embarrassed shock how deeply indebted to this writer I am. When I was working on *Angels in America, Part One,* and having a lot of difficulty figuring out how to proceed, I saw *Tales of the Lost Formicans* in a marvelous staged reading, directed by Gordon Edelstein at New Dramatists. I left the reading sunk deep in that delirious mix of emotions—a destabilizing cocktail of elation, depression, excitement, envy and admiration—that a writer almost always feels at having encountered, in the work of a peer, an unmistakably impressive achievement; at having encountered, unexpectedly, the real thing—not mere entertainment (though that is rare enough), but art.

I sometimes worry that I am more than ordinarily possessed of what most writers have, a magpie memory: it is clear to me now that the Apocalypse in Suburbia of *Formicans* impacted powerfully on the development of my own teleological tale. Connie, I believe, is a genuine pioneer, a truly original writer who first arrived at a new theatrical space, from whence a number of plays and playwrights, myself included, have emerged. I do not mean by this that all her fellow playwrights are the children of Connie

Congdon. But in the early years of the previous decade a discovery was waiting to be made, namely that the theatre's peculiarities made it a particularly resonant space for the staging of the kind of postmodern, collective nervous breakdown American society has been having. Connie, among those of us working within the tradition of narrative dramatic realism, and with all due credit to her forebears, got there first. The discovery was too important to disregard, leaving many of us who adopted her innovations feeling, as Brecht writes in his journals, like the person who wrote the *second* sonnet.

Connie possesses all the virtues a playwright should possess, and she wears them in a pure, almost classical style. Her plays are entirely, unapologetically theatrical, by which I mean that they play the contradictions of the theatre for all they're worth, and it is in the playing of these contradictions that her work derives both dramatic life and meaning. The paradox that an object onstage both is and isn't real; the dialectic of tragedy and comedy, of tackiness and grandeur; the simultaneous elusiveness *and* the imponderable, unavoidable weighty presence of both Time and Place—so fearfully restrictive, so effortlessly manipulated in the theatre; the tension between the script as literature, as poetry, and the script as score for a pretend-spontaneous, kinetic event: this is what theatricality is. The distilled essence of this art is seeing double, pondering and experiencing conundrums, the tension and clash of opposites. You will find this essence in these plays.

You will also find writing that transposes with breathtaking ease from wonderful, mordant comedy to heartbreak, from real poetry to real vulgarity, from beauty to kitsch and back to beauty again. Connie's visions imprint themselves indelibly on the memory: horrifying moments, such as the young woman trying to breathe life into her umbilically attached baby in *Casanova*; tender, elegiac moments, such as the child sleeping on mattresses piled under the first atomic bomb in *No Mercy*; or, my favorite, the hapless paranoiac Jerry falling asleep, a suicide's pistol in his mouth.

This image incorporates in a single instant Connie's sharp humor, abundant empathy, and her great, galvanizing fear for the survival of our species. Our days are more and more frequently, ominously illumined by a long-shadowed, constantly waning, comfortless "dinosaur light." Connie's search, through the rapidly falling "crocodile night" is for escape, salvation, futurity.

American playwrights of my generation are looking for hope. We seem to accept this search—for real hope, not for Reagan-hope, but rather for what Ernst Bloch calls "concrete, knowing hope"—as our moral, civic responsibility. The generation of American playwrights immediately preceding us did not feel this way. Their absurdism is fraught with a vital, exuberant disgust and despair. And there are younger writers now, some only a few years younger, who are quite exciting, thoroughgoing nihilists. These predecessors and antecessors occasionally make me think of myself and my contemporaries as weak sentimentalists, or at best as cowards who can't face up to the ineluctable truth: Armageddon is upon us, and when it comes it will most likely lack even an ameliorative Michelangelan grandeur.

These older and younger dramatists, with their bleak, at times incredibly funny, plays—hopelessness can be very funny, so can pain—may be expressing hope indirectly, through the Beckettian trope: the fact that this work exists at all is all the reason for hope there is. Or, as Heiner Müller, the great German playwright, said in an interview, "The utopian feature is in the form, and not in the content." Or, perhaps, announcing volubly that we're in Hell may be the best way finally to awaken all of us damned to the facts of our appalling predicament.

Those of us who lived on the periphery of the Sixties, witnesses to but not, by reasons of age or geography or upbringing, the battle-scarred participants in a nearly successful cultural and political revolution, have taken from that decade of rage, loss, struggle and astonishment a belief in social resurrection and redemption. The radical possibilities of this country were revealed then, momentarily, before the prevailing counterforces of Nixon and Reagan swept triumphally, calamitously to power. Perhaps one of the worst crimes of the criminals we have established as our leaders is that they have sealed up the borders of Utopia, and convinced far too many of us that our dreams were mere fantasies, and that maundering, cynical, senile nostalgia, rather than dreaming, is what adults do.

But here is a writer who has not lost the understanding we all once had of the awesome power of dreams, a writer who remembers her dreams, and her nightmares, and who possesses great skills in bringing what she learns in the night to life. Even if it is only stage-life, we are privileged to witness it; it gives us hope and power. To spend time with these plays is to spend time with the splendid woman who wrote them; and she's all the reason anybody needs to want to try to save our species, if saving it is possible. Connie thinks it is possible; and I believe her.

TALES OF
THE LOST
FORMICANS

For my father, Ned Congdon

TALES OF THE LOST FORMICANS was workshopped first at River Arts Repertory, under the direction of Gordon Edelstein, and then received its first production there, directed by Roberta Levitow, after a second workshop at the Sundance Institute, directed by Mary B. Robinson.

It was then produced by Actors Theatre of Louisville, starting on March 19, 1989, with the following cast and creative contributors:

CATHY	Lizbeth Mackay
ERIC	Jason O'Neill
JIM	Edward Seamon
EVELYN	Mary Bouchet
JUDY	Jan Leslie Harding
JERRY	Bob Morrisey
ACTOR	Jonathan Fried
DIRECTOR	Roberta Levitow
SETS	Paul Owen
LIGHTS	Ralph Dressler
COSTUMES	Lewis D. Rampino
SOUND	Mark Hendren

This production was chosen as the U.S. entry in the International Theater Festival in Helsinki, Finland.

TALES OF THE LOST FORMICANS was produced by The Women's Project & Productions, New York City, opening on April 17, 1990. The cast and creative contributors were as follows:

CATHY	Lizbeth Mackay
ERIC	Noel Derecki
JIM	Edward Seamon
EVELYN	Rosemary Prinz
JUDY	Deidre O'Connell
JERRY	Michael Countryman
ACTOR	Fred Sanders
DIRECTOR	Gordon Edelstein
SETS	James Youmans
LIGHTS	Anne Militello
COSTUMES	Daniele Hollywood
SOUND	John Gromada

The staging should be relatively seamless, with the stage space shared by all the characters. Furniture and other objects in the world are minimal because they are artifacts.

With the exception of the actor who plays Jerry, the Aliens are played by the human cast members wearing matching sunglasses. They are human in their demeanor, except that they seem overly pleasant and solicitous. (The character of Jim is only effective as an Alien in Act One.)

The Voiceover speeches can be shared by the actors as Aliens (with the exception of the actor who plays Jerry). They need not be hidden while they do the Voiceovers, although sometimes it might be interesting if they were. The play works best, however, when Actor #7 does most of the Voiceovers.

Jerry's "squeak" is a manifestation of his effort to sigh with a throat constricted by tension.

ACT ONE

As the audience files in, Jerry lies on the stage, in darkness, lit only by a hand-held fluorescent lamp beside him. He is looking at the night sky with binoculars. He's lying on a sleeping bag. The chair and table for the next scene are pre-set nearby. After the audience gets settled, the lights bump all the way up and three Aliens enter. They are the actor playing Evelyn, the actor playing Cathy, and the actor playing Jim. Two of the Aliens unfold a star map and the Cathy/Alien finds, with difficulty, a small dot at the periphery and points to it.

CATHY/ALIEN *(To audience)*: You are here.

(As they roll up the map, Jerry gets up and exits, discouraged, crossing near them, dragging his sleeping bag and carrying his fluorescent lamp—he doesn't see them, but they see him. One of the Aliens cues the music and Muzak-like "elevator music" is piped in. Aliens exit, leaving the stage bare except for a chair and table, part of a kitchen ensemble, typical in suburbia but dated by a decade or so. The chair is upholstered with plastic and the legs of both chair and table are of bent chrome. The chair has a hole in the backrest—a design element common to chairs of this type)

VOICEOVER: First item. A situpon. *(Aside, softly)* What? *(Back to mike)* Chair. Chair. For sitting. Sitting and eating or some other ritual. Goes with table . . . which we'll see in a minute. Note the construction. Forward legs (*Aside*)—they call them legs? (*Back to mike*) Forward legs are made as one unit, curving up to provide the rear of the chair. Rear legs are constructed in a smaller curve unit which fits under the seat and inside the forward leg unit, providing a very strong system for the body pads—cushions—and then the body itself. The wobble that some of these chairs exhibit we attribute to climate changes . . . or some other entropic reality.

(An Alien enters and "shows" the chair—sort of like Vanna White on "Wheel of Fortune")

Care was taken in beautifying the chair. The sleek surface of the legs reflects light except, of course, where there are spots of oxidation. And this surface is the substance *chrome*. We have several other examples of that substance—evidently a precious metal used as a surface to apportion many religious objects, specifically the numerous wheeled sarcaphogae used to carry spirits to the next world.

(Alien holds up a small model of an automobile)

The cushions of the chair are covered in a substance made to mimic the epidermis of the sitter, but treated to hold a sheen which is kept polished by friction of the buttocks against the surface. The significance of the hole in the backrest is unknown to us at this time. It was, perhaps, symbolic. A breathing hole for the spirit of the sitter, or even the ever-present eye of god.

(Alien exits. Jim enters, a middle-aged man in work clothes. He is wearing lipstick and has a bandage on his right index finger)

Next, the table. Four legs—the hard surface covered with geometric shapes—decoration or, perhaps, a code?

(Jim lowers head, face down, staring until it slowly touches the table surface, stays there. After a beat, the table wobbles)

JIM: Hmmmm. (*Rests the side of his head on the table—pressing it gently against the cool of the surface*) Ahhh.

VOICEOVER: The table legs also wobble—this leading us to theorize that perhaps both examples of the wobble phenomenon are not random but conscious built-in representations of the unreliable nature of existence for this particular . . . species.

JIM (*To someone offstage*): I'm gonna finally fix the goddam toaster. Evelyn?

VOICEOVER: Wait. Reverse it, please. (*Pause*) Please reverse it— it's too early—something else goes here—

JIM: Nilaveh? Retsote moddag ath skif eelanaif annog mai. (*Reverses his movements very fast and exits*)

VOICEOVER: There.

CATHY (*To audience*): Why would I move back home?

VOICEOVER: This is right.

CATHY (*To audience*): I mean, I have a perfectly nice home of my—wait a minute—(*Stops to listen to something offstage, then back to audience*)—anyway, it's a two-bedroom apartment, rent-controlled—(*Stops again*) Excuse me—(*To someone offstage*) Honey? Mike? Is that you? (*Exiting to check on "Mike"*) Mike? Are you throwing up? (*Sticking her head back in to talk to the audience*) He's in the bathroom. (*Offstage, to "Mike"*) I'm coming in. (*A beat. Sticking her head back in to talk to the audience*) Bad news. Excuse me. . . . (*Offstage, to "Mike"*) What? You *what??!!* And she's *what???!!!* (*Reenters fully, talks to audience*) Life's funny. One minute you're married. The next minute, you're not. One of his students, eighteen years old, "Kimberly," plays the oboe, the baby is his. (*Exits*)

JUDY (*From offstage*): *Home!!* I'm *home!! Jason!! Jennifer!! Somebody* help me get these groceries outta the car!! (*Enters and crosses, lugging bags of groceries, stops near her exit and speaks to audience*) Last week one of the neighbors ran her rid'em mower the entire length of the street, on the grass—one mowed swatch through eight or nine lawns—flowers, toys, garden hoses all mowed into teeny, tiny little pieces—looked like a party. Then she hit somebody's rotary sprinkler and it threw her off course, but she kept on going, her foot flat on the gas, screaming at the top of her lungs until she came to rest, violently, against a garbage truck. Her husband died last year—he used to do all their mowing. I—I—I gotta move outta here. (*Exits*)

VOICEOVER: They reproduce with difficulty.

ERIC *(To Cathy offstage)*: You hear me, Mom? Everything is completely fucked up! I didn't get the fucking divorce. It's not my fucking fault. And now my entire life is fucked! *Mooooommmmm!*

(Cathy enters and looks at Eric)

VOICEOVER: They are grouped in loosely structured units called families. Ring.

ERIC *(Picks up phone)*: Yo. (*To Cathy*) It's someone named Grandma. Wait—is this the Grandma we're supposed to live with? (*To person on phone*) Where is this place? (*Listens to answer—turns back to Cathy*) No. No fucking way. Fuck no.

(Cathy takes phone)

CATHY *(On phone)*: Mom? Yes, they all use that word. A lot.

VOICEOVER: The economic system is antiquated, but communication is excellent, in spite of primitive equipment.

CATHY *(On phone)*: Yes, everything is fine. He's excited about coming. Excuse me—(*To Eric, sotto voce, handing Eric the phone*) *Now, for Chrissake be nicccccccce.*

ERIC *(Into phone)*: Whatsup, Grandma. (*Can't do it, hands Cathy the phone*)

CATHY: I'll call you back, Mom?

EVELYN *(On stage, on the phone)*: No.

CATHY *(On phone)*: No?

EVELYN: It's your father.

(Jim wanders on)

CATHY: What?

EVELYN: He's . . . different. I don't know . . .

CATHY: Should we still come home?

ERIC: This is my home.

EVELYN: Please.

ERIC: This is my home!

EVELYN: Please.

ERIC: *This is my home.*

EVELYN: Please.

(They both hang up. Evelyn follows the wandering Jim off as he exits)

CATHY: Eric, we *have* to go home. We are going home. *And that's final!!!*

ERIC: You're outta control, Mom. You need to get some fucking help.

CATHY: *Listen!!!* I am the mother!! You are the child!! I am in control here!!! *I am the adult!!!*

ERIC: Mom. There are no adults in this world. I just figured that out this year. And this boy's not going to live in any fucking suburb. No way. (*Exits*)

VOICEOVER: No way.

(Judy is standing, looking out over the audience's head, pointing out houses to Cathy)

JUDY: Split level, split level, raised ranch—

CATHY: Those are new. Nice.

JUDY: Ten years at least. (*Beat*) Now that's a new one—a twisted cape. High dollar house—didn't catch on.

CATHY: That was our little hill.

JUDY: It was just leftover dirt from something else. It wasn't, like, a real hill or anything.

CATHY: So what did our side of the street do?

JUDY: Some new siding. Above-ground swimming pools. Trying to be, you know. . . . (*Points at a house*) New garage. It's a kit.

CATHY: Really? Huh. (*About another house*) Boy, that lawn looks like hell. He used to keep it perfect.

JUDY: You don't know?

CATHY: What?

JUDY: Spread newspapers on the living room rug, lay down, and shot himself.

CATHY: Oh my God!

JUDY: Of course, it still soaked through.

CATHY (*Still about the suicide*): Why?!

JUDY: He lay there all afternoon. Say goodbye to that wall-to-wall carpeting. (*About another house*) And over there? She never leaves the house.

CATHY: That was a showplace inside.

JUDY: Still may be. We'll never know.

CATHY (*Another house*): The . . . boys. Those wild boys . . .

JUDY: Killed in Vietnam. Killed in a car wreck. And the other one's a lawyer.

CATHY: Mom never wrote.

JUDY: I thought you knew, or I would've—

CATHY: Yeah.

JUDY: Nobody writes . . .

CATHY: No. (*A pleasant memory of someone*) Oh, whatever happened to Darryl?

JUDY: San Francisco.

CATHY: Is he still alive?

JUDY: I dunno.

CATHY (*About the neighborhood*): Strange.

JUDY: Yeah, it's pure Mars. I had to move back. I couldn't afford my rent plus the Reeboks. Mom's alright with the kids. I mean, that's the way families used to do it all the time. This is a nice place to live. We grew up here. It's not the subdivision that's the problem, it's the society. My mother and I . . . get along. (*Long pause, waiting for Cathy to say something about this—agree with her*) I mean, you're doing all right, aren't you?

CATHY (*Realizing that Judy wants to hear this*):   Yeah.

JUDY: It's only temporary. Until I get a better-paying job. I think I'm gonna start at one of those learning centers they advertise on TV—you can put it on your Mastercard.

CATHY: What are you gonna learn?

JUDY: Radiology. I don't know about wearing all that lead. Can't be good for you. What are you going to do?

CATHY: Something'll come up.

JUDY: Remember that little dog that was in love with you?

CATHY: Oh, the humper.

JUDY: Why don't we call him up for Saturday night? Boy, uh. (*Beat*) Actually, he's dead. They get kidney problems, those dogs.

CATHY (*Thinking about the suicide*):   Why did he do it?

JUDY (*Thinking about the dog*):   He was a slave of love, humping your leg—his little pink thing reaching out . . . with no place to go. So sad.

CATHY: No, I meant Mr. Whatshisname.

(*Cathy puts a finger to her forehead like a gun. Judy moves the "gun" so that the "barrel" is in Cathy's mouth*)

JUDY: Bang.

CATHY: Oh.

JUDY: Yeah, he meant it.

CATHY: But why?

JUDY: Seems so incredible to you? He wasn't happy!

CATHY: Well, who is?

JUDY: But in a house that nice! You know?

(*Judy exits. Cathy stays on the "lawn."*
     Jim enters as before, wearing lipstick, and puts his head down on the table, just as before)

VOICEOVER: This is the correct placement. Thank you.

JIM (*About the coolness of the table against his head*): "Ahhh."
(*To someone offstage*) I'm gonna finally fix the goddam
toaster. Evelyn?

(*He exits, returns with the toaster, sits.
Cathy enters the scene and addresses the audience*)

CATHY: I'd forgotten how small this house is.

(*Evelyn enters, holding a dish towel. To Evelyn:*)

What?

EVELYN: He's in the kitchen. He's just sitting there.
CATHY (*To Evelyn*): What time is it?
EVELYN: Ten a.m.

(*Cathy enters Jim's space, Evelyn following*)

CATHY (*To Jim*): What are you doing home, Dad?
JIM (*Pleasant, oblivious*): Hi. I fixed this damn thing again.
EVELYN: What are you doing home, Jim?
JIM: What's for supper?
CATHY: What you got on your mouth?
JIM: Chapstick.
EVELYN: It's an honest mistake.

(*Evelyn wipes lipstick off Jim's mouth.
Phone rings*)

CATHY (*On phone*): Hello. (*Hands receiver to Jim*) Dad?
JIM (*Takes receiver, then puts it to his ear*): Uh-huh? . . . Hello,
old buddy. . . . Home. . . . What?! (*Looks at watch*) What??!!
(*Stands, drops phone*) No. (*Starts to exit, looks at Cathy*)
CATHY: What is it, Dad?
EVELYN: He's supposed to be at work! Don't you see?! He's
supposed to be at work!!
JIM: I—I don't understand.
CATHY: Want me to go with you?

JIM: To work with me? Why? It's all right. Doesn't anybody think it's all right?! (*Bolts out the door*)

(*Cathy exits after Jim.*
Evelyn notices the phone receiver which hasn't been hung up—she picks it up)

EVELYN: Hello? Jack? . . . He's left. He'll be right there. . . . No, he's fine. Came home to get Cathy. She's . . . visiting. . . . I'm fine, Jack. . . . Bye-bye.

(*She hangs up the phone. She looks at the paper towel with the lipstick on it. The toaster pops—it's fixed. Eric enters in his jockey shorts—he's just gotten up*)

ERIC: Toaster fixed finally? Get some frozen waffles today—okay, Grandma?

EVELYN: No.

ERIC: Jesus, I can't even eat what I want? (*Exiting*) I don't get to live where I want, I can't say what I fucking want to say—

EVELYN: What did you say? (*Exiting after him*) *What did you say?*

ERIC (*Offstage*): *What kind of fucking life is this, huh???*

(*Jerry enters, sits in the kitchen chair and talks to the audience*)

JERRY: First off, they get a warehouse—doesn't have to be all that big, say, about the size of a Safeway. And the first thing they do is spray the walls and the ceiling flat black. And then they bring in about thirty loads of number ten gravel and they cover the floor with it. And then a couple, three loads of retaining wall rock—you know the size I mean—about as big as my fist. And they sprinkle that over this base of gravel. Now you know they've made some mounds here and there, so the floor isn't completely flat. They hang some lights from the girders and set up some big spots, and they got a control booth in a corner. Then they bring in the machines—the lunar lander and the L.E.M. And that's when they set up the cameras, shout "Action!" and make a movie. Then they print it in black and white on crummy film in slow motion and pipe it onto all the television sets. And whammo—all the world sees a man land on the moon and plant the American flag. I mean, "Moon Rocks?" Really. And don't talk to me about Voyager. They got a ride at Walt Disneyworld better than that. Think about it. (*Exits*)

VOICEOVER: He loses three days—no—wait. This is the female bonding scene.

(*Judy and Cathy are talking*)

CATHY: The kids? Your mom?
JUDY: At the mall.
CATHY: A little risky.
JUDY: I wouldn't go near the house—are you kidding me? His apartment. Are you into this? You don't seem into this.
CATHY: Oh—I *love* it.
JUDY: Yeah.
CATHY: I *love* this.
JUDY: Yeah.
CATHY: It's too much.
JUDY: Yeah.
CATHY: God.
JUDY: Right.

(*Long pause as they both smile and nod*)

CATHY: We're talking the same guy.
JUDY: Right.
CATHY: The one.
JUDY: That's right.
CATHY: Amazing. Makes me crazy! Uh! You are my hero. You are definitely my *hero*.
JUDY: There's just one thing.
CATHY: What? What?
JUDY (*Beat*): I said the L-word. (*Pause*)
CATHY: What?

JUDY: I said the L-word.

CATHY: No.

JUDY: Yes.

CATHY: Was he . . . there?

JUDY: Was he there.

CATHY: Are you sure he heard you?

JUDY: Oh yeah.

CATHY: What did he do?

JUDY: It seemed to throw him off rhythm slightly.

CATHY: Then? You said it then?

JUDY: I know.

CATHY: Boy.

JUDY: I know.

CATHY: Was there any discussion . . . later?

JUDY: Nope.

CATHY: An acknowledgment of any kind from him?

JUDY: Are you kidding? (*Beat*) *Are you kidding?* (*Beat*) It would've been easier if I'd farted, frankly. Oh God. Oh God.

CATHY: I know.

JUDY: It's just—been a long time for me.

CATHY: I know.

JUDY: I just sort of, like, lost it.

CATHY: I know.

JUDY: Oh God, what an amateur.

CATHY: It'll be all right.

JUDY: He heard me say it.

CATHY: He'll forget. Men have short memories. Particularly for emotional information.

JUDY: Oh boy.

CATHY: Don't worry about it.

JUDY: I'm fucked. I'm totally fucked. Can you tell me I'm not fucked?

CATHY: Maybe he's different.

JUDY: I wish I could take it back.

CATHY (*To herself*): Oh my God. Starting from scratch.

JUDY: What?

CATHY: Nothing.

(Cathy and Judy exit in opposite directions)

VOICEOVER: This is where he loses three days.

(Jim enters and sits at the kitchen table, and stirs his coffee very carefully, completely immersed in this action. Evelyn enters)

EVELYN *(Ready to go)*: Alright.

JIM *(Pleasantly)*: Okay.

EVELYN: Are you go to the ready store?

JIM: What?

EVELYN *(Annoyed, as to a child)*: Are—you—ready—to—go—to—the—erstoe?

JIM: I—I—

EVELYN: *Yaagh!! Yaagh!!* Are you ready to go to the yaagh?

JIM: Alright!

(Evelyn exits. After a long beat, Jim stands up and begins to look around for her)

Evelyn? Baby?

(Aliens enter and take his table and chair, so when he comes back to where he was sitting, everything is gone. Jim panics and begins to run around. Suddenly a pair of headlights appears right upstage from him—Jim freezes in their light. A loud diesel horn honk. A Trucker enters, having climbed down from the truck)

TRUCKER: *Whatthehelliswrongwithyou?*

JIM: Who are you?

TRUCKER: Are you *blind?!!*

(Evelyn enters with groceries in a couple of bags)

EVELYN: *Jim!!* Good *God!!*

TRUCKER: Is this guy yours???

EVELYN: Jim—you were right there with me at the checkout—
I turn around and you were gone!!

TRUCKER: Keep him out of the street!!

JIM *(To Trucker)*: I'll be with you in a minute.

EVELYN *(To Trucker)*: We're sorry.

JIM: Nice truck. Peterbilt!

TRUCKER *(Exiting)*: Dickhead!

JIM *(To Evelyn)*: Where's my coffee?

EVELYN: Come on, Jim.

(Evelyn exits and Jim starts to follow. Aliens replace his table and chair, but not his coffee. He turns and notices his chair and table again, crosses to it and sits—the coffee is gone. Evelyn enters in different clothes)

Alright. What do you want to do today? *(About his clothes)* Wait—didn't I lay out some clean clothes for you? These are the same ones you wore yesterday, Jim.

JIM: I can't keep track of my damn coffee. Isn't that funny?

(Evelyn gets a fresh cup and puts it down in front of him. Jim puts his hand in it and burns it)

It's hot. *Owwwwwww!!*

EVELYN *(In sympathy and fear)*: Oh *Jim!* That's your hurt hand! *(She tries to get him up)* Come to the sink—I'll pour cold water on it.

JIM: No. Every time I leave this chair, something happens.

EVELYN: I'll get a washcloth.

(She exits. Hank enters—he's a male relative of Jim's)

JIM: *Hank!!*

HANK: Jimmy!!

(Jim puts out his hand—Hank shakes it vigorously and it doesn't hurt. Jim looks at his hand in amazement)

How are you doing?

JIM: What are you doing here?

HANK: I'm collecting for the Sunday paper.

JIM: No kidding. Why?

HANK: That'll be three thirty-five.

JIM *(Looking in his billfold)*: I don't have it.

HANK *(Whispers)*: Get out while there's still time. (*Horn honk. Hank speaks in a normal voice*) Gotta run. I'll be back.

JIM: That's what you always say. Hank? Hank!!

(Evelyn enters, dressed differently again)

EVELYN: I was honking for you, Jim. Didn't you hear me?

JIM: Hank was here, Evelyn!!

EVELYN: Hank is dead, Jim. Jim?

JIM: But he was here.

EVELYN: Jim—the paperboy yesterday—you called him Hank.

JIM: The paperboy is Scott.

EVELYN: Yes, that's right. Scott.

JIM: Scott—I know. I know that.

EVELYN: The doctor wants to check your hand today—
(She looks at his burned hand—the same one that had the bandaged finger at the beginning of the play) Jim!! You took the bandage off again!! Dammit! Come on.

JIM: Wait.

EVELYN: What is it?

JIM: I—I have to find my insurance card.

EVELYN: I left the car running. Don't be long.

(She exits. Jim takes out his billfold and sits down at the table and goes through all the cards and the pictures. As he lays the cards out carefully in a row, an Alien enters and begins to pick them up. Jim doesn't notice—he's become too involved, distracted, looking at some of the pictures he's found in his billfold. The Alien exits with the cards—Jim turns back to go through them, notices that they are gone—pats the table where they were,

*looking for them. Sound of a car horn honking. The honking
becomes a long hum. Jim stares ahead.*

*Cathy and Judy are doing the L-word scene as in the earlier
part of the play—like the tape is running backwards. Jim exits)*

CATHY *(To herself)*: Cha-erks murf geentrats. Dog eyem ho.

JUDY *(Backing in)*: Kab ti kate duk I shiwa I.

CATHY: Tner-ref-fid see eebyaim.

JUDY: Tkuff tawn my eem illet ooya nak. Tkuff eelatote my.
Tkuff my.

VOICEOVER: We've seen this.

CATHY: Ti touba eerow tnode.

VOICEOVER: I said we've seen this. And X-load tape. It's a
zoomer. Thank you.

(Cathy and Judy exit, still in the backwards mode.

*After a beat, Evelyn enters, sits down at the table and makes
a phone call.*

*In another space, Cathy and Jim are in the cab of his pickup.
Jim is humming "That Old Black Magic")*

CATHY: Where are we, Dad?

JIM: In the pickup.

CATHY: I know that.

EVELYN: Hello? Yes.

CATHY: Where are we going? Where's the job?

EVELYN: This is Mrs. McKissick. The doctor saw my husband
last—I'll hold.

JIM: Out . . . out.

CATHY: Another subdivision.

EVELYN: Yes, we have insurance.

JIM: No. It's a—a—great, big place where you shop—

CATHY: A mall?

JIM: A mall. And we're putting in the—the—*Goddammit!!*

EVELYN: When does he get back from his cruise, then?
(Writes something down)

CATHY: Drainage?

JIM: Right.

EVELYN: Thanks. (*Dials another number*)

CATHY: But you're the foreman. What are you running errands for?

EVELYN: Yes. Our doctor gave me your—I'll hold.

JIM: Jack—Jack wants me to.

EVELYN: Yes. Yes, we have insurance.

JIM: You hear something? (*Stops the truck*)

EVELYN: I'll hold.

CATHY: No. Where are we?

JIM (*Still humming*): I hear something—a humming.

EVELYN: Yes, we have insurance.

CATHY: A humming?

JIM: Yeah.

EVELYN: Yes, we have insurance!

CATHY: We've got to get Jack this pipe, Dad. Dad?

(*Jim has phased out, hums again*)

EVELYN: Blue Cross. *Yes.*

(*Trucker enters. Suddenly, he notices Jim and Cathy in the pickup. He stops immediately and crosses to them*)

TRUCKER: Can I help you?

EVELYN: ALL RIGHT.

JIM: I'd like a large root beer. (*To Cathy*) What do you want?

CATHY: Dad—(*To Trucker*) We're delivering some pipe. He's the foreman of the pipe-laying crew.

TRUCKER: Oh shit! Not him again!

CATHY: Listen—this is my father.

TRUCKER: You letting him drive?

EVELYN: *I was just talking to somebody*—oh, sorry.

TRUCKER: You'll have to back out. The street is closed off.

CATHY: Yessir. (*To Jim*) Back out, Dad.

EVELYN: Something's wrong with him. He's . . .

JIM: What? Oh.

EVELYN: Confused or . . .

CATHY: We have to back out. Back out.

EVELYN: *Something.* He's not . . .

CATHY: We *have* to back out. *Please*, Dad.

EVELYN: Himself.

JIM: Oh. Oh. (*Jim seems to be having trouble with the gear shift*)

EVELYN: Thank—you. (*They've hung up on her—she hangs up the phone and writes something down*)

TRUCKER: Back this truck outta here!

CATHY: Reverse, Dad. (*Reaches over, gets the gear shift in*)

JIM: I got it—I got it. (*Gets it into reverse*)

CATHY: Press the gas.

JIM: Right. Right.

> (*Trucker exits.*
>   *Evelyn gets up and exits.*
>   *A beat or two later*)

JIM: Who the hell was he?

CATHY: Shouldn't we turn here, Dad?

JIM: What? Oh. Gotta get this watch fixed.

CATHY: What's wrong, Dad?

> (*Jim is humming, doesn't answer.*
>   *Eric enters, throws down his books. Cathy crosses to Eric.*
>   *Jim exits*)

VOICEOVER: They study the words and lives of the Dead. These hold Great Meaning for them.

ERIC: Fucking stupid American History. Not even in English! Now, Mom, I ask you, I fucking ask you, what the hell good is this for me?

CATHY (*Looking at the book*): This is in English. These are just parts of original documents, that's all.

ERIC: Look! All the fucking esses are effs! (*Reads*) "Feftember 19. He failed on his courfe, and made twenty-fix leaguef, fince it waf calm. Thif day, to the fip came a booby, and in the evening they faw another, and the Fanta Maria failed Weft toward the fetting fun." No way. No way. Not this boy.

CATHY: Eric, you are not quitting.

ERIC: I hate the bus.

CATHY: But you took the bus in New York all the time. It's not different.

ERIC: It's a different bus.

CATHY: *Eric, you are not quitting school and I will not hear another word about it!! Do you hear me???*

ERIC: I'm not deaf. (*Exits*)

(Cathy sits and reads Eric's history book—Evelyn enters, distraught)

EVELYN: *Where is God??!* (*She lurches through the space*) Where is God where is God where is *God??* Where is He where is He where is He?? *Where is God??! Where is God??!!! Where is He where is He where is. . . .*

*(She exits, still distraught.
Jim enters)*

JIM: Did your mother come through here?

CATHY: Yeah.

JIM: How did she seem?

CATHY: Better.

JIM: That's a. . . . That's a. . . .

CATHY: Good?

JIM: Good. Good. Good. Good. (*Exits*)

CATHY (*Reading from Eric's American history book*): And on this corf—course they sailed until after midday of the next day, until it was found that what they had said was land was not land, but only cloud. . . . (*Introducing the next scene, to the audience, as Cathy*) "Possible Explanation Number One."

(Jim enters with blueprints and a field book—he's working on a construction site and knows exactly what he's doing. The Actor

enters, carrying an incomprehensible metal object—he is costumed as a B-Movie Alien. Cathy watches)

B-MOVIE ALIEN *(Approaching Jim)*: Greetings. Your overlord said you could repair any object.

JIM: What?

B-MOVIE ALIEN: It is very fucked up. We are . . . kinda stuck. Old pal.

(Jim takes the object and looks at it carefully)

JIM *(About a part of it)*: This needs to be machined better, I can tell you that.

B-MOVIE ALIEN: No problem. Way to go. Far out. My buddy. Give me some skin.

JIM: Do you have a—a—never mind. *(Takes a small all-purpose knife-pipe tamper tool from his pocket and opens the "knife")*

B-MOVIE ALIEN: I don't understand. Put away your weapon. We come in peace.

JIM: You're not from here, are you?

B-MOVIE ALIEN: What do you mean? I am Earth through and through. I hail from Ohio.

JIM *(Too involved in fixing the object to care)*: No problem. Never—force—anything.

B-MOVIE ALIEN *(Repeats it into a small recording device)*: Never force anything.

(The thing lights up)

JIM: There. *(Hands thing back to Alien)*

B-MOVIE ALIEN *(Into recorder)*: There. *(To Jim)* What is your task here?

JIM: Oh, I'm laying some pipe over there.

B-MOVIE ALIEN: Well, this is top secret. Know what I mean, butter bean?

JIM: Oh, sure—I'm used to that. Corps of Engineers, you know.

B-MOVIE ALIEN: What's your name?

JIM: Jim McKissick.

B-MOVIE ALIEN: Thanks so many.

JIM: Hell, I never even seen one before. I couldn't describe it if I had to.

(Alien places his fingers on Jim's head—Jim is instantly paralyzed)

B-MOVIE ALIEN: Forget. Forget. Forget. Forget. How many? *(Looks in notebook—can't find the answer—does a few extra to be sure)* Forget-forget-forget. *(He's overloaded a bit—burns his fingers)* Whew! No problem.

(Alien exits with gadget. Jim looks blankly at his hand, then exits, nearly catatonic)

CATHY *(To the audience)*: And that night I had a dream.

(Cathy sits next to Jim—they are in the pickup again)

Dad, where are we now? We're going around in circles.

JIM: It's the circle drives.

CATHY: Is this the way to the job?

JIM *(Reading street names)*: Kiowa, Iriquois, Quapaw, Huron—

CATHY: Where are we?

JIM *(Reading street names)*: Saturn, Jupiter, Uranus, Mercury—

CATHY: Dad—what's that ahead? Like a big wall of—

JIM: Dark.

CATHY: But it's daytime. It's noon!

JIM: We ran out of streets.

(Cathy gets out of the pickup)

Watch your step.

CATHY: Where are we?

JIM: This is where the mall goes. See?

CATHY: No, I can't see anything—it's dark.

JIM: They haven't put in the electrics.

CATHY: But what happened to the sky?

JIM: There'll be skylights. They're in the plans.

CATHY: Can we get out of here?

(Trucker enters, but is wearing Alien sunglasses)

ALIEN TRUCKER: Perhaps the little lady would like to see a map?

(He snaps his fingers and two Aliens enter with a large, clear drawing of a rock, a wall and a large arrow pointing in-between. They hold up the drawing—Alien Trucker points)

This is a rock. This is a hard place. You are here.

JIM: Alright. Thank you.

(Alien Trucker snaps his fingers, and he and Aliens exit with drawing)

VOICEOVER: Jim? Thanks for bringing the pipe. It's about time, Jim. You're fired. Please leave the company truck.

JIM: Alright. Thank you.

CATHY *(To invisible voice)*: *What???!!* *(To Jim)* Dad. Dad? Let's get out of here!!

JIM *(Cheerful)*: Alright. Thank you. *(Exits.)*

CATHY *(To her exiting father)*: Alright? Thank you? Alright? Thank you? How do we get home? Dad? *(To the audience)* And I woke up and it was true.

(Evelyn enters, speaks to Cathy)

EVELYN: I can't believe it. I can't believe it. You believe in something and they just take it away from you—they jerk it out of your hand like a toy—like a toy from a baby. Years and years and years and years. Thinking you're part of something and you're *not*. Calling him by his first name—Jaaack. Christmas presents. Being nice to Louise—Loooweeeze, *Loooweeze*. It's not her fault. But I just always liked him better than her. I mean, are we just, just a pair of boobs? I mean—are we just horses?

CATHY: What happened? Mom?

EVELYN: Don't upset your dad.

(Jim enters)

JIM: Jack doesn't want me any more.

CATHY: Oh no.

JIM: I need to get the rest of my tools out of the car.

(He exits. Eric enters)

ERIC *(Surprised to see them)*: Whoooops! *(Exits)*

CATHY: Eric!! Come here!!!

ERIC *(Offstage)*: Why?

CATHY: It's *noon*.

ERIC *(Offstage)*: I came home for lunch . . . *money!!* I forgot my
lunch money. Yeah! I'm—going—back—to—school! *Bye!!*

EVELYN *(To Cathy)*: Well, what are you going to do!! Just sit
there?? He's cut school! He's cut school! He's cut school!

CATHY: I know, Mom. What do you want me to do? *Kill him??*

EVELYN: *Yes!!!!* That's what I would've done to *you!!!* I'm going
to help your father get his tools . . . or something. *Look* at *me.*
I'm doing *something!!!* *(Exits)*

CATHY *(To her absent ex-husband)*: Michael, you sonovabitch,
where *are* you! You jerk! You asshole! *(Notices audience)*
Excuse me. I don't know—I'm much nicer than that, really.
Excuse me. Excuse me. 'Cuse me. *(Exits quickly)*

VOICEOVER: What they call community is, in fact, random
habitational clustering, but those in adjacent dwellings are
labeled "neighbors" and are treated with tolerance.

*(A phone rings at Jerry's and keeps on ringing until it stops. Jerry
just stares at it. Cathy enters, looks at Jerry)*

CATHY: Excuse me. I was ringing the doorbell. I kept ringing
the doorbell. Six, seven times. No one came, but I saw you
standing in here, so I walked in. Excuse me. . . . Sorry.

JERRY: I was watching the phone.

CATHY: I wasn't on the phone. I was ringing the doorbell.

JERRY: But the phone was ringing.

CATHY: Who called?

JERRY: I don't know.

CATHY: It was me. At the door.

JERRY: They hung up.

CATHY: I'm looking for my father.

JERRY: Wow. Are you working it out in therapy?

CATHY: No. I'm asking around.

JERRY: Wow. Sort of street-corner psychiatry? You just blurt things out and take whatever answers people give you?

CATHY: I don't have much choice. I am dependent on what other people have seen, you know.

JERRY: Oh—wow. Like using the wisdom of the world. No bullshit. Other people's experience. Would you like something—?

CATHY: He's been taking walks. He's wearing khaki pants.

JERRY: I love khaki pants.

CATHY: And a shirt. He's been taking walks for exercise and sometimes, he gets . . . confused.

JERRY: I know about that. Would you like something to—

CATHY: There's something wrong with this floor.

JERRY: —drink? I don't get company much, but I have a well-stocked refrigerator.

CATHY: I don't drink a lot of fluids.

JERRY: You should. I know. I'm a nurse. Have you ever had the feeling that something that's just happened has happened before?

CATHY: There's a name for that.

JERRY: Really?

CATHY: Déjà vu.

JERRY: I've heard that before! (*Gasps*) Wow.

CATHY: It's French.

JERRY: France. They know about it, too! See? It's all over the world! Things happen! Things happen!

CATHY: Yes, they do.

JERRY: Another world—but it's this world. I don't know, maybe it's the government, but why do we know these things, if they aren't true? Why do we feel, like, this force, unless it's out there or, maybe, right here in this living room?

CATHY: Why would this force be in your living room?

JERRY: Exactly! You know. You *know*. I knew you would. We feel things that disturb us—right? Right? But why would we *want* to do that? Why wouldn't we just feel the things that make sense? But nooooo, no, no—God forbid we should have a little peace of mind. If we had a little peace of mind, we might think clearly. Noooo—it's give you something, take it away. Give you something—Oooops! Dropped it. Bend over and pick it up now. Are we good and bent over? Goooood. (*Mimes gleefully kicking someone in the butt*) Sur*prise*!

CATHY: Do most people understand you?

JERRY: No, but you do.

CATHY: Not that much—

JERRY: I want to show you some pictures.

CATHY: I don't think so. I really have to—

JERRY (*Takes photos from his pocket*): Here.

(*Cathy looks at them*)

CATHY: Is this Vietnam?

JERRY: No, it's my backyard. Look at the sky, see?

CATHY: It's all marked up.

JERRY: You see them!! I knew you would. Tiny, little metal kites in the sky?

CATHY: You drew them in.

JERRY: No, I didn't.

CATHY: I can tell.

JERRY: We're controlled by aliens. And they're idiots.

CATHY: I'm going now.

JERRY: Oh.

CATHY: You need to find some friends.

JERRY (*Afraid to move his mouth for fear aliens will see him talk*): They're making you do this.

CATHY: No, they're not.

JERRY (*Little mouth movement*): Yes, they are.

CATHY: I have to go. (*Exits*)

JERRY (*Looking up at the sky*): I see you. *I see you.* (*Flipping the bird to the sky*) How's *that?*

VOICEOVER: Hmmmm. There's that gesture again.

(*Jerry exits*)

Next segment: An object may have many uses.

(*Judy enters with a large screwdriver in her mouth. She is watching the street*)

CATHY (*From offstage*): Judy! Hey, Judy! *Judy!!*

VOICEOVER: Vocal intensity is frequently necessary for effective communication.

(*Cathy enters, sees Judy*)

CATHY: What are you waiting for?

JUDY: The skateboard hoard.

VOICEOVER: Offspring are born without wheels and must acquire their own.

JUDY: I'm taking Jason's wheels. He won't use Jennifer's skateboard. It's pink.

CATHY: Sounds serious. What did he do?

JUDY: It's all about power, Hon. And they've figured it out. We never figured it out. We were stupid.

CATHY: It's so windy.

JUDY: Nothing stops them. Even rain. My Ex came by. He's got a new Corvette. And a new girlfriend. She's young. Of course. Her biggest problem is if her blow dryer shorts out. Nature uses us. When I think that if I were watching TV some night and this movie came on where a small head

appears from between some woman's legs and then this
thing that is all wet and bloody comes out, and begins to
bleat, and there's this long slimy tube attached to its body
that comes from inside this sobbing and amazed woman,
I would run out of the room and lose my dinner. And then
I would call up the TV station and say, "What the *hell* is this
horror movie doing on TV where my kids can *see it!*"
So how's the journal?

CATHY: I gave up. I can't write about my daily life.

JUDY: Why? I liked that story about the ant.

*(Sound of a far-off beat box approaching—with about three
kinds of music coming out of it at once)*

Oh, Jesus.

CATHY: What's that?

JUDY: Jagger

CATHY *(Sees him)*: Who's he?

JUDY: Brain surgeon's kid. He's the leader. He's thirteen.

CATHY: I hear the wheels. There they are!! My God, they've got
a sail! They look like a big ship!!! *(Music is closer)* Who *are*
they?

JUDY: *They are our children!!*

CATHY: *Who are they?!!!*

JUDY: *I don't know!!!*

CATHY: Is Eric with them?

JUDY: No, but there's Jason *and* Jennifer!

CATHY: That sail looks familiar.

JUDY: It's my mother's Elvis Presley bedspread!! *Jasonnnnnn!!!!!*

(Judy exits, running. Eric enters, crosses to Cathy)

ERIC *(About the kids on the skateboards)*: Look at those little worms.

CATHY: Eric—I was looking for you.

ERIC: Yeah.

CATHY: Grandma gave me this phone bill. Look at these
charges—*(Reads)*—$35.12—New York—2:45 p.m. $42.10—

New York—3:10 p.m. And this one just last week: $65.37—
three hours and forty-five minutes.

ERIC: Yeah.

CATHY: Have you been calling New York City in the afternoon?

ERIC: Yeah.

CATHY: Are you out of your mind? The rates are sky-high then!

ERIC: I needed to talk to Todd.

CATHY: There's not a conversation in here that's less than two
hours!

ERIC: We always used to talk after school.

CATHY: But not *long distance!*

ERIC: Hey. I'm a long-distance guy.

CATHY: This bill comes to almost two hundred dollars!

ERIC: Hey. I didn't get the divorce. I didn't ask to move here.
I didn't make Grandpa sick or whatever the fuck is wrong
with him. Matter of fact, I didn't ask to be born. You and
"Mike" had all the fun when I was conceived. I was exploding. You think exploding is fun? Doubling and quadrupling
and sixteenth-toopling or whatever the hell it is. You're a
blob, you're a fish, you're some hairless tadpole weird-
looking piece of flesh? Huh?

CATHY: Well, for your information, conceiving you wasn't all
that much fun!

ERIC: Well, don't talk to me about it! Call Dr. Ruth. And if I
can't talk to my friends, then *fuck this world,* you know?
(Exits)

CATHY *(Trying to come up with a parting shot)*: Well—*Eric!*
You know. . . . *(Gives up. To audience:)* "Eric. Possible
Explanation."

(She watches the following scene.
Jim is reading the National Enquirer *and Evelyn is*
knitting)

JIM: Says here that alien beings have been abducting young
girls, having intercourse with them, and then returning

them to society where they, these young girls, bear monstrous babies, fathered by these alien beings.

EVELYN: Hmmmmmm? Ouch!

JIM: What's wrong?

EVELYN: This aluminum is hard to knit. *(Holds up knitting)* Booties.

JIM *(About booties)*: Strange shape. *(Back to paper)* These alien babies grow up to look pretty much like humans but are monstrous in that they have no respect for anything, especially their parents. Or their parents' parents. They hold nothing dear, these alien offspring, except each other. *(Takes the newspaper and exits)*

EVELYN *(To the absent Jim)*: Sounds too improbable. Why do you read that trash? She's naming him Fong Emo Six. It came to her in a dream.

(She exits after Jim.
Jim reenters, without the newspaper, crosses the stage, stops, changes his direction, crosses briefly, stops, changes direction, talks to himself)

JIM: There's nothing wrong with me.

(He exits.
Cathy and Evelyn enter from opposite sides of the stage. They meet at the kitchen table and the argument begins)

EVELYN *(Overlapping the following)*: There's something wrong with that boy! All those years you've been sending those damn pictures—he looked fine! "Eric—fifth grade," "Eric—eighth grade"—big smile and all those thank-you notes. I don't think he wrote them at all—I think you wrote them for him. In the meantime, look at what he's becoming. He looks at me like I was from Mars! Does he appreciate his own grandmother? Noooooo. Of course not. And your friend Judy—*she's gone off the deep end.* She's a complete slut!! I don't know how her mother stands it. I don't know how we all stand anything. Am I the only one that sees that everything is going straight to hell? I talk, talk, talk, and no one listens. Noooo. I asked you to come home for your own good and because I wanted an *adult* to help me because things are completely *impossible, impossible,* do you hear me?

CATHY *(Simultaneously with the preceding)*:   I knew it!! I knew it!! You wonder why I haven't been home—you wonder why we haven't come home to visit? Because I knew it would be like this!! You have no idea what my life is like— what it's like raising a child in the world today. I was a *peach!!* When I think of how *easy* it was for you, it makes me *crazy!!* For your information I sat him down to write all those notes. And do you appreciate it? Noooooo. Of course not. *You could have come visit!!* But no—you were scared of where we lived. *Great!* Makes me feel great! Makes me feel wanted! And Eric, too!! He looks at you that way because he doesn't know you. But you don't know him! And you *don't want to know him!* Can you see how lonely he is? Noooo. Eric was right. This isn't my home. *I gave up my home* to come *here.* Isn't that a riot? I don't know who you are, I don't know who Dad is, I don't know—

(At Evelyn's line, ". . . do you hear me?" they both stop for a beat or two, then start back up. [Cathy's stopping line may vary— Evelyn's line is the only cue])

EVELYN *(Overlapping the following)*:   But instead, you go to work, come home, and only think of your own problems. See? See? That's exactly what's wrong with the world today! It's *me, me, me,* and to *hell* with anyone else! And *that's* why *Eric* is the way he is. *Who* are his models? Hmmmm? It's coming home to roost.

CATHY *(Simultaneously with the preceding)*:   —anything. And *now* you, my own mother hits me where it hurts the most!! But, of course you would—you're my *mother!!* *That's what mothers are for! Go ahead!! Kick me!! In the stomach!!* "Come home, Cathy—please." So I fall for it. And what do I get for it?

(Cathy stops)

CATHY: *Oh, please.*

EVELYN: Yes, it's coming home to roost. Believe me, the world got by when men thought only of themselves, but when women do, we're *dead, dead, dead!!*

CATHY: I don't want to hear it!! Judy's right, no one really gives a *damn* about who is raising the kids as long as they don't have to put in the *fucking* time themselves!

EVELYN: There's that word again!! *See!!*

CATHY: I never use that word. *See what you drive me to?*

EVELYN: I brought you into this world—I can drive you wherever I *want!*

CATHY: I didn't ask to be born! You and Dad had the fun when I was conceived! *(Puzzled, suddenly)* Wait a minute—

EVELYN: It wasn't that much fun!

CATHY: Well, call Dr. Ruth!

EVELYN: What are you talking about?

CATHY: I don't know!!! *(Exits)*

EVELYN: What am I—invisible? *(Exits)*

VOICEOVER: They are fascinated by tools, however primitive.

(It's dark. Judy enters, wearing clear plastic goggles and carrying a small propane torch—she turns on a flashlight, revealing Cathy, also wearing goggles and carrying another small propane torch. Cathy and Judy are trying to be quiet. [Real torches are unreliable on stage—the effect can work with small flashlights in torch bodies])

CATHY: I don't know about this.

JUDY: He says to me—

CATHY: You talk to him?

JUDY: No. He was just standing in the hall.

CATHY: Your hall?

JUDY: My mother's hall—yeah, my hall, my hall . . . now.

CATHY: How did he get in?

JUDY: I don't know—he was waiting for Jason. Jason had his mirrored sunglasses.

CATHY: Jason's just a kid.

JUDY: Don't start with me! I can't pick my son's friends! I can't lock him up! Besides, you know as well as I do—whatever is forbidden, they love!

CATHY: So Jagger's in the hall—

JUDY: "Fire is real." He says to me. "Fire is real." The kid is heavy.

CATHY: I can't talk about kids anymore.

JUDY *(About what they're about to do)*: Come on—it'll get your mind off Eric. And everything. Ready? *(Lights their propane torches)*

CATHY: What a beautiful little flame—*(Sudden realization)* Oh my *God!* What are we *doing?* Oh my *God!!*

JUDY: No problem.

CATHY: No *problem?*

JUDY: It's all fiberglass. It'll melt like sugar.

CATHY: Are you sure this is the right Corvette?

JUDY: Believe me, I know this Corvette. I've dogged him in it for weeks.

CATHY: Are you sure nobody will see us?

JUDY: Make any design you want. Be creative.

(Judy puts flame to Corvette body. Cathy watches, tries)

CATHY: It's melting!

JUDY *(Working away)*: The way I see it, they fucked up in the Sixties, you know? They, like, took away all the values and didn't put anything in its place. You know—so, like, everything just—the whole mess they left—just started to coagulate like it would—I mean, the laws of physics apply to life—Carl Sagan or whoever—those PBS guys have shown us that. Anyway, it, what was left of society, just coagulated like bad pudding, spoiled pudding, you know, like when the egg's separated and can't be put together again completely right. So they make this globular pudding or sometimes it happens to clam chowder. Anyway, it must, like of *formed* and we're stuck with it. There's a piece of God and a clump of law and a lot of lumpy, fucked-up pictures and words that don't hardly mean anything anymore. And—ahh—I made a peace sign but the center fell out, so don't do that. *(Looking at Cathy's work)* Oh, like just a free-formed continuous line. That's great.

CATHY: Thanks. That's enough.

JUDY: No, as long as we're gonna do it. His insurance will pay for it. Just think of no child support payments for six months—and he's taking out his new girlfriend every night—took her to fucking Las Vegas! Restaurants I'll never see the inside of! Buys the kids toys, clothes, whatever shit they want, but no child support for me. He's Santa Claus—I'm the Wicked Witch of the West. Trying to teach values that *nobody believes in anymore!!*

CATHY: Let's do the other side.

JUDY: I'm not into it anymore.

CATHY: Come on. Watergate. And—and all the lies about everything.

JUDY: All the bullshit.

CATHY: Nixon.

JUDY: Marilyn Monroe and John F. Kennedy doing it. Martin Luther King's sex life.

CATHY: Backing dictators—calling them democrats.

JUDY: Fucking with the destinies of other countries. Pardoning each other for criminal acts!

CATHY: Killing presidents—our own!!

JUDY: Selling us!! Selling us!! *(Stops) Shit!!!* I'm out of propane!

CATHY: So am I.

JUDY: *See??!* Nothing fucking *works!!!*

(They exit.

Jim is sitting on the couch, staring at the television. Evelyn enters and watches him)

VOICEOVER: They watch hours of television.

(Evelyn crosses to Jim and comes up behind him and embraces him around the neck. Then she begins to rub his neck. After a beat or so, she sits next to him on the couch and puts her legs on his lap. During all of this, Jim has continued to look at the TV, but responds unconsciously to Evelyn—he doesn't resist her. She kisses him and he responds, but the TV catches his attention again. Evelyn takes Jim by the hand and leads him off into the bedroom. A count of fifty. Evelyn returns alone. She sits on the couch and stares at the TV)

JIM *(Offstage)*: Honey? Honey? My leg's gone to sleep. Isn't that funny?

(Evelyn doesn't get up.

Sound of cheap top forty from a bar. Jerry and Judy are sitting separately—a seat or two between them. Judy checks her watch: She's waiting for someone)

VOICEOVER: Where genders meet.

(After a beat, Jerry begins to speak—to no one in particular. Trying not to, Judy notices him out of the corner of her eye. Jerry sees this and then begins to deliver the speech directly to her)

JERRY: Lincoln was elected president in 1860. Kennedy was elected president in 1960. Both men were involved in civil rights for Negroes. Both men were assassinated, on a Friday, in the presence of their wives. Each wife had lost a baby, a male child in fact, while they were living at the White House. Both men had a bullet wound that entered the head from behind. Both men were succeeded by vice-presidents named Johnson who were southern Democrats and former senators. Both Johnsons were born one hundred years apart—in 1808 and 1908, respectively. Lincoln was killed in Ford's Theatre. Kennedy was killed while riding in a Lincoln convertible made by the Ford Motor Company. John Wilkes Booth and Lee Harvey Oswald were born in 1839 and 1939, respectively, and had the same number of letters in their names. The first name of Lincoln's private secretary was John—the last name of Kennedy's private secretary was Lincoln.

JUDY: *Will you leave me the fuck alone?*

JERRY: Think about it. Life can be understood. You come in here a lot. You like the bartender?

JUDY: I don't like anyone!! I have responsibilities!!!

(Judy exits. Jerry sits for a moment, then squeaks involuntarily and exits.

Judy enters, yelling)

Jason! Jennifer! Jason! Jennifer! *(Sees them, exits—the next several lines are done from offstage.) Get offa her!! Jason!!* Right now!! *(Pause) Don't hit him with that!! (Pause)* Jennifer!! Give me that!! Where did you *get* that?! *(Pause) Jason!!* Leave her alone!! *Jennifer, come back!! Jason—don't run off!! (To some neighbor)* Well, I'm *sorry,* lady!! Go live in a fuckin' convent if you don't want to listen to *kids!! (Back on—to the audience)* You haven't seen a skateboard, have you? Picture of Satan with Mick Jagger's tongue—hanging out? No? Orange wheels—*(Exiting)* I live over there—if you see it. Just leave it in that Blue Pinto—none of the doors lock. *(Pause)* Thanks.

VOICEOVER: The decoding of behavior provides a key to gender identification.

(Cathy is waiting, looking at her watch. Judy joins her—she's late. They sit for a beat)

CATHY: You were so positive!

JUDY: I know.

CATHY: You were so sure.

JUDY: I know.

CATHY: It's incredible!

JUDY: You're telling me. Two Corvettes that much alike! And what the hell did that—that—Cambodian—

CATHY: You said he was from Thailand.

JUDY: Whatever—some skinny oriental guy—anyway, what did he think he was doing parking a car like that on a residential street?

CATHY: He, probably, foolishly, thought it would be safe here.

JUDY: Well, he doesn't know anything—he's just asking questions. What's he doing with a Corvette, anyway?

CATHY: What do we do?

JUDY: Jagger thinks he's got a way into the police computer— if it comes to that.

CATHY: No way!! I'm not encouraging that kid—he's scary enough already.

JUDY: We might be arrested—they know it's two women.

CATHY: They know it's two women! They know it's two women! Oh my god, oh my god, oh my god! How can they know that?

JUDY: They heard giggling.

CATHY: Giggling! Giggling! Who was giggling? I wasn't giggling. You were giggling!

JUDY: No, I wasn't. I was distraught! I still am!

CATHY: You're distraught! You're distraught! I'm the one who's distraught! Look at my life! It's falling apart!

JUDY: And what do you think mine's doing? Singing a little song?

(A beat)

CATHY: What's his plan? Jagger?

JUDY: Zap the records—it's easy, he says.

CATHY: Good. Good. Tell him we'll pay him in cash.

(Judy exits, leaving Cathy. Cathy starts to exit, addresses the audience)

Lately, I've been having trouble breathing. Several times a day, I forget how. I'll notice that I'm running out of breath because I haven't exhaled. So I exhale, and then I'm fine until a few hours later and I realize that I'm out of breath again. So I inhale or exhale, whichever is appropriate.

(Jerry enters. Cathy crosses to join him—they are in his house.)

VOICEOVER: They are concerned with interior decoration.

JERRY: So I'm tearing out that entire wall. Open this all up.

CATHY: Uh-huh.

JERRY: Then I buy good furniture. *(Squeaks)*

CATHY: Uh-huh.

JERRY: I might take out that wall, too.

CATHY: Don't want to take out too many walls.

JERRY: Well, then, no more—just those two. *(Squeaks)*

CATHY: Uh-huh.

JERRY: How's the therapy?

CATHY: What therapy?

JERRY: Right. Right. That's the best kind. In my opinion.
    (Emits a high-pitched rhythmic laugh)

CATHY *(Starts to leave)*: Well, I should—

JERRY: Yes. *(Pause)* Did you enjoy the magazine?

CATHY: It was . . . interesting. *(Returning the magazine to him)*

JERRY *(Giving it back to her)*: Keep it.

CATHY: I'm having a hard time reading, lately. Everything seems to be some kind of message.

JERRY: Message?! Yes. Did you see my ad? Wait—*(Finds it, shows it to her)* Read it.

CATHY *(Reads)*: "Top-Risk Action Group for hire by individuals, organizations, and governments. Rescue a specialty. Call The Watcher, (719) 555-9564. Before noon or after midnight. *(Pause)* But you're not a group.

JERRY: I can be.

CATHY: I have to go. Thanks for the dinner.

JERRY: Next time I'll get the hot mustard sauce instead of the
  sweet and sour. And more fries.
CATHY: Thanks.
JERRY: And a hot apple pie for you. If you want it.
CATHY: Thanks.
JERRY: I wouldn't want to get it if you didn't want it.
CATHY: Thanks.
JERRY *(Squeaks)*: Bye.
CATHY: Bye.

> *(She exits. Jerry bangs his head against something, exits.*
> *In another space, Cathy reenters, reads from the magazine)*

The young Basque terrorist, age 16, walked
Out of the apartment house
On Calle Reina Cristina Street
Heading toward his car.
He froze in mid-stride,
Slapped a hand to the side of his head,
As if he had just remembered something very important,
And fell to the asphalt, dead.

The bullet that killed him
Was fired by a friend,
A fellow terrorist from another faction,
Hiding in the lobby of the apartment building
They shared.
Who are the Basques?

> *(Cathy exits.*
> *Eric enters, dressed in a couple layers of clothing—he carries*
> *a pair of sweatpants, which he puts on over his two pair of pants,*
> *and a full knapsack. Cathy enters with an empty suitcase)*

CATHY: What is this? I found this in your room. What are you
  doing?
ERIC: Getting dressed.

CATHY: Have you gone *crazy???* You're putting on *layers of clothing!!!*

ERIC: Bag is too small. Cheap piece of shit—not even Samsonite—embarrassing.

CATHY: Eric what . . . is . . . this.

ERIC: I'm outta here.

CATHY: You are *not!!!*

ERIC: Yep.

CATHY *(Grabbing him)*: You are *not!!! Not, not!!!* Take *offf* these clothes!!! *Now!!!* Take them *off* take them *off, take them offffff!!!!!*

ERIC: Mom, please. I'm much stronger than you. Just let me go.

(She holds on. He looks at her, then firmly, but gently, removes her arms from his body)

I sold my stereo. Girl I met's taking me to the airport. I'll be at Dad's. This is his number—*(Hands her a scrap of paper)*— just in case you burned it or something. *(Picks up knapsack. He then places his open hand on top of his mother's head in an awkward gesture of affection)* Bye. Say "bye" to Grandma and—him—for me.

(Eric waddles off—his bulk making him look like a toddler. Cathy sits on the floor for a beat, then gets up slowly. Horn honk—she runs to say goodbye—we see her wave, but weakly, because he's already gone and doesn't see her.
Jim wanders through)

JIM: There's nothing wrong with me.

CATHY: *Then it must be us!!! Huh???? We* must be *fucked up!!!* Because it can't be *you!!! Noooooo!!* *(Beat)* Oh, Dad. *(She embraces him and breaks down)*

JIM: Oh, Honey—Shhhhh. Shhhhhh. Shhhhhhh. *(Wipes away her tears)* Who was that fat kid that just went out the door? He go to your school?

(Resigned, Cathy exits)

JIM: Now where was I? Oh—*(Points, offstage)* There.

(He exits.
Cathy exits. Judy enters and sings)

JUDY:
O crocodile night,
You've always been there,
In the thin air,
Or on the dune.
O crocodile night,
You're always waiting,
Tonight you're mating
With the moon. *(Pause)*
The song of the hamper,
The song of the screen,
The song of the dishes,
The song of the green,
The song of the streetlights,
The song of the park,
The song of the lawnchair,
The song of the dark.

(To her offstage children, at the top of her lungs) Now for
Chrissake go to sleep! (Exits)

VOICEOVER: Why they sing is under investigation.

(Jerry is sleeping—suddenly he is surrounded by Aliens. They lift
him up, carry him away—he wakes up during this)

JERRY: *Aaaaaaaaaaeeeeeeeeeeeeee!*

(Aliens exit with Jerry)

VOICEOVER: This is a good place for an intermission.

ACT TWO

To signal the end of the intermission, Jim enters and begins talk-
ing to the audience. He is in possession of all his faculties. After a
few beats of the speech, Cathy enters, drawn by this vision of Jim,
and listens.

JIM: Jack's a smart guy, smarter than me in a lot of ways. I'm
a carpenter by trade and, before the war, I did my appren-
ticeship on stick-built, lath-and-plaster houses. One-inch
boards laid diagonally on studs with sixteen-inch centers.
Hell—pounds of nails. Tens of thousands of nails for one
house. Then I got drafted and when I came home, we
started putting up roof trusses and making walls of three-
quarters- or five-eighths-inch sheetrock. You know
there's no rock in sheetrock—it's just plaster pressed
between two sheets of heavy paper. That's what's in my
home.

CATHY: I dreamed about Dad the way he used to be.

JIM: Jack's getting into modular homes which you buy prefab
in two to four sections which you haul to the site and put
together. Now these have one-eighth-inch paneling made of
wood products that have been fused into a solid sheet and
melded with a surface of plastic photo-reproduction of your

favorite wood-grain. These houses go up very fast, of course, and sometimes come with the curtains already on the windows. People laugh, but why today would you want to build a house that would last a hundred years? Think of the changes in the last hundred years. Can you imagine the next hundred? What will be here—right where I'm standing? All the nails in the world won't keep those walls from cracking when the bulldozer comes. So Jack is right. I mean that.

(Jim exits. Evelyn enters)

EVELYN: I figured it out. We're going to get in the car. And we're going to travel west.

CATHY: What good will that do?

EVELYN: It's worked for our families for two hundred years. We started in New Jersey and Massachusetts. We've managed a state about every two generations.

CATHY: But we're already in the west.

EVELYN: There's more to go.

CATHY: I don't understand how this will help.

EVELYN: I don't believe in medical science. They're making it up as they go along. They laugh at us when we leave the room.

CATHY: Will Dad go?

EVELYN: When I put him in the car. I'll just pack him up. As soon as we start to drive, his brain will start to clear. Memories will come flooding in. Vocabulary, too. Words of songs he's forgotten. Jokes. Anecdotes. Our life together—it's all floating around in the air. We just have to gather, gather it in. I'm gonna keep driving until he's back together. It may take as far as San Diego, but I'm not stopping until every piece is there again.

CATHY: What about Eric?

EVELYN: We'll put a message on the answering machine.

CATHY: We don't have an answering machine.

EVELYN: We'll *get one!!*

(They exit.

Eric crosses to a pay phone, puts in a dime, dials, gets the answering machine message. [The following voices are on the answering machine])

CATHY'S VOICE: Hello. Eric? This is Mom. We've taken a little trip.

EVELYN'S VOICE: For your Grandpa—to make him better.

JIM'S VOICE: Huh? What is this thing?

CATHY'S VOICE: Please come home anyway—a neighbor will let you in. Please.

VOICE OF TELEPHONE OPERATOR: Please deposit fifty cents for an additional minute—please—

(Eric can't get his money fast enough—he gets a dial tone—he beats the phone with the receiver, hangs it up, exits.

Evelyn and Cathy are in the car, traveling. Jim is lying down in the back seat)

EVELYN: Do you have any idea where we are?

CATHY: Where else? The car.

EVELYN: Jim?

CATHY: Mom, we've been traveling in circles—I don't know where the hell we are.

(Evelyn looks in the back seat)

EVELYN: Jim—?

CATHY: On the plains somewhere. Mom? What is it?

EVELYN: We'd better go back.

CATHY: Is he all right?

EVELYN: Please. It didn't work.

(Jim sits up, looks out window)

JIM: There's that old man again. That spindly-legged old guy running against the side of the car.

EVELYN: What?

JIM: Been running alongside me all my life. Look at him go.

EVELYN *(To Cathy)*: He's talking!

CATHY: What're you talking about, Dad?

JIM: That old guy—that long-legged old man. Boy, can he run.

EVELYN: It's working.

CATHY: What old man?

JIM: Look.

CATHY: Oh, him.

EVELYN: Where? Where?

CATHY: Rows of something, Mom. It's rows of corn or something out the window. See?

JIM: Running, running, running. Oh, it's a strange place— this . . . where are we?

(Evelyn and Cathy look quickly at each other, panicked—decide to lie)

EVELYN: Idaho.

CATHY *(Overlapping Evelyn)*: Nevada.

EVELYN: Nevada.

CATHY *(Overlapping Evelyn)*: Arizona.

JIM: Are we lost?

CATHY AND EVELYN: No.

JIM *(Hillbilly voice)*: Hey, hey, HEY! Your boy pissed in the snow outside my cabin. It's frozen there! *(Another hillbilly voice)* It'll thaw next spring—what's your worry? *(First hillbilly voice)* I recognize my daughter's handwriting! *(Another memory comes)* Uh—uh—uh—This is the forest Primeval, the murmuring pines and hemlock, bearded in moss and in garments green, stand like Druids of eld with beards that rest on their—their—*(Trying not to let his memory loss stop him—he sings)* Sometimes I wonder why I spend these lonely hours, dreaming of a song, a melody . . . haunts my . . . memory. . . . *(Speaks)* Stop the car. *(Gets out of car)* Left—loose. Right—tight. Left loose. Right tight. Crying so loud—must be a boy. No, it's a little girl—it's a little, little girl—

(Evelyn gets out of the car—Jim grabs her and takes her to him, as if to dance)

Evelyn—we're making love in the graveyard and scaring the hell out of those kids. They think our sounds are coming from the dead lying below us. *(Scared, breaks from her)* My tongue's stuck on the clothesline! Trying to lick the ice— Mama, Mama, help! *(Really reverting)*

First bath outside in sun.
Fireflies in jar
Night-night. *(Climbs back in the car)*
Warm pee.
Bosom.
Mmmmm. Mmmmm. Mmmmmm.
Shhhhhhh. *(Lies back down)*

EVELYN *(After a long beat)*: Jim?

CATHY: What happened?

EVELYN *(Gets back in the car, upset)*: He was dreaming. I guess. Let's go home.

(Cathy breathes a sigh of relief. Evelyn glares at her)

CATHY: I'm sorry—I'm just so worried about Eric.

EVELYN *(Pretending to forget with a vengeance who her grandson is)*: Who?

CATHY: Mom!

EVELYN: Sorry.

CATHY: Which way?

EVELYN: I don't know!

CATHY: Tell me which way!

EVELYN: For Chrissakes! You're a grownup!! *Pick one!!*

CATHY: We'll go this way.

EVELYN: What are you *doing*? It's that way!!

VOICEOVER: They often dream they have been abducted by extraterrestrials.

(Alien played by the Judy actor is reading a copy of the National Enquirer—*she notices the picture of an alien on the front of it, looks at it closely, then puts it into a large Zip-loc bag and seals it. Other Aliens enter, rolling Jerry in on a dolly—he wakes up and opens his mouth to scream, but can't make a sound)*

ALIEN *(Putting her face very close to Jerry's face and talking very deliberately)*: What—can—we—do—about—your—fear?

(Jerry can't answer—he just stares at them, screaming silently. They massage his jaw and shut his mouth for him. They all begin to pet him roughly to comfort him, like inept children stroking a dog. They proceed with an examination—it should satirize the examination of field scientists on National Geographic *of an animal in the wild. They measure him, take blood, etc.—all with the air of completely dispassionate scientists. One Alien finds a pair of clip-on sunglasses in Jerry's pocket, holds them up for other Aliens to see, and they all laugh rhythmically. An Alien produces* Playboy *magazine, opens it to the centerfold, and moves it in front of Jerry, trying to arouse him. Another Alien unzips Jerry's fly, looks inside and waits for an erection. After a beat, Alien takes out a Dustbuster and inserts it into Jerry's pants through his fly and turns it on briefly. Jerry reacts as the semen is sucked from him. This finishes the exam. An Alien tags Jerry on his ear, zaps him unconscious, and they lay him down gently and exit.*

Evelyn and Cathy are looking at snapshots of their trip west)

EVELYN: Here we are at the Blasted Pine. *(Pause)* Here's that rock that looks like a—

CATHY: —baked potato.

EVELYN: Yes. *(Pause)* Here we are at Glen Canyon.

CATHY: Full of water.

EVELYN: They filled it in. *(Passes through several pictures quickly)* That's the rest of Utah. He wouldn't let me stop the car, so these are all blurry.

CATHY: He seemed to be in such a hurry.

EVELYN: No, he still knows he hates—

CATHY: —the Mormons. Yeah.

EVELYN: Here's—

CATHY: —Reno.

EVELYN *(Correcting her)*: Las Vegas. *(Pause)* Here's—

CATHY: Death Valley.

EVELYN *(Correcting her)*: Barstow. *(Pause)* Here's San Bernadino. *(Pause)* Here we are at . . . at the zoo.

CATHY: Where?

EVELYN: San Diego.

CATHY: Who's this guy with the wet drawers, walking out of the picture? He's looking off to the right, like he doesn't notice . . . he looks so . . . old . . . he's lost, completely lost. *(Exits)*

EVELYN: Here's the other Blasted Pine. *(Pause)* Here's the Pacific Ocean. *(Pause)* Here's a shell on the beach. *(Pause)* Here's a piece of shell. *(Pause)* Here's a sliver of driftwood. *(Pause)* Here's. . . . *(Exits with the snapshots)*

VOICEOVER: They seem to enjoy what is called dreaming—

(During the voiceover, Cathy joins Judy outside—they are smoking dope)

—and spend one-third of their lives in this comatose state, allowing their minds to make stories of whatever stimuli are left over from the day or the life. Significance is then divined from these neural and electronic collages and the process is deemed therapeutic.

JUDY: I found this in Jason's drawer.

CATHY: What? No—all of a sudden I feel so weird smoking this now.

JUDY: I grounded him for life.

CATHY: That's a long time when you're his age. This is good.

JUDY: Imagine what it does to the brain of a twelve-year-old?

CATHY: So, anyway, you were Eve? Man.

JUDY: I can't control my subconscious, alright? Would you rather hear the Spider Dream?

CATHY: No!

JUDY: Okay. I was naked in the Garden and I was looking at all the leaves and stuff and, suddenly, it really began to grow right before my eyes—you know, like that speeded-up photography on nature programs of the opening of a flower or whatever? But this was closing up—you know—the leaves out of control, covering up the sky.

CATHY: Like kudzu.

JUDY: Yeah. Like some paradisiacal kudzu—some mojo kudzu—

CATHY: —of Eternity.

JUDY: No, not Eternity—don't say that.

CATHY: Okeedokee.

JUDY: And the fruit got real big and started hanging lower and lower on the trees. Ever seen a cow that needs to be milked and the farmer's on vacation or something? Mooo. Moooo. Ridiculous, man. I mean, moooooooo. I'm a cow.

CATHY: You're not a cow.

JUDY: I don't want to be a cow.

CATHY: You don't have to be a cow.

JUDY: What is this? Some feminist accusatory bullshit? I know I don't have to be a cow.

CATHY: Listen—are you listening? What was I talking about? I mean, it's not belief. It's feeling. You feel things. And maybe they are assholes. But it's love. How can love be bad? I mean, love is good.

JUDY: Love is very good.

CATHY: Yes, we love and that's good.

JUDY: But we're fucked.

CATHY: Oh, yeah. Go on, I am listening.

JUDY: At that very moment—

CATHY: What moment?

JUDY: In this Garden. Keep up.

CATHY: The Snake.

JUDY: No. No Snake. The Snake was in the next grove, helping Adam—

CATHY: Helping Adam name things.

JUDY: At that very moment—

CATHY: Like the Blue-Footed Booby.

JUDY: I hear this something—sound. Ssssssssss.

CATHY: It is a snake!

JUDY: No snake. Get off of this snake thing!

CATHY: Then what was it?

JUDY: Pressure.

CATHY: God.

JUDY: No. The Tree. The Major Tree. The whole place.

CATHY: What? This is the Knowledge?

JUDY: Yeah. It was all about to bust—*open!* So I just sort of jumped—like Superman? And it worked! So—whoosh—I flew up through the limbs, through the Mojo Paradisiacal Kudzu, and—whoosh—broke through all the Green stuff. *(Pause)* And I was *free!* And the light poured in—

CATHY: And then you woke up.

JUDY: What?

CATHY: You woke up. You were dreaming all this.

JUDY: Oh yeah. I woke up—I woke up.

CATHY: Alone.

JUDY: No—he was there. The guy—you know.

CATHY: You lucky . . .

JUDY: I'd been flying. I had felt so free. And I looked down and what did I have in my hand? The Fruit of the Tree—still sticky, the little bishop, its one eye staring blankly at me.

CATHY: Oh, that fruit, the passion fruit, the forbidden fruit, the fruit of forgetfulness.

JUDY *(Long pause)*: I finally told him I loved him—love him. You know, just sitting there—not in the throes of passion or anything.

CATHY: Not again.

JUDY: Different guy—they don't know each other.

CATHY: What did this one say?

JUDY: "We don't have time for abstractions." And then he said, "Be here now."

CATHY: So that was it.

JUDY: Oh no, I'm seeing him next Sunday. I love him. Really. Everything's gonna be fine.

CATHY: Wake up, Jude.

JUDY: Well, at least I'm trying. You're not even *trying*. At least I'm trying to be *alive*.

(Judy exits. Evelyn enters)

EVELYN: I'm leaving for the ah—

CATHY: Oh, Mom! Judy just left—I—Should I go?

EVELYN: No, it's my day. Thursday. Thursday is my day.

CATHY: I took him the—

EVELYN: Good. Did he ah—

CATHY: Yeah. Well, a little. His eyes seemed to . . . a little.

EVELYN: Oh, well, then he must've known—

CATHY: Oh, he knew. He—Sure.

EVELYN: Well, I've got some new—*(Holds up one of those plastic bags from a mall store)*

CATHY: Great

EVELYN: So—*(Exits)*

CATHY: Tell him—*(Waves instead. To herself)* Get straight. Get straight. Wake *up!*

(Jerry wakes up. Cathy doesn't notice and exits)

JERRY: Hmmmmmmmm. *(Stretches)* Oh my God, I'm outside!!! Oh my God, I'm lying *in my driveway!* *(Looks around to see if the neighbors see him—checks his watch)* Oh my God, I've got to get to work! Oh my God, my fly is open! Oh my God, I hope I'm an alcoholic!

(He exits.
    Cathy is on the phone)

CATHY: Finally.

    Yes. May I speak to Eric, please.

    Well, then, let me speak to his—his father.

    Yes, "Michael." *(Waits)* Hello, Mike?

    Where's Eric—is he there or over at Todd's?

    You *what?????*

    Well, he's not!! He's *not* here!!!! When did he leave?

    A week ago!!! A week ago!!! We've been gone for a week and a half!!!!

    You put him on the *plane* and *never called me?????*

    OhmyGod ohmyGod ohmyGod ohmyGod. *Didn't* you *worry* when you didn't *hear from him???*

    I know he doesn't call *a lot!!* Well, *ever*—alright—*but why didn't you call me to see if he arrived!!!!*

    Hello?? Hello!!

    This is *who???*

    Nice to *meet me??? Where is my son!!!!*

    What do you *mean,* "He can take care of himself!!" How do *you* know? You're only eighteen yourself!!! *Go practice your fucking oboe!!!*

    Mike? *Mike!!* What are you doing!!! Our *son* is lost somewhere between New York and Colorado and you put your *child girlfriend* on the *phone????*

    "Only the Midwest?" What do you think the Midwest is— Rhode Island? *Look at a map, you imbecile!!!* It's *huge!!!*

    No, I will *not* calm down. *You will* call the airline and check the passenger list and find out if he had to change planes. And if he did, *where*—and *pray* he didn't land at *O'Hare*—that's in Chicago, by the way.

    I'll wait up for your report! *(Hangs up)* Mom? *Mom! Moooooooooommmmmmmmmmmm!!!!! (She crosses, looking for Evelyn, runs into Jerry)*

JERRY: I'm looking for my sunglasses.

CATHY *(Turning and crossing away from him)*: Mooommmmmm!

JERRY: Are you looking for your mother now?

(Cathy exits)

And sometimes therapy just makes things worse. I know. I understand. *(Speaks to the audience)* I talk to her so much better when she's not here.

(He exits.
  Jim and Evelyn are looking at menus)

JIM: I'm gonna get the country chicken. I know that's boring, 'cause I always get it.

EVELYN: Wait—how did we get here! Oh my god—something . . .

JIM: No—sometimes I get the liver and onions. That's good. Their liver and onions is good.

EVELYN: Jim—where's the desk? Where's the . . . nurse? I was holding a straw for you, I—

JIM: They have *some* good things here.

EVELYN: You're so much better all of a sudden.

JIM: You know you're at Big Boy. The table is sticky.

EVELYN *(Feeling the table)*: It is! It is! Oh, it *is!!*

JIM: Look at those plants.

EVELYN: Are they—

JIM: Real. They're real. Those are real plants.

EVELYN: It's beautiful in here. The Big Boy is beautiful.

JIM: How do they water all these plants? They probably stand on the booths. *(Beat)* I'm gonna get the salad bar.

EVELYN: Me, too.

JIM *(About the plants)*: Maybe that *is* the salad bar.

(Evelyn is staring across from them at something, doesn't respond)

Do you think? Baby?

EVELYN: Look at that couple over there.

JIM: What.

EVELYN: Over there.

JIM: She looks sort of like you.

EVELYN: No, *him.* He reminds me of you—kind of.

JIM: Am I that skinny?

EVELYN: He's not skinny.

JIM: He's skinny.

EVELYN: And she looks like—

JIM: Oh no, you're much prettier than that, Baby.

EVELYN: Don't look!

JIM: Did she see us? It doesn't matter. She's probably thinking
    the same thing we are.

EVELYN: Oh my God—Don't look.

JIM: Damn! I'm missing something good. What's wrong?

EVELYN: I don't know.

JIM: What's *he* doing?

EVELYN: He's just sitting there, staring.

JIM: Are they having a fight?

EVELYN: No. She's holding a straw for him—ohmyGod.

JIM: What?

EVELYN: Wait. *(Moves her hand up very slowly and moves it back
    and forth, watching the woman while she does it, as if she is
    checking her reflection in a mirror)*

JIM: What are you doing, Evelyn?

EVELYN: Shhhhh. *(Moves her body back and forth, watching the
    woman, then does one quick hand movement, turns away, thinks,
    looks back at woman—stops, stares, bewildered and afraid)*

JIM: I can't take you anywhere.

EVELYN *(Grabbing Jim's hand)*: Let's get out of here.

JIM: I don't care. I'm looking. *(Looks at woman, looks away)*
    She's crying and looking at us. What's wrong?

EVELYN: She's remembering—she's remembering—

JIM: *What?*

EVELYN: She's remembering *now*. Oh *God*, let's get *out* of here!

JIM: Evelyn, Baby—

(Evelyn drags Jim by the hand)

EVELYN: Come on—while we've still got some *time!!!*

(She exits, pulling him—he laughs, following her, still not understanding.
Female Alien enters and gives report in a smooth documentary style. It is juxtaposed with the actions of Jerry, who is fantasizing about Cathy)

ALIEN: Hello. This segment of our presentation is about masochism.

(During the following speech, Jerry sits and imagines Cathy. He begins to become aroused. His Fantasy Cathy swoops in and kisses him passionately—she swoops away and he still can feel her there. He continues to imagine lovemaking, laughter and himself being witty. The fantasy is broken, when the real Cathy enters after the masochism speech is over. Then Jerry returns to his state of nervousness and fear with her)

Masochism is a rather disorganized but, nevertheless, grow-ing religion with many followers of both genders. It seems to be a form of worship of the Mating Process by celibate non-participants and centers on, usually, the idealization of the Worship-Object. The ceremonies are held in private and usually include solitary fertility rites. Prayer is also solitary and silent and can be observed several times a day, depend-ing on the devotion of the Masochistic supplicant.

(Fantasy Cathy enters. Pause)

The Object is called up through telepathy, conversations and encounters are constructed by the supplicant, and the mating act is imagined silently. The experienced Masochist can pray at any time, anywhere. Once the Worship-Object has been selected and a true masochistic state has been achieved, the Masochist eschews contact with the real Object—

(Fantasy Cathy exits)

—communicating only when necessary, and then through broken sentences or a high-pitched rhythmic laughter. This action is designed to repel the real Object, thereby protecting the contemplative life of the now securely celibate Masochist.

(The Alien presenter has exited and the real Cathy enters, sees Jerry)

CATHY: Hello.

(Jerry emits a high-pitched, rhythmic laugh)

CATHY *(Starting to exit)*: See you.
JERRY: Excuse—
CATHY *(Not seeing him)*: Huh?
JERRY: I've avoiding you—been—Me—sorry.
CATHY: I just came to talk.
JERRY: Thank—thank you. A lot on mind—my mind. Things . . . happen . . . to . . . me. *(Exits, laughing with his high-pitched, nervous laugh)*
CATHY: Me, too. You're not the only one things happen to! You know?! I'd like to be weird! I'd love to have permission to be weird! *(Exits)*
VOICEOVER: They wash their clothes in public places.

(Jerry and Evelyn are in a laundromat—they've never met, but Jerry begins talking)

JERRY: Black eggs, warm rocks, gelatinous material falling from the sky—I mean, were these people all crazy? Think of the toads! Great storms of toads, falling in deluges, piling up on the roads. Fish! In Singapore, it rained fish. And Ed Mootz of Cincinnati had his peach tree destroyed by red glop that fell from some strange-looking cloud—there's a picture of him standing by his dead tree in a book I have at home. Angel hair and star jelly—scientists always laugh at these—but people have picked this stuff up. I'm not kidding! Not to mention the weird metal shit that falls from the sky and the ice—brains some old lady or destroys her television. And you hand 'em the goddam thing and they put it in one of those giant baggies and take it away. And that's the last you ever hear of it!

(Long beat as Evelyn looks at him)

EVELYN: People—people on game shows buying vowels because they don't know the most commonest phrase. I mean—ignorance.

JERRY *(After a beat)*: Baron Rodemire de Tarazone of France was assassinated by Claude Volbonne—twenty-one years earlier, Baron Rodemire de Tarazone's father had been assassinated and by a man named Claude Volbonne. But it was a different Claude Volbonne and they were not related!!!

EVELYN: And that second dryer is *shot!*

JERRY: I know—I lost a quarter in it last week.

EVELYN: They say they're working on these things. They say, "We're working on it!" "Lady!" But are they? I mean, where are the results?! And for that matter, where are they? Huh? When was the last time you actually saw someone in charge? I mean, in the flesh?

JERRY: On television.

EVELYN: Exactly! On television.

JERRY: On television.

EVELYN: When was the last time you saw the person who owns this laundromat? I mean, *who is in charge? Who is running this place? Huh?!*

JERRY *(Grabbing Evelyn)*: That's what I want to know!

EVELYN: That's what I want to know, too!

JERRY: I really want to know that.

EVELYN: So do I.

JERRY *(Letting go of her)*: Excuse me.

EVELYN (*Quickly folding a piece of her laundry*): I usually do this at home.

JERRY: Not me. I do it in public all the time. I think it's job stress.

EVELYN: My dryer's broken.

JERRY (*About the incompetency of the world*): Of course. Is someone working on it?

EVELYN: My husband's boss. I mean, his ex-boss, came over and tried, but . . .

JERRY: An *ex*-boss, of course. Power just . . . leaks.

EVELYN (*Thinking about Jim and everything*): How can a country that sent a man to the moon—

JERRY: Maybe they didn't. Maybe he didn't go.

EVELYN: You mean he didn't go?

JERRY: Maybe.

EVELYN: But we saw it.

JERRY: Where?

EVELYN (*Gets it*): On television! (*Pause*) How did I used to know things? I mean, when we first came here, it was just a bunch of houses built on concrete slabs. The contractor's wife named all the streets. My husband helped build it. And now you're telling me it was all a dream?

JERRY: No—no, we're awake! I know that.

EVELYN: I can't sleep.

JERRY (*Coming to her, very tender*): You need to sleep. You should sleep.

EVELYN: I'm afraid to close my eyes. Change happens so fast.

(*Jerry and Evelyn sit silently next to each other, watching the clothes turn in the dryer*)

VOICEOVER: Change happens.

(*Sound of country music—Evelyn arises from her chair in the laundromat, leaving her laundry. She crosses and exits with purpose. Jerry picks up her laundry and tries to pursue her*)

JERRY: Wait. Wait!! Wait!! Come back!! *(To audience)* Why do people always say that? Like—someone steals your car and you yell, "Hey, come back here!" like they're going to put on the brakes, back up, and give you back your car. I mean, if they wanted to come back, they would.

(Evelyn has reentered and is lying on the floor of a shower in her panties. She is curled into a tight knot. Sound of a shower dripping. She's asleep. Upstage is a bed with a large lump in it and a chair with a pile of clothes by it)

EVELYN *(A drip from the shower hits her)*: What? *(Half wakes up, shivers, reaches for something like someone who's thrown off the covers, finds a shirt, puts it on, sits up, looks up at the shower)* I'm in a shower.

VOICEOVER: She is in a shower.

(Evelyn stands, burps, waits, burps, crosses to a chair, sits. She finds a man's boots and puts them on. She finds cigarettes and lights up)

EVELYN: These aren't my boots.

VOICEOVER: Motel. Mo—tel. When a traveler is tired, a motel is used.

(Evelyn crosses to curtain, shuffling in the boots, parts the curtain, reads a neon sign)

EVELYN: Ang-La. Ang-La. Ang-La. Angri—Shangri—

VOICEOVER: She doesn't know where she is.

EVELYN: Shangri-La. Oh.

(A large mound of blankets sits up and speaks)

JACK: Baby? Where are ya?

EVELYN: Who is that?

JACK *(The mound lies back down)*: Jack. Jack. Hey, I'm a little queasy—okay, baby?

(Evelyn starts to gather her stuff, frantically)

EVELYN: What am I doing? What am I doing? Oh my God. That's it—I'm alone. *(Looks off in space for a beat while her aloneness hits her, then exits in Jack's shirt and boots)*

JACK: Evelyn? Evelyn? It wasn't charity. *(Beat. No answer)* I knew it. Damn.

(Cathy is sitting in the house, surrounded by maps—the TV is on. Jerry enters with Evelyn's laundry—he puts it down beside Cathy. Cathy looks at him and he exits. After a beat, Cathy hears someone else entering the house from the opposite direction)

CATHY: Mom?

EVELYN *(Offstage)*: Yeah?

CATHY: Where you been?

EVELYN *(Still offstage)*: Oh—out with some friends. I ran into some people I knew at the—the—they asked about your dad, so I—I. . . .

VOICEOVER: Never force anything.

CATHY: Anybody I know?

(Evelyn enters, her coat on and wearing Jack's boots, carrying a grocery bag)

EVELYN: No. Heard anything from Eric?

CATHY: No.

EVELYN *(Sits on the couch)*: Did Mike check on the planes?

CATHY: Yeah. He never got on. He cashed in the ticket. He's a missing person, Mom. *(Rattling the maps)* Look at this! Look at this! This is America. How did it get to be so enormous?

EVELYN *(Simple statement of fact)*: We took it from the Indians.

CATHY: That's not Eric's fault! I mean, what are we supposed to do with all this land?! Didn't anybody think about that?!! I mean, didn't anybody think back then that people could get *lost?!!* Didn't anybody think about the *goddam future?!*

EVELYN: What's an APB?

CATHY: I tried to get one. He's not a criminal. I'm gonna go to bed—I'm gonna sleep with this telephone.

EVELYN: Stranger things have happened.

CATHY: What's in the bag?

EVELYN: Clothes.

CATHY: Should I leave the TV on?

EVELYN: Uh-huh.

CATHY: Nice boots.

EVELYN: Thanks.

(Cathy exits with the telephone. Evelyn lies down on the couch, her head on the grocery bag, and stares at the TV. After a beat, Cathy reenters and looks at her mother with curiosity. Evelyn doesn't notice her. Unable to figure out what it is exactly that bothers her about Evelyn, Cathy quietly exits again. Evelyn flicks through the channels with the remote and finds the "Tonight Show" theme)

Heeeeeere's Johnny.

(Eric is asleep in a mall at night. Suddenly, a Muzak version of "Raindrops Keep Falling on My Head" comes over the P.A.)

VOICE ON P.A.: Hey, Haircut.

ERIC *(Waking up with a start)*: Where—where—where?!!

VOICE ON P.A.: Up here. The eye.

ERIC *(To the source of the Voice)*: Listen—they told me this was a DEAD mall. They specifically said this was a *dead* mall.

VOICE ON P.A.: "They"?

ERIC: Nobody.

VOICE ON P.A. *(Knowing that Eric is withholding names)*: Yeah. Right.

ERIC: I'm outta here. *(Starts to go)*

VOICE ON P.A.: Says who?

ERIC: I didn't touch nothin'. I didn't do nothin'.

VOICE ON P.A.: Yeah yeah. Listen, Wonder Bread. Get out of here—alright. But you tell the other "Nobodies" to stay away from here, too. And to stop sleeping in the Goodwill Box.

(Eric tries to get himself to leave—the reality of being outside alone hits him)

ERIC *(To the source of the Voice)*: Well, boy, I'm goin'. I'm outta here. *Dude.* I'm hittin' the road. I'm hittin' the fuckin' road, man. I am *out o' here. (Begins to cry.)* Mr. Eye? I'm lost.

(Static on P.A. Eric exits.

Cathy is standing, feeding Jim in the cafeteria of a nursing home. He is standing, doing a kind of frenetic bounce, like someone whose shoes are stuck to the floor would do to get free. He is staring at a door that sunlight is leaking through. He's lost a great deal of weight—we can see this because his pants are much too big for him. The shirt he's wearing isn't his own—the sleeves are a little too short. And his hair has been slicked back—the effort of a nurse's aide to make the patient look tidy)

VOICEOVER: We used to be nomads.

CATHY *(About the spoon she's holding up to his face)*: Here, Dad. Over here. Over here, Dad. Look, Dad. Please. Please, Dad. Eat. Eat something. Dad—

(He takes a bite and goes back to looking at the door and dancing)

Good! Want some more? Here's some more. Dad? Dad? Dad? Daddy? *(Holds the spoon out for a couple more beats, then lowers it to the plate)* They'll put you on an IV, Dad. In your arm. *(Takes his arm and tries to show him)* They'll put an IV in your arm. Here. If you don't eat. Do you hear me? So you gotta eat—

(Jim is staring at the door)

What's out there? It's just an old alley. It's just an old dirty alley, filled with garbage cans. And falling-down fences. And oil spots. And junk. Stay here and eat. Please.

(Jim crosses to the door in a kind of scooting walk)

No, Dad! Stay away from the door!

(Jerry enters)

JERRY: Don't worry. You have to hold something down and then pull—he won't be able to figure it out. *(About the tray)* Is he done? Well, I gotta take it anyway. *(Takes tray—shouts to Jim)* Jim! There's nothing out there! What do you want to go out there for? Here's your daughter to feed you!

CATHY *(To Jerry)*: I didn't know you worked here.

JERRY: I told you I'm a nurse.

CATHY *(To Jerry)*: Why are you so calm?

JERRY: Am I? Don't worry about the door. He'll get tired of trying. Then we'll put him to bed. *(Exits with tray)*

CATHY *(Afterthought, to Jerry)*: Wait! My father's a mechanical genius! He can figure out how anything works. You don't understand! Hey!

(Cathy gives up, looks at Jim. He's trying the door with no success. She sits and watches him as he continues to try the latch. The lights change to night, and Jim slides slowly down the door, exhausted, still holding onto the door handle)

VOICEOVER: Light change. Night.

(Jerry reenters)

JERRY: My shift's done. I thought I'd help put him to bed. *(Crosses to Jim and helps him up, removing his hand from the door handle)* Jim? Hey, you're my buddy. *(Getting him up)* That's a boy. *(Straightening out his trousers)* What you want to go out there for anyway? That big, bad world—whew, listen to the news. *(Winking at Cathy)* It's better in here. *(Presenting Jim)* Say goodnight to your daughter.

(Jim looks over Cathy's head—he doesn't seem to see her)

He says "Goodnight."

(Jerry exits with him. Cathy crosses to the door that Jim was struggling with. She opens it with ease and exits.

Cathy sits in the chair in Jerry's house. Jerry is there and they are listening to Mozart)

This music came with the house. But I would've bought some, anyway. It's nice to have you here.

CATHY: I've been here lots of times.

JERRY: You never sat down.

CATHY: Oh yeah. *(Beat)* How can you work there?

JERRY: I like to help people. I like to comfort people.

CATHY: I could use . . . that.

JERRY: Well, the world is round. And we're all on it together. Take off your blouse.

(Cathy unbuttons and takes off her blouse. Jerry crosses to her, amazed)

You're so. . . . How can you live in the world with this skin? Look at this beautiful skin.

CATHY: I'm cold. I'm cold.

(Jerry embraces her)

This is beautiful music.

JERRY: It's Mozart.

CATHY: He understood, didn't he? He *knew*.

JERRY: Yes, he did. He saw everything—

CATHY: —so clearly. It's like his heart—

JERRY: His *eyes* were open to—

CATHY: —understanding—

JERRY: —that he was being poisoned. He was being poisoned and he *knew* it.

CATHY: What?

JERRY: Mozart was being poisoned . . . what?

CATHY *(Putting on her blouse)*: I—I have to go.

JERRY: Why?

CATHY: This isn't what I meant. You don't understand.

JERRY: But I thought you finally understood. I thought that's why you were here.

CATHY: No, no—it was something about—about just trying to be alive. *(She is exiting)*

JERRY: But John F. Kennedy, Marilyn Monroe, Martin Luther King—someone murdered them, too.

(Cathy has gone. Jerry stops, looks at the audience)

It's not funny, is it? Think about it. *(To himself)* Think about it. *(Exits)*

VOICEOVER: Death and flying.

(Cathy enters, carrying two milkshakes to go. Evelyn enters)

EVELYN: Oh, honey. . . .

CATHY: What?

EVELYN: He's dead.

(Cathy just stands there, not moving for a long beat)

CATHY: But . . . I have the milkshakes.

EVELYN: I have to call people.

(Evelyn exits. Cathy crosses to the right, then to the left, then to the right, then she stops. Jim enters and talks to her, but she can't see or hear him)

JIM: I just had the most incredible dream. Honey? I dreamed I was flying, surrounded by light. But it was so real. I could feel this hot . . . wind on my neck. The tops of trees were just whizzing past below me. And, I'm not kidding, the sound of wings! I reached back to rub myself. And that's when I saw the nest and the open mouths. *(Grabs onto something that seems solid at his sides and then bends his head up and back to see what is above him. Realizes that something is clutching him.*

Looks at the audience) Oh. I get it. Beyond the light.
Angel meat. Noooo.

VOICEOVER: We hear the sound of sirens.

CATHY: Wait a minute.

(Actor/Alien enters, speaks to Cathy)

ACTOR/ALIEN: We hear the sound of sirens.

CATHY: *Not yet.*

(Cathy and Evelyn are looking at a plate of Jell-O with fruit salad suspended in it)

EVELYN: Good. Eat that. We don't have any more room in the refrigerator.

CATHY: I was just looking at it. Wondering how Judy's mom got it to . . .

EVELYN: Yeah. It's all even—the cherries and the grapes didn't go to the. . . . I don't know what to do next. We used to be nomads, you know.

CATHY: Women did all the work.

EVELYN: But it kept your mind off everything. Your husband says it's time to leave and you leave. The baby you lost, whatever, you have to leave it. Someone is always making you do something. You don't have to find a reason to go on.

CATHY: What's that? *(Sound of far-off arguing)* Judy and her mother.

EVELYN: This whole street—it's practically all women now. I thought my father knew everything when I was a girl. And then the President.

CATHY: I thought you knew everything when I was little, Mom.

EVELYN: Oh, let's not lie—after everything we've seen. *(Exits)*

CATHY *(Sensing something)*: Somebody there? *(No answer)* Somebody there?

(Eric enters)

ERIC: Whatsup, Mom.

CATHY: Oh my God! (*Stands—afraid to touch him—a long beat*)
Are you all right?

(*Eric nods*)

Grandpa's dead, Eric. And you weren't even here.

ERIC: I know.

CATHY: How did you get here?

ERIC: I called Kim for money.

CATHY: Kim?

ERIC: Kim. You know—Dad's . . . girlfriend.

CATHY: You didn't talk to your dad?

ERIC: I thought he'd be mad. (*Pause*) You look mad, too.

CATHY: You don't care about anybody but yourself!!

(*Evelyn enters*)

EVELYN: Oh—

ERIC: Hi, Grandma.

CATHY: So Kim knew where you were and didn't call me?!!!

ERIC: Only for twelve hours or so. Mom, give her a break—she's
pregnant and she's only eighteen, and—

CATHY: Oh, big deal—that's how old I was when I had you, and
you turned out just— (*Stops, unable to say "just fine"*)

ERIC: You can't even say it! It fuckin' pisses me off!! This fuckin'
life!!!

EVELYN: Eric, for crying out loud!!

ERIC: *Gramma, get off my fuckin' back!!!*

EVELYN (*Overlapping*): *Eric, how can you talk to your grandmother
that way!*

ERIC (*Overlapping*): *Leave me the fuck alone!*

EVELYN (*Overlapping*): *As long as you live in this house—*

ERIC (*Overlapping*): *Am I in this family or not?!!!*

CATHY: Wait—Wait—Come here. Both of you. There's something.

EVELYN: What?

ERIC: What, Mom?

CATHY: Something—a moment of . . . peace.

VOICEOVER: Oh—She finally has a Moment.

ERIC: Where?

EVELYN: I want that.

CATHY: Listen.

EVELYN: I hear the traffic on the interstate.

ERIC: I hear a TV.

CATHY: Listen

EVELYN: I can't hear anything.

CATHY: Something—It's going. It's gone. Never mind.

ERIC: What was it?

CATHY: I don't know. I just had this feeling that everything—

EVELYN: Will be all right? How can it?

ERIC: No shit.

CATHY: No, that everything *is* all right.

ERIC: Well, that's fucked, I can tell you that.

EVELYN: Goes double for me.

(Eric and Evelyn exit into the house)

CATHY *(After a long beat)*: Dad?

(Alien crosses right up to Cathy and looks at her face, particularly her eyes. He is puzzled by the tears he sees there)

Daddy?

(Cathy listens for Jim, decides she's missed him somehow, starts for Eric's bag. Seeing that she's disturbed, Alien gets it for her and hands it to her—she takes it as if it were levitated, and exits. Alien tries to feel the moment of peace with his hands—can't find it, gives up)

VOICEOVER: We hear the sound of sirens.

(No objection—Alien makes siren sound.
Cathy and Evelyn stand on a hill overlooking the mall.
We hear the sound of sirens)

CATHY: Look! It's Elvis Presley flying overhead.

EVELYN: Yeah. He's really burning.

CATHY: Uh-oh.

EVELYN: He'll catch those shake shingles—they'll go like— *(Snaps her fingers)*—that.

CATHY: They should've used fake ones like Denny's.

EVELYN: Is that the Pizza Hut that just went up?

CATHY: No, Mom, that's the somethingorother church.

EVELYN: Too near the mall. Big mistake.

CATHY *(Just noticing)*: The dumpster at Roy Rogers! Look, it's caught the roof!

EVELYN: There goes the Flea Market! Those booths go up fast.

CATHY: The wind is carrying it. Look! All the recliners are smoldering.

EVELYN: It's getting very close—They won't be able to keep it out. They won't be able to keep it out. Look at the sparks—

CATHY: Down the air conditioning vents.

EVELYN: Only a matter of time.

CATHY: Flaming gas running into the redwood flower boxes.

EVELYN: It's surrounded.

CATHY: It's glowing from the inside. It went up so fast.

EVELYN: The mall is burning.

CATHY: The mall is burning.

(Judy enters, carrying a small paper bag. She takes round ice cream sandwiches out and gives one to Evelyn and Cathy)

JUDY: Have a Dilly Bar.

EVELYN *(Sudden realization—the Dairy Queen has burned)*: Not the Soft Serve?

JUDY: Yes, it just blew up. Jagger helped it along. I wonder where he got the money for the gas.

(Judy and Cathy give each other a sidelong glance, then turn back to watch the fire. To Cathy:)

I was hoping you could get past your pain into Despair and/or Terror.

CATHY: You're a fine one to talk.

JUDY: Despair and Terror are intolerable.

CATHY: Yes, they lead to action. Pain is gentle. Pain is the River of Life, and you can ride it to the Sea.

JUDY: You are very introspective And somewhat articulate. You are On to Yourself. *(Pause)* You'd better eat your Dilly Bar.

CATHY: Alright. Thank you.

JUDY: Is that all you've got to say? Alright. Thank you?

CATHY: Where are the kids?

JUDY *(Points down at the site of the fire)*: Disneyland. *(Judy gives them each sunglasses to wear)* For the glare.

(They put the sunglasses on and become Aliens)

ALL *(In relief)*: Ahhhhh.

EVELYN/ALIEN: That's better.

(Cathy/Alien talks to audience—as she does, Eric/Alien enters and "shows" the kitchen chair from the beginning of the play and sets it near her. He waits while she talks)

CATHY/ALIEN: There were so many Formicans long ago. Fifteen erts ago I lived with a small group. Their culture was complex, yet strangely intangible and the artifacts are a constant source of . . . wonder. *(About the chair)* I used to know what this was for. Several of these survived.

(She and the Eric/Alien look quizzically at the chair, then at the audience.

Cathy/Alien and Judy/Alien sing—the song Judy sang as a lullaby at the end of Act One. After a few lines of the song, Jerry enters and spreads newspapers on the floor. He lies down on them, takes out a pistol, checks to see if it's loaded and puts the barrel into his mouth—he pauses. The Aliens try to soothe him with the lullaby, even though he can't see them)

JUDY/ALIEN:
O dinosaur light,
How death becomes you,

And oozes from you,
Red as Mars.
O dinosaur light,
The sky is turning,
Each night you're burning,
With the stars.

The dream of the screen door,
The dream of the stoop,
The dream of the clothesline,
The dream of the hoop,
The dream of the dirt road,
The dream of the bird,
The dream of the big tree,
The dream of the word.

O crocodile night,
You've always been there,
In the thin air,
Or on the dune.
O crocodile night,
You're always waiting,
Tonight you're mating
With the moon.

Goodnight,
Goodnight,
Goodnight,
Silence—

Goodnight.

(Judy/Alien and Cathy/Alien exit, tiptoeing to be quiet. Jerry has fallen asleep with the pistol in his mouth. He snores contentedly)

VOICEOVER: Goodnight.

NO MERCY

NO MERCY *is for my son, Sam Johnson.*

NO MERCY was presented at Actors Theatre of Louisville, March 14–22, 1986, as part of the tenth annual Humana Festival of New American Plays. The cast and creative contributors were as follows:

ROY LAYTON (YOUNG ROY)	Robert Brock
GENE PROBST	Bruce Kuhn
ROBERT OPPENHEIMER	Jonathan Bolt
JANE NEWELL	Melody Combs
ADAM NEWELL	Jeffrey Hutchinson
ROY LAYTON	Bob Burrus
RAMONA LAYTON	Adale O'Brien
JUSTIN	Joshua Atkins
JACKIE	Beth Dixon
DIRECTOR	Jackson Phippin
SETS AND LIGHTS	Paul Owen
COSTUMES	Ann Wallace
SOUND	David Strang

NO MERCY was commissioned and first presented in workshop during February 1985 by Hartford Stage Company as part of their "First Drafts," funded by a National Endowment for the Arts Special Projects grant.

CHARACTERS

ROBERT OPPENHEIMER, age 40
ROY LAYTON (Young Roy), age 20
GENE PROBST, age 20
ADAM NEWELL, age 25
JANE NEWELL, age 20
ROY LAYTON, age 60
RAMONA LAYTON, age 58
JUSTIN, age 6
JACKIE, age 35

TIME

1945 and 1985

PLACE

The West

1945 and 1985 exist simultaneously on an open and fluid stage.
The play's various locations are minimally suggested: a recliner
facing a TV set on a stand establishes Roy and Ramona's living
room; a swivel chair, Jackie's TV studio; a double bed, Adam and
Jane's bedroom. Rooms, doors, windows, mirrors, other things
referred to in stage directions to motivate actors' movements are
not meant to be actually present on the set. A sense of space, of
light and sky, must predominate.

When Jackie is speaking on camera, the actor always speaks
live, addressing the audience. When Roy and Ramona's TV is
tuned to Jackie's program, her voice is also heard coming from
their set.

Oppenheimer is lost in time. He does not appear gratuitously
or wander aimlessly, but follows a purposeful path which leads
him offstage and brings him on.

Outside on the Trinity site in the Jornada del Muerto area of southwestern New Mexico. Before dawn, July 16, 1945. Total darkness.

YOUNG ROY *(Singing)*:
 I saw the light, I saw the light,
 No more darkness, no more night.

 (Near him, someone starts to pee. Young Roy continues, but louder)

 Now I'm so happy, no sorrow in sight,
 Praise the Lord, I saw the light.

 Gene, don't be doing that while I'm singin'. Don't you have any respect?

 (Half-light up on two young soldiers. Around them on the stage, barely visible, are: a gray-haired man sitting in a recliner and holding a guitar; a nicely dressed woman sitting in a plush executive chair, her back to the audience; two sleeping forms in a double bed upstage)

GENE *(Finishing and zipping up)*: I didn't think we were in church, Roy. Hey, but you're good. You really are.

YOUNG ROY: Well, I'm getting the guitar part down really good. Hey, wait a minute. There he is.

(They look upstage. All that can be seen there is the red tip of a lit cigarette. Oppenheimer coughs several times, takes a drag of the cigarette, and then crosses quickly and exits into the offstage control shed. A bright light washes onstage briefly before he shuts the door behind him)

GENE: That the guy?

YOUNG ROY *(In admiration, bordering on awe)*: Yeah.

GENE: Rolls his own?

YOUNG ROY: Oh yeah. In the dark.

GENE: Well, once you get used to doing it. *(Takes out a pack of Lucky Strikes and lights one)*

YOUNG ROY: They had the thing on the dining-room table— in what used to be the ranch house? They were rolling it around with a stick, looking for little holes, filling them with Kleenex. Then polishing it and polishing it.

GENE: Experts.

YOUNG ROY: Then they were putting the whole *gadget* together at the tower. That's what they call it—the gadget.

GENE: The gadget.

YOUNG ROY: And that's when the storm hit.

GENE: Didn't it get all wet?

YOUNG ROY: They pitched a tent around it. And then he made them so nervous they asked him to leave.

GENE: Kicked out, huh?

YOUNG ROY: And then the thing that held the thing wouldn't fit.

GENE: Army engineers.

YOUNG ROY: No, it was all machined perfect, but it all got too hot, see? So they had to leave it to cool down.

GENE: This thing gets hot?

YOUNG ROY: Oh yeah. You shoulda heard those Geiger-counter things—going like a bunch of rattlesnakes.

GENE: You mean to tell me that this thing—whatever they call it—

YOUNG ROY: The plug.

GENE: This plug gets hot by itself?

YOUNG ROY: Yeah.

GENE: Well, where did it come from?

YOUNG ROY: They made it.

GENE: Do you think these guys really know what they're doing?

YOUNG ROY: Gene, these guys are the smartest and the best in the whole goddam country—and a few other countries thrown in. We got Germans, we got an Italian, and that Russian guy that climbed the tower and held the flashlight so they could set the cameras—

GENE: They're taking a picture of it?

YOUNG ROY: I guess. I was getting the mattresses—to put under it all in case it fell, you know.

GENE: Well, I hope they had a lot of mattresses.

YOUNG ROY: Oh yeah. Sixty-seventy, at least.

GENE: And I hope they were from the officers' quarters.

YOUNG ROY: The lightning was the worst. He asked a guy to go up and, you know, babysit it.

GENE: It?

YOUNG ROY: Yeah, *it*, all put together in the tower.

GENE: What was he supposed to do if lightning had hit it?

YOUNG ROY: I don't know. Warn us all, I guess

(The offstage door opens again, spilling light. Young Roy and Gene snap to attention)

General.

(The light disappears. The soldiers relax again)

GENE: Hey, it's gotten lighter. What time is it?

YOUNG ROY *(Looks at his watch)*: Not dawn yet.

GENE: Looks like it's clearing up.

YOUNG ROY (*Suddenly noticing the sky*): Look at that star! Boy, you can't get much brighter than that! I'm gonna tell 'em.

(*He runs toward the control-shed entrance, is met by Oppenheimer, who passes by him and enters the open area, looking at the sky*)

Are we going to go ahead now, Dr. Oppenheimer?

(*Suddenly Oppenheimer turns and exits quickly*)

GENE: Boy, he really knows who you are. Are you sure you even met him?

YOUNG ROY: Last night. I was pulling in the first load of mattresses. I caught him in the light of my flashlight. He was just sort of standing around—worrying, I think. I *recognized* him. And then he *talked* to me. He told me how he named this project—it comes from two poems.

GENE: Two poems? It took two poems?

YOUNG ROY: I told him how we came out here on the train. I mean, he *listened* to me. And he shook my hand.

GENE: Well, I don't think you're gonna make it in his memoirs.

(*Sound of a far-off and scratchy radio playing "The Star Spangled Banner"*)

YOUNG ROY: What's that?

GENE: Somebody's got a radio somewhere, I guess.

YOUNG ROY: They playing that for us?

GENE: Can't be. This is all top secret.

YOUNG ROY: Well, I'm sure they would if they could.

(*They listen in silence*)

GENE: Where were you last?

YOUNG ROY: Berlin.

GENE: I was sure I'd be in Japan by now.

(*Young Roy takes out a bottle and begins to put the contents on his face*)

GENE: What's that?

YOUNG ROY: Suntan oil.

GENE: Have you gone nuts?

YOUNG ROY: Dr. Teller gave it to me.

GENE: To wear at night?

YOUNG ROY: It's for the—explosion. It might burn.

(Young Roy offers Gene the bottle. He ignores it)

GENE: You and those longhairs.

("The Star Spangled Banner" ends)

RADIO VOICE 1: Good morning. This is KCBA, your Voice of America station. We're opening this morning with Tchaikovsky's "Serenade for Strings."

(The "Serenade" begins. The soldiers put on their welder's goggles)

YOUNG ROY: Hey, soldier, you've got a crack in your goggles.

GENE: Huh? Oh, it don't matter.

YOUNG ROY: Here. You take mine. *(He switches goggles with Gene)* You're the one who's gonna be back there with all the brass. You want to look good.

(Over the P.A. system comes a long mechanical wail)

That's it!

(Gene and Young Roy exit quickly in opposite directions. Silence for five seconds except for the sound of Tchaikovsky on the faint radio. A blinding flash. Blackout. Silence. A woman's voice)

JANE: Adam?

(Adam wakes up and kisses Jane, puts his head gently on her stomach. She is pregnant. His clock radio comes on)

RADIO VOICE: —attributed to Shiite Muslims a spokesman said today.

(Jane exits)

This is KOMA, your sound of the Eighties. Hey, if you get a chance, check out the sunrise—it's absolutely beautiful. And now for our next half hour of uninterrupted mus—

(Adam shuts the radio off; gets up, naked; goes to the window, looks out. The sunrise is particularly beautiful. He opens the window to have a better look. The sunlight hits his face)

ADAM *(Under his breath)*: My god.

JANE *(Reentering)*: Adam—

(Jane comes to Adam with a bathrobe, covering him. He exits. During the next scene, Jane makes the bed and then sits down on the end of it, exhausted, staring at herself in the mirror

    Lights up on the living room of a small tract house. A gray-haired man, dressed up except for a coat and tie, sits in the recliner and sings, accompanying himself on the guitar, which he does not play well. He wears glasses with one dark lens. This is Roy, forty years later)

ROY *(Singing)*:
I saw the light, I saw the light.
No more darkness—

(Has trouble with the chord change on the guitar, stops until he gets it, continues)

—no more night.
Now I'm so happy, no sorrow in sight.
Praise the Lord, I saw the light.
(Talking to himself) I hope they got a piano player down there. *(To Ramona, who is offstage)* Baby?

RAMONA *(Entering from the back of the house, carrying two ties)*:
What tie are you gonna wear?

ROY: I hope they got a piano player down there.

RAMONA *(About one of the ties, a striped one)*: I think this one
is good.

ROY: They told me no stripes. It does something to the cameras. (*Taking the other tie, handing Ramona the guitar*) I wish you'd come down there with me.

RAMONA (*Wiping off the guitar*): You really gonna try to play this? It's been a helluva long time. These strings look rusty.

ROY: I know, but I gotta try.

RAMONA: Now what time will you be on?

ROY: I don't know. They run all day. I could be on any time.

RAMONA: You mean I have to watch this show all day long?

ROY: Baby, if they like me, I might could be on more than once even. Wouldn't that be something?

RAMONA: Roy, you're getting your hopes up.

ROY: Better comb my hair. I don't know about this tie.

(*Roy exits to the back part of the house. Ramona is putting the guitar in its case, still shining it*)

RAMONA (*Thinking Roy is still there*): I wish you wouldn't go.

(*She goes off after Roy.
Oppenheimer reenters. He stares at Roy and Ramona's living room, Adam and Jane's bedroom, stops, thinks*)

OPPENHEIMER (*Shaking his head as he crosses*): No. No no no no no.

(*Laughs to himself, exits.
Adam reenters, wearing slacks and a shirt—his tie is untied. He's finishing a bowl of cereal. Jane ties his tie for him as they talk*)

ADAM: I have to go in a few minutes.

JANE: I know.

ADAM: We have to believe the doctors. They know what they're doing.

(*A six-year-old boy—Justin—enters, carrying a Tinker Toy construction and a box of Ivory Snow. He runs to Roy and Ramona's*

house, goes straight to the TV and turns it on. He stares at the
TV and plays with his toy)

JANE: I'll be all right.
ADAM: You'll be all right. I wish it weren't my first day.

(Jane finishes his tie)

Hey, you're getting good at that.

(Adam exits to finish getting dressed. Jane sits down on the
bed. Still in dim light, Jackie swivels to face the TV camera
and begins speaking in a pleasant, low-key and sincere
manner, almost chatty. Her voice comes from Roy and
Ramona's TV.)

JACKIE: He goes on to say that we can tell when we see all these
signs that have been predicted, like the leaves appearing on
the fig tree say what season it is to people in Israel. When we
first see these signs, that's the tribulation, when they start to
accelerate, He says that we will know that He is near, that
He is right at the door, right at the door—

(Although Justin changes the channel, Jackie continues her talk
as lights come up on her area. She has the sophistication in man-
ner and dress of a female executive. She occasionally swivels her
chair to a different camera angle.)

—ready to return. But the punch line comes next—

(Justin switches the channels very fast, finally decides on a
violent car chase and sits down in front of the TV, stares at it,
still fiddling with his toy)

—verse 34. He says, "Truly I say,"—now when Jesus says,
"Truly I say," He means to really pay attention, to stop, look
and listen. He says, "Truly I say, this generation shall not
pass away until *all* these things shall take place." Of course,
the generation He is talking about is the generation that

would see the signs begin to appear. Who would that be? Yes. Us.

(As Jackie speaks, Adam is finishing dressing for work. He comes into full view, looks into the mirror, adjusting his Air Force uniform. He puts on his hat)

We—are—that—generation.

(Adam exits)

And what does He say would happen? He says, "The generation that sees all the signs come together will be the generation that sees them all fulfilled."

(During the following, Jackie's speeches occasionally overlap Roy and Ramona's conversation)

RAMONA *(Entering and seeing Justin)*: Now what are you doing here?

JACKIE: Now, I am glad to be a part of that generation. Why?

RAMONA: Did you even knock?

JACKIE: Because I want to be part of all this famine and war and suffering?

RAMONA: You walked right in.

JACKIE: Because I want to see the world go through its worst tribulations?

RAMONA: I wish you'd talk to me sometime. Why won't you talk?

(Justin takes the Tinker Toy he's been working on and shows it to Ramona)

JACKIE: Because I want to see the nations of the world begin what most certainly will be *the* Armageddon?

(Roy enters the living room. He's wearing a Western string tie and carrying his guitar in its case)

ROY: I decided on the bolo tie.

(Justin runs out of the house, leaving his toy and Ivory Snow box)

RAMONA *(To Justin)*: Don't go!

ROY: Don't that little boy have a home?

JACKIE: No. I'm glad that I'm part of that generation Jesus talks about—the Last Generation—because I get to see the Lord in my lifetime.

RAMONA *(About Justin)*: I wonder where he lives.

JACKIE: I will get to see the Lord face-to-face in that final moment.

(Roy switches TV channels and finds Jackie)

ROY: There she is.

(Roy sits to watch Jackie. Her voice now comes through the TV speaker again, as well as being heard from her own space)

JACKIE: The Greek word for "moment" is atomos— A-T-O-M-O-S, which is the word from which we get atom—A-T-O-M, which means "that which is indivisible."

ROY: Listen to that—she really knows all this stuff.

RAMONA: No oomph.

ROY: She doesn't need oomph—she's got brains.

JACKIE: Think about it—two thousand years of waiting and *we* are the ones who will see the prophecy fulfilled at that one indivisible moment when we will see Jesus. Praise God.

ROY: This woman's got two college degrees—two of 'em.

JACKIE: So no matter how bad it gets—and it gets pretty bad sometimes—it's just birth pangs.

RAMONA: What does she know about birth pangs.

ROY: Now, baby.

JACKIE: The birth pangs of a world that's about to begin.

(Music comes out of the TV speaker. Jackie holds and then turns upstage in her swivel chair, a segment of the show being over. Ramona turns the TV off)

RAMONA: That music sounds like what you hear at the dentist's office.

ROY: Well, I guess they're trying to do something about that.

RAMONA: It's not the kind of preaching you or I was raised with.

ROY: I'm surprised you remember.

RAMONA: Roy, now don't start with me on that.

ROY: Everything she says is from the Bible. Not enough people preach the entire Bible—they just preach the parts they like.

RAMONA: Well, she doesn't sound like she likes any of it—she just drones on and on.

ROY: She's written a book, you know, about all this stuff. She knows Greek—*Greek*.

RAMONA: Roy, you always think everyone is smarter than you are.

ROY: I wish you'd come down there with me.

RAMONA: No...

ROY: We could walk around downtown.

RAMONA: No, it's too far.

ROY: You gonna leave the house today?

RAMONA: I've got too much to do.

ROY: Baby, I'm worried about you.

RAMONA: I'm worried about *you*. You can't play that guitar. You haven't sung in years. I don't know what you're doing.

ROY: It's been two months you haven't left this house.

RAMONA: That's not true.

ROY: By yourself? When was the last time you went to the grocery store by yourself?

RAMONA: I like it better when you drive me.

ROY: You hardly even go out on the lawn anymore.

RAMONA: I have trouble breathing when I get out there. I think I'm developing an allergy.

ROY: To what? What's out there? This neighborhood's beautiful—always has been.

RAMONA: It's been known to happen.

ROY: Well, I gotta go. Wish you'd change your mind. (*No answer. He kisses her*) See you later, baby.

(Roy crosses to exit with his guitar, stops to wave at Ramona. Oppenheimer enters, sees Roy and stops to stare at him, as if Roy sparked some memory. Ramona waves back and Roy exits. Confused, Oppenheimer exits the way he came, crossing near but not seeing Adam, who is entering with his briefcase. Ramona settles down in her chair to read the Sunday papers. Jackie swivels to the camera)

JACKIE: Paul tells us: "In the twinkling of an eye, we shall all be changed." Now how quick is that? *(Not moving)* 'Bout *that* quick. Want to see it again?

(She holds a smile, then swivels away from the camera, takes off her body mike and looks through her notes.
   Adam enters his bedroom, with briefcase, ready to go)

ADAM: Did I tell you about my console?
JANE: Part of the best computer system in the world. Yes.
ADAM: Did I tell you about my chair?
JANE: Better than the President's.

(Adam kneels in front of Jane and massages her legs as she talks)

ADAM: There'll be pressure.
JANE: Well, being cooped up for twenty-four hours . . . and everything . . . else. Adam, how close are you to the ah—the ah—thing.
ADAM: I never see it. Not my job, really. Hey, it's a lot better than being cooped up for nine months.
JANE: More than nine months. Adam, I can't stop worrying.
ADAM: He must like it in there.
JANE: She.
ADAM: Once I'm sealed in. You can't talk to me.
JANE: I know.
ADAM: No communication with the outside world—except NORAD in Colorado.
JANE: If you can call that the outside world.

ADAM: One of the guys said it's built on giant springs, so if there's
ever a direct hit, the whole complex sort of goes boing. It's
kinda brilliant, really. When you think about it.

JANE: How long do you have to wait for the van?

ADAM: It's always early. Because you can never be late. It's nice
down there.

JANE: You told me.

ADAM: Launch Control is one of the best assignments in the
whole Air Force. We're very lucky. We're set for life now.

JANE: Yes.

ADAM: The doctors on this base are some of the best in the
world. They're experts in their field.

JANE: Yes.

(Adam goes to the mirror. Horn honks)

You have to go. *(Holds on to him)* You have to go.

*(Adam removes her arms, turns, kisses her—she breaks it. He
leaves, looking back for something from her. She doesn't respond.
To herself:)*

You have to go.

*(Justin enters and runs to Ramona's living room. He stares at
Ramona, waiting for her to wake up)*

RAMONA *(Awake, to Justin)*: Oh, you're back! *(Getting up)* Do
you want a cookie?

(Justin nods, reaches for the cookie. She moves it away from him)

Where do you live?

*(Justin just stares at her, not speaking. She gives in, hands him the
cookie and takes him to the window)*

Can you point the direction? I bet it's up there in the circle
drives, right? Do you live on a street with a star name? An
Indian name? Why won't you talk? Hey, show me.

(Oppenheimer enters from the control shed)

OPPENHEIMER: It can't be New Mexico because I'm walking on grass. And there's a woman . . . and a child. . . . I—I can't see more . . . it's too blurry. Their movements are so slow.

(Oppenheimer crosses upstage, looks one way, considers, then exits in another direction, again near Adam, who doesn't see him. Adam crosses to wait for the elevator into the silo. During Ramona's speech, we hear the elevator arrive. Adam gets in; we hear it descend)

RAMONA *(To Justin)*: Look at this street. I used to know who lived in every single house. Everybody. We used to play Scrabble and gin rummy with those people—they're gone. We used to have barbecues with this half of the street. Now I don't know a soul there or anywhere else, for that matter. I really wonder if anyone lives in any of these houses. I see lights on in the evenings, but it seems I never see anybody come and go. Trash cans appear in the early morning and somebody carries them away. Nobody beats rugs or shakes out dust mops, any of the things that got people outside. It's like the houses are the only things that are alive. Might as well be on Mars. Mars.

(Adam steps out of the elevator and exits. Roy enters and Jackie stands when she sees him)

JACKIE: Oh—Roy Layton.

RAMONA *(Puts Justin down)*: Now, you stick around for a little while at least. Okay?

(Ramona and Justin exit to the kitchen to get more cookies)

JACKIE *(Coming to Roy)*: I heard you sing many, many years ago. It was at your church. My Aunt Dorothy introduced us.

ROY: My church?

JACKIE: Pillar of Fire. On Maple Street.

ROY: That's not my church, ma'am. I just used to sing there.

JACKIE: Oh. I'm so glad. They're exactly the opposite of what I'm trying to do here. This must be your guitar. May I . . . see it? (*Opens his case*)

ROY: You don't have a piano player, do you?

JACKIE (*Taking out the guitar, looking at it with awe*): I was twelve or thirteen. You stood in front of the altar. You sang an old hymn I'd never heard before—about the ending of the day and then the dawn?

ROY: That was the song with all the B-flat chords. They're hard.

JACKIE: I was wearing a yellow pants suit—I was the only girl there in pants. Afterwards I asked you if I could strum your guitar. You talked to me quite a while.

ROY: Uh-huh.

JACKIE: You *do* remember.

ROY: No ma'am, I don't.

JACKIE: Well, it doesn't matter. Really. Do you need to tune this . . . or anything?

ROY: If you want me to. Ma'am, I'm pretty nervous.

JACKIE: Oh, here. (*Hands the guitar to him*) Sorry. It was wonderful to see it again.

ROY: Ma'am—

JACKIE: I know—out of the clear blue I call you up. Well, I asked you here because—well, I've received some criticism that this program is rather . . . cold.

ROY: Uh-huh.

JACKIE: You *do* think it's cold.

ROY: No ma'am. I watch it every day.

JACKIE: Well, then you know what I'm trying to do here. They make me furious. And all those holy-roller churches with their falling on the floor, laying on of hands, are fooling around with something that is not in their domain.

(*Oppenheimer enters, very agitated, crosses behind Roy and Jackie and exits. No one notices him*)

Trying to bring down the power of God, attract the Holy Spirit like it's something that can come down a lightning rod if you wave it in a bad storm. A church should be built on the Word. The Word is the Church's domain. The Word. And it has to stop with that.

ROY: Really—I just used to sing there.

JACKIE: They did have the best music.

ROY: Yes ma'am.

JACKIE: What is this around your neck?

ROY: Bolo tie.

JACKIE: Oh, is this one of your hobbies—making these?

ROY: No ma'am. I bought this. New.

JACKIE: I'm sorry I got so vehement. The one thing I don't want to get is preachy.

ROY: No, I wanted to say it's been a while since I played . . . this guitar.

JACKIE: Well, we are on again in a couple of minutes. Now I'm using your song to end the program—kind of like the benediction. I'll introduce you and then I'll have to hurry around to the studio door—I'm going to stand and shake hands as the audience leaves. Now when the red light on that camera goes out, you're off. But just finish the song anyway, like you would normally. By the way, please sing something other than "I Saw the Light"—the new Hank Williams biography has really devalued him for Christians. You understand. Nothing personal.

ROY: Ma'am. I don't want to do this.

JACKIE: Why not?

ROY: I can't. I can't play this guitar anymore. Simple as that.

JACKIE: Oh. My. They wanted—specifically asked for a guitar. You know, to increase the . . . warmth factor.

(*Jane is sitting on the bed talking on the phone. She is upset*)

JANE: Yes, that's who I mean. He's a new Launch Control Officer—

ROY: Well, I guess that does it. (*Puts his guitar back in the case*)

JANE: Yes, L.C.O.—whatever. (*Pause*) His wife.

JACKIE: Wait. Wait. I'll think of something. Sit here. I'll come up with something.

(*Roy puts his guitar down and sits off-camera. Jackie returns to her chair and waits for her camera cue*)

JANE: I know his duty just started, but this is kind of an emergency. No, I'm not in labor—that's the problem. Yes, this is our first baby. Thank you. Are they sealed in the control room yet? I thought it took longer. No. I—I just need to talk to him. I understand. I understand.

JACKIE: I want to talk to you today about something that most preachers never speak about although it's found throughout the Bible.

JANE: I understand.

JACKIE: I'm talking about what will happen to each one of you on that day at that last moment.

JANE: I understand.

(*Sits holding the telephone receiver for several beats, desolate, not knowing what to do.*

Ramona, looking at her watch, enters with Justin. They have a plate of cookies)

RAMONA: Better turn the TV on—don't want to miss Roy.

(*Ramona turns it on. Jackie is heard through the TV*)

JACKIE: Today we're looking at the Rapture, that moment when "we shall be changed, in the twinkling of an eye." Now the word *rapture* means—this is from Webster's Dictionary:

RAMONA: I wonder who does her hair? (*Sits down*)

JACKIE: —"the state of being transported by lofty emotion; ecstasy or the transporting of a person from one place to another, especially to heaven." So plane, bus, train, or Rapture—all forms of transportation.

RAMONA *(Takes a small snapshot out of her pocket and shows it to Justin)*: This is my boy.

JACKIE: What it is is the coming of Christ for the Church in which He instantly catches up all living believers to meet Him in the air and translates them into perfect and immortal bodies without them experiencing physical death.

(Justin gives snapshot back to Ramona)

So you could be Raptured, like that, and someone is standing there looking at a pair of your empty shoes.

(Ramona turns the volume down)

There are signs leading up to the Rapture, of course. And these I was describing earlier this morning. But they are all part of the Tribulation—Armageddon being the climax of many years of suffering, war, natural disasters, droughts, world famines. And can any of us deny that these signs are present and increasing? All we need to do is watch the news, read the paper. And any of us then might pray that we might be Raptured before we have to witness any more suffering.

I, myself, many times think it should happen now because the world has had enough. When I see the faces of children who are starving because a drought has ravaged their country, or a war has ravaged their country, or I see bodies being removed from the site of an earthquake and people wandering, looking for a lost father or a daughter, I—planes with bombs over our heads right now! The leaders of the world . . . no one is doing anything, no one is listening. IT'S COMING. WHO'S READY? DEAR GOD.

(Disoriented by this sudden burst of emotion, Jackie finds herself on her feet. She looks briefly at Roy, confused, sits down and finds her place in her notes. Roy stares at her)

The word *rapture* comes from the Greek *harpazo*, which is translated as "caught up." That moment of Rapture is prophesied by Matthew: "For as the lightning comes from the east, and flashes even unto the west; so shall the coming of the Son of Man be."

(Roy experiences a sharp pain in his blind eye. He snatches off his glasses and covers his eye)

And now the final word will be a benediction sung by an old friend of mine, Roy Layton. I've asked Roy to sing a cappella so that we can all carry just the words away with us. And I'll be at the studio door ready to shake hands with all those who worshipped here with us today. Roy? Roy—

(Roy comes to and stands. Jackie signals to the booth and exits quickly)

RAMONA: That *is* Roy! But where are his glasses?
ROY: *(Singing)*
The sun is slowly sinking,
The day is almost gone,
Still darkness falls all around us,

(Oppenheimer crosses laterally, stops when he hears Roy's singing, watches him)

And we must journey on.
The darkest hour is just before dawn,
The narrow way leads home,
Lay down your soul at Jesus's feet,
The darkest hour is just before dawn.

(During the song, Jane leaves her bedroom and walks straight across the stage to Roy. He doesn't see her until the end of his song, when she is right in front of him)

JANE: Help me.
ROY: What?
JANE: Please, I'm overdue. I'm scared.
ROY: Ma'am, I think I'm on television here.

(Ramona stands up in front of her TV. Roy looks up helplessly at the control booth, gets nothing)

Don't you need a doctor?

JANE: I have doctors at the base. But they won't help me. They won't even tell me anything. *(Takes Roy's hands and puts them on her stomach)* Please. Please. You can start now.

ROY *(Taking his hands away)*: I'm not a faith healer, ma'am.

JANE: I have faith. *(Putting his hands back)* Please. I know it will help.

ROY: I—I bless thee in the name of the Father, and the Son—

JANE: No! That's for when it's born. I need something for now. *Please.*

(Jackie enters)

ROY *(Closing his eyes in panic)*: Dear Jesus.

JANE: I—I feel something!

ROY: Dear God.

JANE: I FEEL SOMETHING! I FEEL SOMETHING! I—

(Jane collapses in Roy's arms and he lowers her to the ground. Jackie runs to help. The TV program goes to static and Ramona pounds the TV and switches channels, trying to get Roy back)

RAMONA: Damn TV! Dammit!!

(Justin picks up his toy and Ivory Snow box and is gone before Ramona can stop him. Oppenheimer stares at Roy)

OPPENHEIMER: Something about him. Something about him.

(Roy stands up. Jackie stays with Jane. Oppenheimer moves to Jane's bed and sits on it, after testing it to make certain it's real. He remains very interested in what he can see in the TV studio.
Ramona sits on the edge of her chair, staring at the empty television. After a moment she begins looking through the phone book. During the following action, she finds the number, dials, gets a busy signal, dials, until she finally gets through)

JANE: What happened?

JACKIE: You fainted.

JANE: No. No. It was wonderful. I felt something—I felt tingly and then just floated away. That's the first time anything like that has ever happened to me. (*To Jackie*) Do you think the feelings I had went down to the baby?

JACKIE: I—I don't know. Do you feel alright?

JANE (*Interrupting*): I'm not really, that religious—no offense. I was just so desperate—all I wanted was to just know I tried. So I could have a little peace. But this—

(*Gets up—Jackie helps her—and crosses to Roy*)

I just want to say. That you're a real preacher.

(*Jane takes Roy's hand and kisses it, then exits, ignoring Jackie's efforts to help her. Jackie signals to someone offstage to help Jane*)

RAMONA (*On the phone*): Hello? I'm looking for my husband. Roy Layton. The singer. Can you have him call his wife? His *wife*.

(*Oppenheimer begins to roll a cigarette, not taking his eyes off Roy*)

JACKIE (*To Roy*): What happened?

ROY: I don't know. We aren't still on, are we?

JACKIE: No, thank God. Did she just faint?

ROY: I don't know.

JACKIE: You don't know?

ROY: I never done it before in my life. Honestly. She took my hands, put them on her stomach. What could I do?

JACKIE: You could take your hands away!

ROY: How could I? She looked up at me and said "I have faith." When people have that much faith, what do you do? Don't you give them what they want?

JACKIE: You could just pray for her.

ROY: I did. That's what I did.

(Phone rings at Ramona's. She answers it quickly)

JACKIE: And then she fainted. *(No answer from Roy)* And then she fainted. Pregnant women faint.

RAMONA: Yes?

ROY: I guess so.

RAMONA: I was hoping you were someone else.

JACKIE: That's all it was then, wasn't it?

RAMONA: Can't you keep track of that little boy?

ROY: I'm just a singer. And not a very good one.

RAMONA *(Still on the phone)*: Well, I understand that you're just the babysitter, but—. Yes, he usually drops in once a day. A couple of times today. Listen, I'm expecting an important phone call.

(Jackie crosses to Roy, takes both his hands and looks at them. Oppenheimer stands)

JACKIE: When I heard you sing that time you don't remember. I didn't tell you—you made me cry.

ROY: Baby doll, that was the song. It was the song.

(Jackie exits)

RAMONA: Uh-huh. Well, it's nice to finally know where he lives. No, I'll be here. I'm always here. Right. *(Hangs up the phone, crosses to the picture window and stares out)* This world. *(Turns the TV on)* I dunno. I dunno.

(Alone, Roy stares at his hands)

ROY: Like electricity coming down my arms.

(Ramona sits in the recliner)

RAMONA: Little boy. Little boy.

*(Ramona closes her eyes.
    Roy senses the presence of someone)*

OPPENHEIMER: Something about him.

ROY *(Not seeing Oppenheimer)*: Who's there?

(Ramona is asleep in her chair, the TV on but nothing on the screen except light. It is now late at night. Justin enters and goes to the kitchen cupboard, looking for cookies. Instead he finds a box of Ivory Snow and brings it back into the living room. He likes the picture on the box—it's a mother holding a baby. He curls up with it beneath the light of the TV screen. Ramona sleeps through the next scene. Roy exits, passing Young Roy, who enters pulling a large cart filled with Army-issue mattresses secured with ropes. He shines a flashlight in Oppenheimer's eyes)

YOUNG ROY: Who's there?

(Oppenheimer finds himself at Jornada del Muerto, the Trinity site, in the shadow of the tower that holds the gadget. It is the day preceding the test, just before dawn)

OPPENHEIMER: What?

YOUNG ROY: Dr. Oppenheimer?

OPPENHEIMER: Yes, yes. Can—can you turn that light off?

YOUNG ROY *(Turns it off)*: Sorry, sir.

(Young Roy approaches the tower base, walks under it cautiously, looks up at where the gadget is suspended and rolls the cart to what he thinks is a spot directly under the gadget. With shaking hands, Oppenheimer starts to light a cigarette he rolled while watching the previous scene.

About the proximity of the gadget to the match:)

You gonna light that here? Sir?

(Oppenheimer looks at Young Roy for a beat, then at his own hand, as if he never saw it before)

OPPENHEIMER: I don't remember rolling this. *(Lights his cigarette. This brings on a bad coughing spell. When he's done, he looks at his watch)*

YOUNG ROY (*About the mattresses*): They're bringing some more. In a truck. From Base Camp.

(*Pause. Oppenheimer nods, distracted*)

They think ten to twelve feet. Will that do it?

OPPENHEIMER: Do what?

YOUNG ROY: Cushion the fall. Just in case.

OPPENHEIMER: Just in case?

YOUNG ROY: It falls.

OPPENHEIMER: It?

YOUNG ROY: The gadget. Are you all right, Dr. Oppenheimer?

OPPENHEIMER: I'm just kinda tired. I think I nodded off . . . I was in the control shed and then I wandered—no, this is the tower . . . I was up on the tower checking the . . .

YOUNG ROY: Gadget.

OPPENHEIMER (*Snapping to*): The gadget? It's not going to fall. It's secure.

YOUNG ROY: Well, as they say, better safe than sorry, sir.

OPPENHEIMER: Who are you exactly?

YOUNG ROY (*Coming to attention and saluting*): Corporal Roy Layton, sir.

OPPENHEIMER: How do you do. (*Looking at watch again*) Where is everybody?

YOUNG ROY: Getting the mattresses.

OPPENHEIMER: Oh. Right. That's good. I'm—I'm waiting . . . here. Here.

YOUNG ROY (*Readjusting the cart, looking up at where the gadget would be*): Excuse me, sir, but what do you think? Is this a good way to do it? Or should they be just laid on the ground? Maybe in a wide circle? Or just piled up every whichaway? What do you think? Sir?

OPPENHEIMER: What?

YOUNG ROY: What do you think about this configuration of mattresses here?

OPPENHEIMER: That will probably be fine.

YOUNG ROY: Yes, sir.

OPPENHEIMER: Where *is* everybody?

YOUNG ROY: Any minute now. They only went ten miles.

OPPENHEIMER: What? Oh.

YOUNG ROY: Everything going all right, sir?

OPPENHEIMER: I think I need to get to my next . . . stop.

YOUNG ROY: All the vehicles are gone.

(*Oppenheimer crosses to Roy's guitar, left from the previous scene, and picks it up*)

Oh, that's mine. (*Takes it and puts it upstage, near the mattresses*)

OPPENHEIMER: I've just been so tired. We've been working so hard. It's been very hard, particularly these last few months. Hornig called in for the weather report yesterday—fell asleep on the radio, waiting for the answer. I just now nodded off myself. Had a dream—classic—like running for a train, never catching it. I was in a place, a lot like here, but different. . . . There was a woman and a child. Strange. Even now, I feel groggy. In parallax, like a camera. You look up here at an image that's coming through down there backwards and upside down. You look familiar. I feel like what you say, you've said before. What we do is. . . . Even those goddam mattresses . . .

YOUNG ROY: I'd be glad to drive you anywhere you want to go. Drove Dr. Teller the other day. He's a helluva guy. He's famous, isn't he? Not that you're not, sir.

OPPENHEIMER: That's all right. I'm not. Fermi is the famous one. *Fermi. Fermi.* Yes, I talked to him last night! (*He's relieved—a familiar name*)

YOUNG ROY: Everything is all right, isn't it, sir? I mean *it's*— (*Motioning to the gadget*)—okay, isn't it?

OPPENHEIMER (*Patting Young Roy's shoulder and arm to establish that he's real*): Everything's—going—as—scheduled. Yes, that's right. I'm certain of that. I had a bad night last night— coughing. That's why I'm so tired.

YOUNG ROY: I was there at the ranch house, you know. When they were putting the two halves together and polishing it.

OPPENHEIMER: So you are—somebody I work with . . . ?

YOUNG ROY: I was there in one of the jeeps.

OPPENHEIMER *(A memory comes)*: With the motor running? With the motor running!

YOUNG ROY: We were ordered to do that, sir. So you all could make a quick getaway in case it blew.

OPPENHEIMER *(Joyous)*: In case it blew! Right!

YOUNG ROY: So that was a close call, huh? I wondered about that. I did. Boy, it was pretty scary, I can tell you now. Sitting out there, waiting, not knowing if the whole thing was gonna go blewey or not!

OPPENHEIMER: Go blewey?

YOUNG ROY: Blow up! Explode! And take alla us with it.

OPPENHEIMER: The plug would never blow up by itself.

YOUNG ROY: Right. What?

OPPENHEIMER: Would never happen. What do you think we've spent all this time on? I mean, we're worried sick that this goddam firing mechanism isn't going to work. *Yes.* YES!! That's it! That's what's next! Oh, thank God. WE'RE TESTING IT NEXT. THE FIRING MECHANISM!

(Oppenheimer laughs with relief. Young Roy, as excited as Oppenheimer, whoops in joy. Exhilarated, they scramble to the top of the mattress pile)

YOUNG ROY: Great. Great! I'm excited, too. I have to tell you, sir, ever since I got here—there's something about this place.

OPPENHEIMER: Do you really think so?

YOUNG ROY: There's something about it.

OPPENHEIMER: It is beautiful, particularly right now, for some reason. Some people find it barren.

YOUNG ROY: No place in this country is barren, sir.

OPPENHEIMER: They call this place the Jornada del Muerto, you know.

YOUNG ROY: What's that—Spanish?

OPPENHEIMER: The conquistadores. Cheerful bunch.

YOUNG ROY: What's it mean?

OPPENHEIMER: Journey of Death. I'm suddenly so happy. I don't know why.

YOUNG ROY: I thought this was called Trinity.

OPPENHEIMER: No. That's just the project and the buildings and all that.

YOUNG ROY: I just wondered what the name meant.

OPPENHEIMER: Well, the Trinity—

YOUNG ROY: I know what the Trinity is, sir. I was just wondering what all this has to do with the Father, the Son, and the Holy Ghost.

OPPENHEIMER: Nothing—I—I named it that. I never thought that it might offend anybody.

YOUNG ROY: No offense taken, sir.

OPPENHEIMER: Of course, I realize now how it might—

YOUNG ROY: Oh, it's a nice title, sir. Don't get me wrong. I just wondered, you know.

OPPENHEIMER: They called me in Berkeley for a name. And I had been reading a poem by John Donne—he was a *minister*, you know:

As West and East in all Flatte Maps are One,
So Death doth touch the Resurrection.

YOUNG ROY: Uh-huh.

OPPENHEIMER: Death *touches* the Resurrection.

YOUNG ROY: Uh-huh.

OPPENHEIMER: And it's quite flat out here.

YOUNG ROY: Okay.

OPPENHEIMER: And I thought of my favorite poem by this same minister:

Batter my heart, three-person'd God—

(Skipping to the last two lines)

Unless you enthrall me, I never shall be free,
And ne'er be chaste unless you ravish me.

(Young Roy really doesn't get this one at all. He waits, instead of replying)

Batter my heart, *three*-person'd God.

(Young Roy just continues to look at him)

We needed a name.

YOUNG ROY: Well, it's sure better than Journey of Death.

(They laugh)

OPPENHEIMER: Last night Fermi was taking bets on whether the explosion would just suck all the oxygen out of New Mexico or out of the entire Northern Hemisphere. He looked up at the Oscuras—that mountain range—at sunset—they were never more beautiful. And all he could say is, "Ah, the earth on the eve of destruction." Just then, a tarantula sidled up next to him. He ran in *real* terror then. Oh shit. I shouldn't be telling you that.

YOUNG ROY: Oh, that's all right, sir. I'm not afraid of tarantulas. I'm really not afraid of anything out here. Two months ago, if I thought I'd be here in New Mexico, well, I would've laughed. I got my orders home in Berlin, and they told us we'd get a month off then go back to, you know, clean up. But when I reported for duty, they put us on this train and the next thing I know, we're heading west. A whole train full of soldiers heading west for no reason. Seemed like then. And we stopped in Nebraska—*Nebraska*—for three days and played baseball to kill time. And still we have no idea where we were going or why. And then, and then, back on the train and further west, and the ground starts to change. My buddy wakes me up and presses my face to the window. Lord! There's a herd of antelope galloping alongside the train and I look up and got my breath took away again!

Mountains! Blue-green, almost black the pine is so thick. They are so still and big, they look painted on. Well, that's when I knew I was going somewhere important. Something about the speed of that train—I swear once we got close to here, we went faster and faster—I think those guys could've lost control like *that*. (*Snaps fingers*) I mean, that prairie blurred into the desert and the day went *by*. And then, bang, we were stopped. 'Cause we were here. Stopped. Dead. And it was so quiet. The sky was full of stars. And I could feel that train moving inside me for the whole next day.

OPPENHEIMER: Then you've been away in the war quite a while.

YOUNG ROY: Yes sir.

OPPENHEIMER: Three years?

YOUNG ROY: Yes sir.

OPPENHEIMER: And they send you home for just thirty days and then out here?

YOUNG ROY: I'm not complaining. This is just about the most exciting thing that has ever happened, sir. I mean, I missed the invention of the motor car, I missed Christopher Columbus, I missed the time when Lord Jesus was walking around on earth, I missed the invention, no, *discovery* of electricity. I was beginning to think that absolutely nothing was ever gonna happen to me. You know?

When I think that the smartest men, why, in the whole world are here. And all the knowledge that's went into this, from way back there. When the first guy got an idea, like a little light bulb going on over his head, and, wham, he invents that light bulb. And then another guy makes it better. And another guy says, "We got a light bulb, we need a socket." And, wham, we got a socket. And then a lamp. And then, the next thing you know, the whole world is lit up. Lamps everywhere! No more darkness.

OPPENHEIMER:

If the radiance of a thousand suns,
Were to burst at once into the sky—

YOUNG ROY: Was that from the Bible?

OPPENHEIMER: It's from something called "The Song of the Lord."

YOUNG ROY: Our Lord—Lord Jesus?

OPPENHEIMER: An ancient prince—that kind of lord. He's supposed to go into battle. All his enemies are assembled. But he won't go—he has doubts. But *his* god, Krishna, appears to him. Blazing and radiant with light and with many arms, all holding weapons. And then Krishna shouts, "I am become Death—"

(Oppenheimer stops. Long pause)

YOUNG ROY: Is that how it ends?

OPPENHEIMER: No . . . no . . . Krishna shouts, "I am become death—the shatterer of worlds."

YOUNG ROY: And that does it, huh? That's all it takes, I bet.

OPPENHEIMER: He goes into battle. He goes and—

YOUNG ROY: Wins? Right? He wins. There's your happy ending. You see? You see, now that's what we call a good omen where I come from. Like when you open the Bible with your eyes closed and you read whatever verse your finger falls on? And that verse has meaning for you right then? You were meant to read it. Like now, you were meant to think of that poem.

OPPENHEIMER: I remember now. I remember this.

(Horn honks offstage)

YOUNG ROY: Hey, they're here! With the mattresses! (*Jumps down off the mattresses*) I'll be there tomorrow morning, sir. I get to be in one of the trenches. A kind of forward observer.

OPPENHEIMER: You haven't seen it. You haven't seen it yet.

YOUNG ROY: That's right! That's exactly it! 'Cause you can't even begin to imagine. 'Cause you just know it's gonna be incredible. Oh, sir, it's gonna go great. And then you'll be able to get some sleep, you'll see. Can I shake your hand? I want to tell my kids someday.

(Oppenheimer leans down from the top of the mattresses and shakes Young Roy's hand. Oppenheimer tries to hold on to Young Roy briefly, but he disappears into the darkness. Oppenheimer lies back on the mattresses, confused and desolate.

At Roy's and Ramona's house it is now morning. The TV is still on. Justin is gone. Ramona wakes up suddenly in her chair)

RAMONA: Oh my God. *(Gets out of the chair)* Oh my God. What time is it? *(Goes to the back bedroom)* Roy? Roy! You let me *sleep* in my chair! Roy? Roy—*(Reenters the living room looking for him, then goes into the kitchen, growing more frantic)* Roy? ROY! *(Stands bewildered at her front door)* Maybe it's a binge. Maybe he just went out on a binge—

(Young Roy appears, inebriated and trying desperately to cover it up. He is in uniform and carrying a duffel bag. One eye is covered with a bandage)

YOUNG ROY: Hi, baby. I had an accident. Didn't want to tell you when I called you from New Mexico. They sent me home on a plane! An airplane! *(Coming to her)* I saw something incredible in New Mexico. Something incredible. But I can't talk about it. I can't talk—*(Kissing her gently)* I'm sorry I'm late. I lost track of the time. Okay? Okay? I lost track of the time.

RAMONA: Roy—

(Young Roy passes Ramona and crosses into the house. He stops and puts his hand on his bandaged eye—the pain stopping him. Roy, age 60, approaches the house)

ROY *(Starting to talk the moment he sees Ramona)*: It's like something you always knew, deep inside you. You *knew*.

(Young Roy exits into the back of the house)

And one day someone says it and *wham*! It all breaks loose! Of course. Of course, death *meets* the Resurrection.

RAMONA: Where have you been? Where are your glasses?

ROY: Now I know. There was some reason why I was there, some reason why this—(*Points to his blind eye*)—happened to me. With this eye—(*His good eye*)—I see this world. And with my blinded eye, I got to see the next.

RAMONA: I remember—I remembered.

ROY: I been walking all around. Looking at everything. Just in case. Saying goodbye.

RAMONA: And you never talked about it again.

ROY: 'Cause it can happen any moment—"In the twinkling of an eye, we shall all be changed." Like that.

RAMONA: What happened, Roy?

ROY: Do you know how many neighborhoods there are around us? Islands of houses everywhere. And each house has people in it, and God watches over every single one of them. How does He keep track? How does He keep track?

RAMONA: Where's your guitar?

ROY: Oh, I don't need it anymore. I sing by myself. I make people *cry*.

RAMONA: Roy, honey, come in now. Come on in.

ROY: I hate to. I hate to. Come to me.

(*Ramona comes to him. He puts his arm around her shoulder*)

Look. (*He's still looking at the world*) It's a shame, isn't it.

(*Blast of light and, this time, a rumble that grows until it simulates the real blast at the Trinity site. When it stops, Roy and Ramona stand still and Oppenheimer stands on top of mattresses, looking at the mushroom cloud of the test. Cheers and shouts can be heard everywhere: "It worked! It worked! Oh my God, it worked!" Gene comes running in, his goggles around his neck. He sees Oppenheimer, but not Roy and Ramona. He acts as if it's natural that Oppenheimer is on top of the mattresses. He's very excited*)

GENE: It worked!! It worked!! Hey, Dr. Oppenheimer! The war is over for sure now, huh? Colonel Kisto—, Kistow—, the Russian guy? Says you owe him ten dollars.

OPPENHEIMER *(Climbing down, looking in his billfold)*: I—I'll have to pay him tomorrow.

GENE: Tomorrow! Right! We got a million of 'em now the war is over! I have to admit, I never thought it would work.

(Gene grabs Oppenheimer's hand and shakes it. Oppenheimer sees Roy and Ramona and runs after Gene as he exits)

OPPENHEIMER: Help me! *(Exits)*

RAMONA: I can't breathe. I have to go in.

ROY: Stay. Stay with me. My whole life makes sense now. I see it all.

RAMONA: Roy, when our boy was killed, you did this. You stayed up for two days figuring it all out. Do you remember?

ROY: I even figured that out now. You see, Danny was conceived right before I went to work on the bomb. Maybe right at the time—when the die was cast, and I was going to be there. So he had to die, you see.

RAMONA: He did not have to die! You can't tell me he had to die! Roy, you've gone too far. People die all the time and none of it makes any sense!

ROY *(With increasing agitation)*: His father conceived him and went immediately to a place called Journey of Death which was also called Trinity. You see? Father, Son, and Holy Ghost. And finally, the last piece is there. I healed somebody, Ramona. The Holy Ghost came down my arms and into this woman's body. I could feel it, Ramona, like electricity coming down my arms. It was real. And she could feel it, too. And she wasn't even religious. I know that's what the Holy Ghost is, then—electricity, coming down my arms. God's like lightning coming through us into the world.

RAMONA *(Trying to bring him out of it)*: Roy, you're not part of the Trinity. Or some place called Journey of Death. Some person named those places, not God. You're my Roy—that's who you are.

ROY: But I'm trapped there, Ramona. I'm caught.

RAMONA: Roy, that was forty years ago!

ROY: Forty years ago I saw with my own eye what everybody's been waiting for since the world began!

RAMONA: What? What?

(Oppenheimer enters, still chasing Gene, but finds himself back where he started. He stops when he sees Roy and Ramona)

ROY: The end! I saw it! For real with one of my eyes! And then the power of God came down my arms. So it does all make sense!

RAMONA: No. No!

ROY: You see, Ramona, I was never really sure that God existed. I believed it, of course. But I didn't *think* it. But now I have proof. I have a fact. So that means—that means it's all true. The Bible, Revelations, Hell—it's really gonna happen. Trinity. Trinity. Baby, we're caught.

RAMONA *(Running into the house)*: NO.

(Roy stays outside. Oppenheimer watches him during the next scene. Ramona notices something out the picture window. It is Jackie coming up the walk. She is carrying Roy's guitar in its case. She's dressed in the same clothes, looks disheveled. She looks through the window of the front door. Ramona opens the door and looks at Jackie)

JACKIE: Is Roy here?

RAMONA: He's at work.

JACKIE: I—I need to talk to him.

RAMONA: He's not here.

JACKIE: I have to tell him something.

RAMONA: Oh?

JACKIE: This is his guitar.

RAMONA: I see.

JACKIE: We were at the hospital all night, Mrs. Layton. That woman came down during the program yesterday and asked

for the laying on of hands . . . I don't do that. I didn't want
my church to be a carnival, accent on the carnal.

RAMONA: Well, that's a comfort.

JACKIE: And then her water broke, and the baby started to
come. We made it to the hospital all right. (*Breaks down*)
I'm sorry. I've been up all night.

RAMONA (*Taking the guitar*): Why don't I take this now.

(*Jane enters her bedroom. She is in the dress she wore at the
TV studio*)

JACKIE: They called the base and her husband was on his way.
He'd just gotten off duty—they couldn't get hold of him.
She wouldn't stay, so I took her home.

(*Jane crawls onto the bed painfully and curls up on her side*)

Roy doesn't know. The baby died.

(*Roy enters*)

The baby died, Mrs. Layton. (*She and Roy see each other*)
You have to tell him.

(*Jackie exits quickly. Ramona turns and sees that Roy has heard.
She tries to touch him, but he turns from her and crosses numbly
to the door and goes outside. She exits into the back of the house.
Adam enters his bedroom, still in his uniform*)

ADAM: NO!!!!!

(*Adam crosses and looks at Jane in bed. She doesn't look at him.
Oppenheimer crosses to Roy and speaks to him*)

OPPENHEIMER: It was like a wheel that somebody started
rolling a long time ago. As a discovery, it was beautiful, as all
pure knowledge is. It's the same wheel that transported us
this far, and into—

ROY: —Rapture.

OPPENHEIMER: When you're at the door, don't you go through it? Particularly when you turn around and see there's a line forming behind you? You can't stop reaching for mystery.

(During this, Adam climbs into bed behind Jane, his uniform still on)

ROY: You can leave. You can put your hands in your pockets and just go home.
OPPENHEIMER: I know you now.
ROY: I carried the mattresses.
OPPENHEIMER: Yes. *Yes.* You helped me that day. You had such faith.

(Roy looks at Oppenheimer for a beat, then crosses to his house and enters. He turns on the TV, keeping the volume low. The music for Jackie's program begins. Roy sits down. Oppenheimer lights a cigarette, turns and exits, coughing. Jackie enters the TV studio, carrying a Bible. She is in the same clothes. She motions for the booth to cut the music. She addresses the audience, not the camera, and doesn't sit in her chair)

JACKIE: I'm unprepared. This won't be a lesson. For those of you who got out your world maps, I'm sorry—I don't want to talk about history tonight . . . or prophecy.

    (Jumping to something she knows, reading) Matthew: "And in the fourth watch of the night, Jesus went to them, walking on the sea. When the disciples saw Him walking on the sea, they were terrified, and said it is an apparition and cried out for fear. Thereupon Jesus spake to them, saying, 'Take courage, it is I. Be not afraid.' And Jesus called to Peter, saying, 'Come, Peter, come.' So Peter came down out of the ship, and walked on the water, to go to Jesus. But perceiving that the wind was strong, he began to sink, and cried out, saying, 'Master, save me.' And Jesus immediately stretched forth His hand and took hold of him, saying, 'O ye of little faith, why didst thou distrust me?'"

I've been thinking a lot about Peter. Out in that boat.

I had to sit somewhere last night and wait. There was nothing else I could do. It seemed I had done everything I could do, and it wasn't enough. I'd never had a time quite like that. I guess I'm inexperienced.

I got into this because I was touched a long time ago by a human life, by the life of one man, Jesus. He was the first really friendly person I ever met in the Bible, and I felt I knew Him. I never really understood the mystery of His life, I never really figured out, even with all my study, how He could die for my sins. And, frankly, no one has ever really explained to me how that really works. But now, even talking about it in front of all of you—I feel very moved.

I think we're the brightest animal that God made. In fact, we're God's spoiled brat, sometimes. We're so smart, so bright, so intelligent that we don't *think* we believe in anything anymore. We *think* we don't have any faith. The one thing that most people do have faith in is how much faith they *don't* have.

So . . . where was I? Peter, yes. (*Reading from the Bible*) "So Peter came down out of the ship, and walked on the water, to go to—" (*Stops for a second, looking hard at the page*)

Peter "came down out of the ship" and he "walked on the water." Maybe it was only a couple of steps, but he did walk on water. Peter was *walking* there . . .

(*Roy crosses to the TV*)

So how much faith do we need?

(*Roy turns the TV off*)

How much faith do we need?

(*Roy sits in the recliner. Jackie exits. After a beat, Justin's toy is thrown up on top of the mattresses, then the Ivory Snow box. Justin appears, climbing up. He arranges the Ivory Snow box so he can see the picture, then lies down on top of the mattresses and goes to sleep. Ramona enters from the back of her house, talks to Roy)*

RAMONA: I thought you were laying down.

ROY: Couldn't.

RAMONA: Grocery store's open late tonight. We could get a head start on the week.

(Roy gets up numbly)

ROY: Okay.

RAMONA: Roy, please. It's like living with a dead person.

ROY: I'm sorry, baby.

RAMONA: Roy, we just had a bad time. Everybody has them, sometimes. (*Embraces him*) Lookee here—bet you thought I forgot this one.

(Ramona sings and rocks Roy. Jane gets up out of bed and goes to the mirror, leaving Adam asleep)

What a fellowship,
What a joy divine,
Leaning on the everlasting arms.
What a blessedness—

(Roy stops Ramona)

ROY: No more.

(Phone rings. Ramona answers it. Roy puts his glasses on)

RAMONA: Yes. No, not today. Oh no. Oh, don't. Don't. Of course I will. Yes. (*Hangs up the phone*) He's been lost before.

ROY: Who?

RAMONA: Little boy. Justin. But he always comes *here*.

ROY: Oh, that little boy.

RAMONA: Every day he comes to see me.

ROY: Oh baby, he'll be all right.

RAMONA: It's just so late, Roy. That was his mother on the phone—she's home for once. She was crying.

ROY: It is late. Well, they'll call the police.

RAMONA: She said the police are looking. They've been looking most of the day.

ROY: They'll find him. They're experts at it. Those guys know what they're doing.

RAMONA: Roy, you always say that.

ROY: I do? (*Pause*) I do.

RAMONA: Yes.

ROY: I'll get the flashlights. (*Exits to the back of the house*)

RAMONA (*Taking the afghan from the back of the recliner*): I'll take this—just in case he's gotten wet. I'll leave the TV on for him.

(*Roy returns with the flashlights*)

ROY: We'll have better luck if we split up.

RAMONA: Outside . . . by myself . . . in the dark?

ROY: I know, baby. What's his name again?

RAMONA: Justin.

(*They go outside*)

It's so dark, Roy.

ROY: I know.

RAMONA: Well . . . you go that way. And I'll go this way.

(*They separate*)

Oh Roy, tell me we're gonna find him.

ROY: We'll find him, baby.

RAMONA: Do you really believe that?

ROY: I have to.

(*They exit calling "Justin!" Not moving from the mirror, Jane wakes Adam*)

JANE: Adam? Adam?

ADAM: What? Are you all right?

JANE: It's so cruel, Adam. My body doesn't know. Everything is working the way it should. It's just going on, as if everything was fine.

ADAM: Maybe you should've stayed at the hospital.

JANE *(Crosses to the window)*: Hold me.

(He comes to her, embraces her from behind. His hand touches one of her breasts)

It's so amazing, Adam. I have milk.

(After a beat, they exit. The sound of birds just before dawn. Justin wakes up on the mattresses. He climbs down. As he takes down his toy, it breaks. He hears someone coming and crosses away from the sound. Oppenheimer enters, crosses to him)

OPPENHEIMER: Are you lost, too?

(Justin turns, nods his head yes, and hands Oppenheimer his broken toy. Oppenheimer sees immediately what's wrong with the toy)

I see. *(Fixes it, hands it back to Justin)* How's that? *(The door of the control shed opens, spilling its light onto the stage.)* Oh thank God! *(Runs toward the door, stops and looks back at Justin)* You'll be all right.

(Oppenheimer exits into the control shed. The light is shut off with the closing of the door. Justin looks after Oppenheimer, then lifts his toy into the air and flies it as he exits into the dark, making a flying noise with his breath)

JUSTIN: WHOOOOOOOOOOOOOSHHHHHHHHHH.

CASANOVA

For John Seitz and Jeff Weiss

CASANOVA premiered at the New York Shakespeare Festival, Joseph Papp, Producer, May 28, 1991. The cast and creative contributors were as follows:

ACT ONE

ROUSSEAU'S GIRL	Erika Alexander
THERESE	Margaret Gibson

In Paris

SOPHIE	Kaiulani Lee
BOBO	Jeff Weiss

The Hague

GIRL SOPHIE	Liana Pai
GIACOMO CASANOVA	John Seitz

On the Road

UTA	Erika Alexander

Casanova's Childhood (Venice)

GIRL THERESE	Martha Thompson
YOUNG CASANOVA	Ethan Hawke
THERESE'S MOTHER	Erika Alexander
GRANDMAMA	Marylouise Burke
PRIEST	Jack Stehlin
MAN AT FESTIVAL	Robert Stanton
ZANETTA, CASANOVA'S MOTHER	LaTanya Richardson
GRIMANI	James Noah
DEAD GAETANO	Robert Stanton
SORCERESS	Marylouise Burke
WOMAN WEARING HOOPS	Liana Pai

At the Seminary

PRIEST   Robert Stanton
LADY   LaTanya Richardson
OLD COUNT   Jack Stehlin
GIRL   Liana Pai
BELLINO   Martha Thompson
SALEMBINI   Jack Stehlin
MONSIGNOR   James Noah

Bobo's Childhood (Paris)

BOY BOBO   Martha Thompson
COUNTESS   Marylouise Burke
FRENCH FOP   Jack Stehlin

Home from the Seminary

OLD SERVANT   James Noah
VENETIAN FOP   Robert Stanton
CATERINA   Liana Pai

At the Convent on Murano

LAURA   Marylouise Burke
IDIOT WOMAN   Martha Thompson
MARINA   LaTanya Richardson

At the Riddoto, Venice

BERNIS   Jack Stehlin
SBIRRI #1   Jack Stehlin
SBIRRI #2   Robert Stanton
MANUZZI   James Noah
WOMAN PASSING BY   Martha Thompson

Act Two

At Piombi Prison

JAILER	James Noah
INQUISITOR #1	LaTanya Richardson
INQUISITOR #2	Jack Stehlin
INQUISITOR #3	Robert Stanton

On the Way to Paris

TRAVELER #1	Jack Stehlin
TRAVELER #2	James Noah

In Paris

DANCING MASTER	Robert Stanton
LADIES AT DAMIENS' EXECUTION	LaTanya Richardson, Martha Thompson
MARCOLINE	LaTanya Richardson

At Versailles

PARIS-DUVERNY	Robert Stanton
EMACIATED WOMAN	Martha Thompson
COURT LADY	Liana Pai

In the Ballet Box

LADY	Liana Pai
MAN	James Noah
MADAME D'URFE	Marylouise Burke

Charpillon's Rooms

CHARPILLON'S MOTHER	Marylouise Burke
CHARPILLON	Erika Alexander

Mariucci's Home

MARIUCCI	LaTanya Richardson
MARIUCCI'S HUSBAND	James Noah
GUILLELMINE	Martha Thompson
JACOMINE	Liana Pai

In the Opera Box

DA PONTE	James Noah

In Sophie & Bobo's Rooms

ALAIN	Robert Stanton
JULIEN	James Noah

At the Ball

FOOTMAN	Robert Stanton
GUESTS	The Company

DIRECTOR	Michael Greif
SETS	John Arnone
COSTUMES	Gabriel Berry
LIGHTS	Frances Aronson
MUSIC AND SOUND	John Gromada
MUSICAL DIRECTION	Jill Jaffe
CHOREOGRAPHY	James Cunningham
DRAMATURG	M. Elizabeth Osborn

CASANOVA was a recipient of a grant award for New American Plays from the W. Alton Jones Foundation.

CHARACTERS

(Note: Postproduction rewrites resulted in a revised character list.)

ACT ONE

YOUNG WOMAN, age 15, Rousseau's mistress
THERESE, a wraith

In Paris
SOPHIE, age 42, Casanova's daughter
BOBO, age 60

On the Road
CASANOVA, age 70+
UTA, young and overweight

The Hague
YOUNG THERESE, age 16 to early twenties
GIRL SOPHIE, prepubescent

Casanova's Childhood (Venice)
YOUNG CASANOVA, boy to young man
ZANETTA, mother of Casanova
GRANDMAMA, mother of Zanetta
SORCERESS
WOMAN WEARING HOOPS

At the Seminary
PRIEST
OLD COUNT, aged

LADY, mother of the Girl
GIRL, age 14
BELLINO, female androgyne
SALEMBINI, Bellino's teacher
MONSIGNOR
TWO YOUNG WOMEN, nonspeaking

Bobo's Childhood (Paris)
COUNTESS
BOY BOBO, pubescent
FRENCH FOP

Home from the Seminary
PAOLO, servant of Zanetta
VENETIAN FOP
CATERINA, age 14
HAPPY WOMAN
WOMAN READING A NEWSPAPER

At the Convent on Murano
LAURA, not a young girl
IDIOT WOMAN
MARINA

At the Riddoto, Venice
BERNIS, the French ambassador
SBIRRI #1, Venetian policeman
SBIRRI #2, Venetian policeman
MANUZZI
WOMAN PASSING BY

Act Two

At Piombi Prison
JAILER
INQUISITOR #1
INQUISITOR #2
INQUISITOR #3

In Paris
LADY #2
MADAME D'URFE, middle-aged
MAN
CAPTAIN
MARCOLINE
CHILD CHARPILLON, prepubescent

Charpillon's Rooms
CHARPILLON'S MOTHER
MADEMOISELLE CHARPILLON, age 16+

Mariucci's Home
MARIUCCI
MARIUCCI'S HUSBAND
JACOMINE, age 9
GUILLELMINE, age 13

In the Opera Box
DA PONTE, the age of his writing of *Don Giovanni*

Paris
OLD WHORE
ALAIN

At the Ball
FOOTMAN
VICTOR, age 35–45
GUESTS, the Company

CASANOVA is best done with an ensemble of actors and can be done with a total of seven women and six men. The following parts, however, should not be doubled: Therese Imer, Sophie, Bobo, Casanova, Young Casanova. Suggested doubling follows:

Young Woman, Uta, Mademoiselle Charpillon, Happy Woman

Girl Sophie, Girl (at seminary), Caterina, Woman Passing By, Lady #2

Zanetta, Lady (at seminary), Marina, Marcoline, Mariucci

Grandmama, Sorceress, Countess, Laura, Old Whore, Madame D'Urfe, Charpillon's Mother

Bellino, Boy Bobo, Idiot Woman, Child Charpillon

Old Count, Monsignor, Paolo, Jailer, Man, DaPonte

Salembini, French Fop, Bernis, Mariucci's Husband, Victor

TIME

The years of Casanova's life, 1725–1798

PLACE

Various European cities

ACT ONE

In the dark, the sound of a young woman's passionate breathing, as in serious lovemaking. As the breathing grows with intensity, little cries are heard and she speaks.

YOUNG WOMAN: Oh God. Oh God.
Oh God! *(The breathing reaches an orgiastic level)* Oh God! GOD!
(Lights up on a Young Woman, but she isn't in bed with a lover—she's lying on the floor in labor)
What—*(Gasp)*
—is—*(Gasp)*
—love?!

(The Young Woman's appearance calls up the wraith of Therese Imer. She appears, as if sitting up from the grave, her hands folded over her breast, still holding some very dead flowers. She is alert, excited and pleased)

THERESE: It's time! *(Stands and brushes herself off, looks at what she's wearing)* Who buried me in this! Look at these sleeves! I'll find *him*, too!

(She is gone. Lights down on Young Woman.

In another space, Sophie, age forty, enters with a candle. She is in her nightgown. Bobo, age sixty, is in bed)

SOPHIE: Bobo?

BOBO: What?

SOPHIE: Rousseau had these rooms.

BOBO: What are you talking about?

SOPHIE: Did you hear something? A moment ago?

BOBO: No.

SOPHIE: I heard breathing. Heavy, passionate breathing.

BOBO: Well, it certainly wasn't coming from in here. Are you sure it wasn't coming from your room?

SOPHIE: Let's not be cruel, Bobo. *(About the sounds)* And then crying.

BOBO: That was you, I believe.

SOPHIE: Bobo. That was last week—I'm much better now.

BOBO: You haven't been out of these rooms in days and days. You've spent the whole time in your nightgown.

SOPHIE: I've put on clean ones.

Do you believe in ghosts?

BOBO: Only living ones, darling. Like me. And anyone else with style.

Why are you talking about Rousseau?

SOPHIE: He had these rooms.

And my father said he was notorious.

BOBO: How ironic.

Where did your father say such a thing?

SOPHIE: Oh, I heard it.

People tell me things. People who know.

Goodnight.

(Sophie exits. Lights up on Therese in another space. She is brushing soot off herself, coughing, looking around)

THERESE: I materialized in a fireplace. *(Sniffs)* Something's burning—must be me. *(Cracks herself up)* I'll find you yet— my stallion!

(She exits.

Lights up on the Young Girl and the sound of her labored breathing again. It continues through Sophie's lines. Sophie reenters)

SOPHIE: Bobo!

BOBO: Whatwhatwhat?

SOPHIE: Listen.

(They listen. The breathing continues)

There. Can you hear it?

(Breathing stops. Vision of Young Girl disappears)

BOBO: You've obviously become unhinged during the night and should be turned over to the authorities or whomever is running France at the moment. Who can it be I wonder ho hum. Come on, get in Bobo's bed. Come on.

(Sophie crosses to him)

Watch for the pot.

(Bobo opens the covers and lets her in. He then gets out and crosses to where Sophie left the candle burning and starts to blow it out)

SOPHIE: Don't put out the candle!

BOBO: Bobo is putting the candle right here where Sophie can see it. Can Sophie see the candle?
Good.
You were such a lovely child. We should have exposed you on a hillside in Greece.

SOPHIE: Bobo?

BOBO: Yes, darling?

SOPHIE: If he comes, I won't see him.

BOBO: Who? Victor? Vincent? Whatever that leggy swain's name was with all the natural hair and no wig, ever.

SOPHIE: No. Not him.

BOBO: Who?

SOPHIE: My father.

I won't see him, Bobo. I'll refuse him.

BOBO: Dearest, he hasn't seen you in thirty years. Why do you think he will come to see you now?

SOPHIE: Because I am his.

BOBO: Hush, hush hush. Go to sleep.

He's in Germany, God help him, and he's much too ill to travel—that's what I hear.

Not that I care.

Of course.

(Lights up on Casanova, age seventy-plus, outside in the dark. He is holding his luggage. After a beat, Uta, an overweight, young serving woman, enters. She is eating a sausage and carries a lantern. She puts the sausage away and takes Casanova's hand)

CASANOVA: Mademoiselle, I am not convinced that you have any idea what you are doing.

UTA: Don't stop now. Come on.

CASANOVA: I think we're being pursued already.

UTA: We can't be.

CASANOVA: I heard someone shouting for me. It was a woman's voice.

UTA: What woman would want you? Listen for the count—he's the only one who cares and that's because no one will take care of his library if you go.

CASANOVA: This underbrush is tearing my shoes.

UTA: Jakob said the coach would be down by the tree.

CASANOVA: Which tree? We're surrounded by forest!

UTA: I'll know it.

CASANOVA: I have to relieve myself.

UTA: You just went.

CASANOVA *(Pain in the groin)*: Uhh.

UTA: Nappies for you. Come on.

CASANOVA: Did you bring a chamber pot—for the trip?

UTA: I brought a bottle.

Come on!!!

CASANOVA: Mind the hat box!!!

(She leads him off.

A match is struck, revealing Therese. She is holding the match)

THERESE *(Sniffs)*: Sausage. Germany! *(Match burns out)* Damn! *(Lights another—it burns out)* Damn! *(Lights another—it goes out)* God. *(Lights another, but this time it's her finger—it continues to burn. She looks around in the darkness, tripping over some things)* I hate disorder. *(Finds the lamp, lights it with her flaming finger)* There. *(Blows out the flame on her finger, then reshapes the end of her finger)* Still perfect.

Now, where are you? Darling? I have a surprise. I heard a woman, so I know you must be here. Darling? It's Therese. It's Therese. Imer. I'm back! *(Looking for him)* I'm back, darling! *(Looking for him)* I said I have returned! *(Sets the lamp down and gestures at it—the room glows and she can see everything)* Gone!?????

Where is he? Where is he where is he where is he where is he!!??? *(Runs around the room, searching madly, like someone possessed. Then she sniffs for odor)* I'LL FIND YOU!!! *(Turns into a wild thing sniffing for his scent and growling, crawling on the floor. She finds two chamber pots, then some papers, then suddenly she catches a scent in the air—she follows it and stands up, reaching to smell it. It leads her offstage)* WHERE ARE YOUUUUUUUUU!???

(Therese exits.

Back to Bobo and Sophie. She is still in his bed)

SOPHIE: You aren't going, are you?

BOBO: Where would I go—this is my room.

SOPHIE: I meant, to the ball.

BOBO: We can't afford it. I'm too old.

SOPHIE: I saw you working on a gown.

BOBO: For one of our clients—Madame Scott. *She* is going to the ball.

SOPHIE: You were expanding the waist.

BOBO *(Knows she knows it's his gown)*: My waist measurement hasn't changed in thirty years!

SOPHIE: Aha.

BOBO: I have to go, Sophie. I need to have some glorious beauty and majesty come back into my life.

SOPHIE: Victor says that kind of thing is sinful because it's paid for by the labor of the poor.

BOBO: Didn't they kill Robespierre for saying that? No, wait a minute—he killed other people for saying that. Or both. Or neither. Oh, anyway, it's finally over and we can make our way around the blood and entrails and rolling noggins and have a fabulous night which is exactly what I plan to do. *(Pulls an invitation out from under his pillow and reads it aloud)* "The Chevalier D'Eon is invited to attend a ball to celebrate the event of Citizen Robespierre losing his head in the treacherous and syphilitic menage of Mademoiselles Liberté, Egalité, and Fraternité." Wit has returned, and on his arm his attractive companion, Irony. A welcome couple at any function. Huzzah.

You should go, too, darling. You could go as my escort.

SOPHIE: No. Victor might call.

BOBO: Oh, the fabulous Victor—he is without peer.

SOPHIE: I realize that I love him, Bobo—in spite of everything.

BOBO: Uhhhhhn.

SOPHIE: I do.

BOBO: Yes. Julien was peerless, also.

SOPHIE: That was so long ago.

BOBO: Months, at least.

Oh, Sophie, why do you have to have a man in your life? God knows, I've lived without one for years, decades, eons.

SOPHIE: I don't know. They court me and I fall in love. And
     then I desire them. And then I can't live without them, and
     then they leave me. And then I die and they never come
     back, not wanting to sleep with the dead.
BOBO: Do what I do, darling. Hold a celebration of desire, by
     yourself, in your boudoir—with lots of candles, several of
     your imaginary friends, and some fruit.
SOPHIE: And then you resurrect me, and then I'm courted, and
     the whole ridiculous cycle starts over again.
BOBO: You are so much like your mother—one man after
     another. But no one got the better of her. No man got the
     better of Therese Imer. Well, except one.

*(In Bobo's memory. Young Therese, an attractive woman of
thirty or so, enters)*

YOUNG THERESE: Sophie? Your papa is coming at any minute.
     Sophie! *(Fiddling with her attire)* Look at the sleeves on
     this gown—ridiculous! *(In the mirror)* No white face—it
     shows the wrinkles when it creases. Just a little powder.
     Bobo?
BOBO *(Answering from his space)*: Yes?
YOUNG THERESE *(About her toilette)*: What do I need?
BOBO *(Entering the memory)*: More money, Madame.
YOUNG THERESE: Sophie will warm his heart and he will help us.
     She resembles him—he can't deny her.
     She is his, you know.
BOBO: I know.
YOUNG THERESE: I will do anything, Bobo.
     And can.
     Because I don't love him any more.
     And the first recipient of any funds will be you, Bobo.
     I'm sorry you haven't been paid in months.
BOBO: It doesn't matter, Madame.
YOUNG THERESE *(Sees his form behind a curtain)*: He's here.

(Bobo primps her slightly—she exits behind the curtain.
Girl Sophie enters from where she's been hiding and listening.
She carries her doll, "Mamzell")

GIRL SOPHIE: Bobo?

BOBO: Yes, my love?

GIRL SOPHIE: I forgot my words.

BOBO: That's alright.

GIRL SOPHIE *(Very upset)*: No, it's NOT! I have to make Papa like me!

    It's very important.

(We see the silhouettes of Young Therese and Casanova on the curtain. She is trying to arouse him sexually. Girl Sophie and Bobo see it, too. Bobo tries to protect Girl Sophie from seeing it)

CASANOVA *(In silhouette)*: Therese! Therese, for heaven's sake!

BOBO *(Trying to distract Girl Sophie)*: Look at Mamzell. She's dancing! *(Continuing through their lines)* Dance! Kick! Dance! Turn! Plié!

YOUNG THERESE *(In silhouette)*: My darling. You know I love only you. You are my greatest love.

CASANOVA *(In silhouette)*: Now, stop it! You're humiliating yourself.

(Young Therese comes out from behind the curtain)

YOUNG THERESE: Sophie? Papa is ready for you.

(Young Therese pulls the curtain to reveal a healthy Casanova, age thirty-eight. Girl Sophie turns around to see him—she is transfixed)

THERESE: Your child, Giacomo. *(To Girl Sophie)* Curtsey.

(Girl Sophie, still transfixed, doesn't move, just sings loudly. Bobo coaches her a little)

GIRL SOPHIE:

> In the green wood
> Lay a fallow deer
> Her dying words were these
> Only say that I am beautiful
> And I shall be love's slave
> Only say that I am beautiful
> And I shall be love's slave.

CASANOVA: You are beautiful, my daughter.

> You have my eyes.

THERESE: There's a dance that she was supposed to do.

> But . . .
> Go on, Sophie.
> *Kiss* your papa.

GIRL SOPHIE *(A prepared bit she's learned)*: Oh, Papa!

> May I sit on your lap?
> May I have a kiss?
> Mama says I have a mouth like a flower.
> See? *(Pooches out her mouth)*

CASANOVA: Therese, may I see you for a moment? *(Pulls the curtain)*

GIRL SOPHIE: What did I do?

YOUNG THERESE *(In silhouette)*: She adores you.

GIRL SOPHIE: I love you, Papa!

> I want to be with you, Papa!
> I'll do the dancing part now!

CASANOVA *(In silhouette)*: Therese, I'm going to strike that child.

GIRL SOPHIE *(Doing the dance with the song)*:

> In the green wood
> Lay a fallow deer
> Her dying words were these—

YOUNG THERESE *(Sticking her head out from behind the curtain)*:
Sophie! Not now!

BOBO: Come away, ma petite.

GIRL SOPHIE: I didn't do it right, Bobo!

CASANOVA (*In silhouette*): Therese, you have made an actress out of my child! She is nothing but a little—little dissembler! Oh, the mincing, the baby syllables, the—

YOUNG THERESE (*In silhouette*): Sophie will do just fine in this world—she will be a lady and marry well! I have seen to it!

GIRL SOPHIE: And now they're both angry!

YOUNG THERESE (*Opening the curtain again*): Please—I know you can see how difficult it is for us here. I've been organizing subscription balls and Bobo is multi-talented, but unless we can have help from you, I'll even have to let Bobo go. (*To Bobo*) Bobo, practice a French song with Sophie.

(*Bobo takes Girl Sophie aside and whispers a French song in her ear*)

Sophie's French is impeccable because of Bobo. He was a chevalier at court but someone humiliated him in front of Louie and he descended violently. You of all people should understand the capricious cruelty of . . . those . . . in power.

BOBO: We're ready.

CASANOVA: What's that supposed to mean?

YOUNG THERESE: Just that you know what it means to be ill-treated—you forget how long I've known you, my darling, dearest Giacomo. I can send Sophie away for the afternoon and we can reignite, we can explore *whatever* you want—

GIRL SOPHIE (*Doing the dance again*):
Only say that I am beautiful
And I shall be love's slave
Only say—

CASANOVA: I don't know if she is my daughter, but she is, most certainly, yours.

GIRL SOPHIE:
—that I am beautiful—

CASANOVA: And you can keep her! *(Exits)*

YOUNG THERESE: Sophie will get what she wants from this
  world of *men*. I have seen to it.

GIRL SOPHIE *(About her father)*: Don't leave me! DON'T
  LEAVE MEEEEE!!!

YOUNG THERESE: I used to undress opposite his window and
  wash my arms and my breasts—I wanted him so badly.
  Oh, he couldn't get enough of me then.
  Maybe someday he'll see you—when you're grown.
  Don't forget him.
  You only get one father, Sophie. Only one.
  My father was a great actor in Goldoni's troupe.
  My father was a great actor and *never* turned his back
  on me!

BOBO: Mamzell looks hungry—why don't you feed her—there's
  pudding. I'll be along.

(Girl Sophie exits)

YOUNG THERESE: I will never forgive him!

*(Young Therese exits. Bobo leaves his memory and goes back to
his room where Sophie is in bed)*

SOPHIE: I'm not going, mind you.
  But it would be interesting to see him.
  Just to see if he'd recognize me.

BOBO: He won't come.

SOPHIE: Not that I care.

BOBO: He won't come.

(In the coach. Casanova and Uta are traveling. Uta is sniffling)

CASANOVA: Uhn!
  One more bump and I shall die of the pain. *(Takes a drink
  from a small bottle of laudanum)* Why are you crying? Oh,
  that will drive me to insanity.

UTA: What am I doing with you? I thought Jakob would say, "No, Uta! Don't go!" But he didn't. He just held the traces, quiet, until we got on.

CASANOVA: But one more day in this horrible country and I would have become an ox or worse—one of those rude comedians who farts and brays and hits people over the head with a bladder—like that disgusting jester at the Count's last dinner.

UTA: And then he shuts the door, nods to the coachman, and we go!

CASANOVA: Of course, I was eating with the house staff. Egad. Someone of my importance. And the food—I find worms in my cheese half the time and the noodles!

UTA: WHY DID I COME??? CAN YOU TELL ME THAT???!

CASANOVA: You begged me to take you.

UTA: That didn't mean I wanted to go!

CASANOVA: Why don't women ever know what they want? Can someone explain that to me? Eh? *(Another bump)* UHN!!! *(Takes a swig from the little bottle)*

UTA: I know what I want. I just don't know how to get it. I'm hungry. *(Takes out the sausage)* Want some? *(Sings to it)*

"I'm a handful, I'm a handful,
Mama, please take care of me."

(Bites into the sausage and begins crying again) This is really good sausage.

CASANOVA: I'm in hell.

THERESE *(Appearing attached to the coach somehow)*: Not yet, Darling.

CASANOVA: What?

THERESE: Found!
Joy!

UTA: Maybe Jakob will miss me tomorrow, after I've gone many more miles with you. And then he will be riding after and fetch me.

THERESE *(About Casanova)*: He's aged. One shouldn't live past one's attractiveness.

CASANOVA: How absurd. Absence does not make one remember—absence makes one *forget*. How odd for me to say that when I'm writing my memoirs.

THERESE: Memoirs?! I'm just in time.

UTA: What do you know about it? What do you know about love? You're an old French book man and dried up, too.

THERESE: She's so young.
　　And stupid.

CASANOVA: I am from Venice, Mademoiselle—La Serenissima —a kingdom with its own and much greater language than French.
　　And I know a great deal about love.

UTA AND THERESE: Ha.

(Music. The stage fills with people—it is the Venice of Casanova's memory. He drinks from the small bottle. Young Casanova appears, holding a rag to his nose)

CASANOVA: I was young once. I was a boy.

(Grandmama enters, finds Young Casanova)

GRANDMAMA: Giacomo! We have to hurry!

(Grandmama takes Young Casanova by the hand and leads him off. We hear her fervent voice echoing offstage)

Hurry! Hurry! Hurry! Hurry!

CASANOVA: I know all about love—particularly its absence.

UTA: Were you an orphan or something?

THERESE *(To Uta, who can't hear or see her)*: Keep your head.

CASANOVA: I am the son of actors—two excellent—

THERESE: Mediocre.

CASANOVA: —actors in Goldoni's troupe. But we were destined to be separated. The streets of Venice are a great home for a boy—you can walk the entire country in an hour—but I suffered terrible hemorrhages of the nose, so I spent much of my time looking up and the hemorrhages transformed my speech in grotesque ways. Yes, I was alone in a strange land called "home," as all children are.

(Lights up on another space. Women are washing the dead body of a man. One of them, Zanetta, is still wearing her white face from the commedia—this is Casanova's mother)

ZANETTA *(Grabbing the rag)*: Let me wash his groin, Amelia. That is MINE.

(Young Casanova enters with his Grandmama. To her dead husband)

I couldn't make my last entrance, Gaetano.
    They called me out of the play. *(To Young Casanova)* Your father never missed an entrance in his life.

YOUNG CASANOVA *(His nosebleed transforms his speech)*: What's wrong with Papa?

GRANDMAMA: Has the priest come?

ZANETTA: Yes.

GRANDMAMA: Kiss your father goodbye, Giacomo.

YOUNG CASANOVA: Goodbye, Papa. *(Kisses him)* What's happened?

GRANDMAMA: He's dead, Giacomo.

YOUNG CASANOVA: No! Mama—

(He reaches for Zanetta who has collapsed sobbing on the body of her husband)

ZANETTA: What—what are you doing you *BOY*! Don't you understand that I have lost my *husband*?!

GRANDMAMA: Come to me, Giacomo—come to Grandmama.

YOUNG CASANOVA: I'm sorry. Mama—

ZANETTA: Why can't you SPEAK!?

(Young Casanova exits)

GRANDMAMA: Zanetta! What did I raise when I brought you up?

ZANETTA: He's my son and I'll do right by him, Mother! He's going to seminary.

GRANDMAMA: You're getting rid of him?

ZANETTA: Who better than God to take care of a son?

GRANDMAMA: Like He took care of His own?!

ZANETTA: Mother! How can you talk that way? *(Loud whisper)* There's death in this house.

(Grandmama exits one way, Zanetta the other.
In another space, a Sorceress is singing, shouting and chanting over a trunk)

SORCERESS:
> By sieve and shears, by a crystal,
> By a cock picking up grain,
> By dreams, by salt, by stones,
> By wax, by the letters of a name,
> Shadows, urine, sticks,
> Herbs, arrows, smoke,
> By the flights of birds, by the shoulder blades of animals,
> May I know it and see it in the bones.
> Eko, eko, Azarak . . .
> Eka, eka, Zamalak . . .
> Fortune is a pancake.

(The Sorceress opens the trunk and helps Young Casanova out.
His shirt is soaked with blood)

Boy? Boy!! *(Slaps him awake, then wipes his nose and looks closely at it)* Grandmama will be back for you soon.
> No new blood.
> You have quite a jaw on you—and eyes.
> This divination is for your eyes only. *(Lays out tarot cards)*

YOUNG CASANOVA (*Nose still full*):   This is blasphemous! I can't!

SORCERESS: Blasphemy? Your parents are with the theatre! Sit down. (*Reading the cards*) You will have a wonderful life. You are blessed. Believe it!

YOUNG CASANOVA: I don't believe it.

SORCERESS: You will live by your nose.

YOUNG CASANOVA: I hope not.

SORCERESS: You follow a mystery, say—you catch it, say—and when you unveil it, your heart beating, your mouth dry—when you rip off the veil—

YOUNG CASANOVA: What!?

SORCERESS: —nothing. Ha ha!
I read the cards. I know nothing myself. I am ignorant.

YOUNG CASANOVA: My nose is bleeding again.

SORCERESS (*Giving him a rag*):   All right. (*Tells the real truth she sees in the cards*) You will be a librarian. You will spend your last years with Germans. You will be incontinent. You will live in a world you no longer recognize.

YOUNG CASANOVA: No! You're making that up!

SORCERESS (*Looking at him*):   There's something about you, some magic that makes me look and look. . .

YOUNG CASANOVA: I don't know what it would be.

SORCERESS: Are you a wolf?

YOUNG CASANOVA: No.

SORCERESS: You will be, I think.

(*She grabs his balls—he gasps. She lets go. He drops the rag, touches his nose*)

YOUNG CASANOVA: I'm not bleeding. (*Nasal blockage is gone*) Listen to the sound of my voice. My voice!

SORCERESS: Come to me—I want to tell you something.

(*Young Casanova approaches cautiously, covering his groin*)

Someone will visit you tonight, while you lie in your bed. Do not mention her visit to anyone as long as you live—or the bleeding will start again. *(Stuffs a book in his shirt)* Here. Take this book. Save your life. Lunatic times. Learn a trade. *Knowledge*, not belief. *Knowledge* will save you.

(Zanetta enters, still in her commedia makeup, smeared from crying)

ZANETTA: I thought so! WHERE IS MY MOTHER? I will KILL HER!!

(Zanetta grabs Young Casanova away from the Sorceress)

SORCERESS: Devil woman!!!

(The Sorceress spits three times and then starts an incantation to ward off Zanetta)

ZANETTA: I am La Buranella, you heathen!!

SORCERESS: Wipe off your makeup! You frighten people!

ZANETTA: This is from *grief*! This is from *respect*! This is the *truth*!

YOUNG CASANOVA: Mama, I'm better. Listen to my voice.

ZANETTA *(Finding the book in his shirt)*: And what is this?!!! *(Throws it at Sorceress)* You are too late! This child belongs to Christ!

SORCERESS: Anyone who asks can belong to Christ, isn't that true? If Christ had been a woman, he would have been called a whore.

YOUNG CASANOVA: What is that smell? It's everywhere. Is it the sea?

SORCERESS: It's me, little love. *(Takes his head, puts it in her crotch)*

ZANETTA: What are you doing??!!

YOUNG CASANOVA: Wonderful.

SORCERESS: Now he'll never forget where he came from.

(Zanetta is taking him away)

Remember what I told you—the woman will come to you.

(Back to Casanova and Uta)

CASANOVA: That night—someone did come to me.
 I've never told anyone about it.
 I can't still.
 Because I know the day I tell, I'll be finished with life.
 I'm still faithful.
UTA: To what?
CASANOVA: My innocence.

(Therese laughs and laughs at this one)

 Who's laughing? Who is it?
UTA: Not me. It was a beautiful story.
THERESE *(Into Uta's ear)*: Don't fall for it.
UTA: There's a fly bothering me.

(In Casanova's memory and in another space, Young Casanova is asleep in his bed. Suddenly, a window opens)

YOUNG CASANOVA: Jesus! Mary! Grandmama! HELP!

(A Woman Wearing Hoops enters. She is in a homemade costume but looks magical and shining to him. She comes to his bed and whispers something in his ear and then exits, singing something. Young Casanova and Casanova stare after her)

YOUNG CASANOVA AND CASANOVA: Come back.
THERESE *(Following after the woman in hoops, also singing)*:
 Be careful what you wish for, darling.
UTA: What is it?
CASANOVA: Woman—whoever you are!
 Get out of my head!
UTA: All right. Take care of yourself.
CASANOVA: Don't go—.
YOUNG CASANOVA: I'm blessed.
THERESE *(Seeing Young Casanova)*: Yes, you are.
 My God, he was beautiful.

(He exits as she tries to touch him)

But what will you do with that blessing? Huh? That's what I need to remember. I threw mine away on *you* and a thousand other lies. By the time I died my heart was as dry and empty as a tunnel. But those young eyes of yours—I'd forgotten—so full of need and attention. Your supple passion—like making love to myself sometimes. Oh, how odd—this liquid feeling that's come over me, like materializing in the sea. Skin. Hair. Tongue.

Having a body is so confusing. Life is so much clearer when you're dead.

(Young Casanova enters, dressed as a novitiate. Priest enters and throws Young Casanova a fig)

PRIEST: This is all I could find.

(Young Casanova bites into it enthusiastically)

THERESE: I'd forgotten how ravenous he was—his appetite. I'm in trouble. *(Exits)*
PRIEST: Why are you so hungry all the time? Didn't they feed you at the seminary? Now hold this—it's the marriage contract—and be silent.

(Lady and well-dressed aristocratic gentleman who is an Old Count enter from opposite directions. Old Count stops dead when he sees Lady. She rushes to him. Old Count is shown to a chair by Priest)

OLD COUNT: She is well-disposed of me?
LADY: Oh, yes.
OLD COUNT: Because I cannot agree unless she is well-disposed of me.
LADY: She is.
OLD COUNT: She must accept me. Every night.
LADY: Of course.

OLD COUNT: I am still vital.

LADY: Any woman could see that.

OLD COUNT: Don't flatter me. You needn't flatter me. As my
future relative, I want you to be sincere with me.

LADY: I will, Sir.

OLD COUNT: You answer too quickly.

LADY: Only because I am sincere, Sir.

OLD COUNT: You must call me "son."

LADY: I—shall. "Son."

OLD COUNT: I want to see her now.

(Lady crosses to exit)

Wait— *(Stands, then sits, then stands and sits again, arranging
himself as handsomely as he can. He is anxious)* All right—
bring her in.

*(Lady lets in a very young Girl, age fourteen at the most. Girl
looks around the room and runs to Young Casanova, flinging her
arms around him)*

GIRL: Oh Sir, I am so happy!

(Old Count stands and walks out. Priest runs after him)

LADY *(Grabbing Girl off of Young Casanova)*: Get off!!! Let go
of her!!! *(Hits Young Casanova, shakes Girl, as she yells at her)*
WHAT HAVE YOU DONE?!! WHAT HAVE YOU
DONE?!! YOU STUPID, LITTLE IDIOT! That's not the
MAN!! That's a *BOY!!* I said, "Run to the well-dressed
MAN AT THE END OF THE ROOM!!"

GIRL: He's a man! He's a man, Mama!

LADY: WHAT ARE WE GOING TO DO??! I have no
DOWRY for you, you stupid little cow!! That's it—you will
go into orders tomorrow!! No grandchildren for me!! *(Lady
begins to hit her daughter)* No estate for me!! I will die in the
GUTTER because you are so STUPID!! YOU HAVE
DESTROYED US!!

YOUNG CASANOVA: I don't think you should hit her.

LADY: And who are YOU?

YOUNG CASANOVA: Nobody.

LADY: Well, Mr. Nobody, you'd better learn how the world works. And mind your own business!

(Priest reenters and Lady looks at him with hope—he shakes his head "no")

Noooo! *(Exits to find Old Count)*

PRIEST: Stay here, Giacomo. And don't *touch* her.

YOUNG CASANOVA: What do you mean, Father? I didn't do anything. I never saw her before.

PRIEST: I don't understand it. You're not that good-looking. *(To Girl)* You are wanton. *(To Young Casanova)* Watch her. *(Exits after Lady)*

GIRL *(Calm)*: I wish I was dead.

YOUNG CASANOVA: That's a sin, I'm sure.

GIRL: If I could kill myself, I would.

Right now.

YOUNG CASANOVA: That's a mortal sin.

GIRL: Hell can't be as bad.

YOUNG CASANOVA: What are you saying? Hell is very, very bad. You BURN there, eternally. There's no END to it.

GIRL: I'll be cloistered.

YOUNG CASANOVA: I'm going to be a priest.

GIRL: Priests aren't cloistered. No one even cares if they're celibate.

YOUNG CASANOVA: They don't?

GIRL: I should be married, I suppose. I'm fourteen. The womb moves around in your body unless it's weighted down with a baby. It can choke you—the womb.

YOUNG CASANOVA: I've heard that.

GIRL: Let's . . . go.

YOUNG CASANOVA: Go?

GIRL: Right up those stairs is the bell tower. It's private. No one ever goes there. Come on.

YOUNG CASANOVA: No. No no no. I—I have to give back the
    marriage contract.
GIRL: Then I shall go up there and hang from the clapper until
    I die!!

(She exits. Lady enters)

LADY: Where is she? WHERE IS SHE?
YOUNG CASANOVA: She's run away.
LADY: Oh my Christ! Where's the priest? Am I completely
    deserted?? I am! I AM!! WHERE IS MY BABY??? Where
    is that stupid little cow??!! *(Turning on Young Casanova)* You
    saw her leave!!
YOUNG CASANOVA *(Pointing in the wrong direction)*: She went
    that way.

*(Lady goes that way. Young Casanova drops the marriage
contract and exits after the Girl.
    Blackout. A lot of church bells ringing.
    Lights up on Priest, Old Count and Lady. Old Count is sitting
as before. Young Casanova enters with quill in an inkwell. Priest
hands marriage contract to Young Casanova to hold)*

OLD COUNT: And you are certain her hearing will return to
    normal.
LADY: Yes, my son.
PRIEST: The doctor said the deafness was only temporary—that
    she escaped the bell tower before her eardrums were
    completely burst.
OLD COUNT: I am deeply attracted to her—I cannot help myself.
    That is the only reason I am enduring this humiliation.
LADY: A man as grand as you can never be humiliated by a
    young girl's silly emotions.
OLD COUNT: Madame, your insincerity is only outweighed by
    your complete lack of wisdom. A man as grand as I can be
    destroyed by a young girl's emotions. *(Pause)* So she is calmer
    today.

PRIEST: Much calmer, my Lord. She has matured several years
in one day.

OLD COUNT: Let's see her.

*(Lady crosses to bring in the Girl. The Girl walks very quietly
over to the Old Count, kneels and puts her head on his lap. He
strokes her hair)*

I will sign.

PRIEST: Giacomo? The marriage contract.

(Young Casanova doesn't seem to hear. The Priest leans closer)

Giacomo?

(No response from Young Casanova)

LADY: You STUPID BOY!! GIVE US THE CONTRACT!!
OH, I can't BEAR him, Father!! He infuriates me!!

PRIEST: GIACOMO!!

*(Priest takes the contract from Young Casanova who suddenly
notices that people seem to be talking to him. He becomes active,
supplying the quill, etc., to the Old Count)*

OLD COUNT: One more stipulation. Her mother is to visit only
on high holy days and at the birth of children.

(Old Count signs. Girl makes an "x" as a signature. Lady signs)

Say farewell— *(Into Girl's ear)* SAY—FAREWELL—TO—
EVERYONE—DEAR.

GIRL: Goodbye.

*(She kisses her mother, curtsies to Priest and then to Young
Casanova, careful not to look at him. Old Count and Girl exit)*

LADY: Wait! I shall not be shut out from the wedding!!

(She exits after them.

After a beat, Priest comes up behind Young Casanova with a stool and drops it right behind him. It makes a loud noise, but Young Casanova can't hear it.)

PRIEST: HEY!!

(Young Casanova can't hear that, either. Priest touches Young Casanova on the shoulder—Young Casanova turns to face him)

YOUNG CASANOVA *(Too loud because he can't hear himself)*:
  YES, FATHER?

PRIEST: Never mind. *(Turns him back around, so Young Casanova's back is to him again. Whispers to the back of Young Casanova's head)* You are beautiful. I love you. I watch you all the time. I want you. Come to me tonight. I know you want to.

(Young Casanova turns to find the Priest right behind him)

YOUNG CASANOVA: OH, FATHER, DID YOU WANT ME
  TO DO ANYTHING ELSE?

PRIEST: No . . . no.

YOUNG CASANOVA: MAY I LIE DOWN? I HAVE A
  HEADACHE.

PRIEST: Yes. Go.

(Young Casanova exits, checking his nose for blood. Priest exits the other way.

Bobo's bedroom. He is at his vanity, putting on white face. Sophie isn't there)

BOBO: He humiliated me in court, the Venetian brute. He'd just escaped from prison and didn't we hear THAT story until we were all ready to scream. I was dressed as a man that day and was a person to be taken seriously. There was talk that I was going to be ambassador to England! He came up to me in front of the entire court at the Palace and proceeded to smell me from head to . . . my nether regions. Well, I was stunned, to say the least. I just stood there amazed! And then he said in the worst French I have ever heard: *(In an Italian accent)* "This man is not a man. This man is a woman!" *(Back to his own voice)* And everyone froze—believe me, when every second of one's life is controlled by rules of decorum, an incident like this is cataclysmic—and then, Louie, King Louie—thank God he didn't live to see the horrible things, unspeakable things that happened to his grandson at the hands of barbarians, *beasts*. The world is a dreadful, horrible place, my sweet. And, if I could take us both to the moon tomorrow, I would! *(Pause. He's remembering the French Revolution)* Paris—you are despicable.

You have been made despicable.

It's a shame his makeup's become politically incorrect—yea, even dangerous. But I'm going to wear it until the day I die.

(Sophie enters, carrying a gown. She is still in her nightgown)

SOPHIE: You shouldn't put on your makeup now. It'll get all over your gown.

BOBO: I can't bear to look at myself without it.

SOPHIE: Why all of a sudden?

BOBO: You mean, I've looked terrible for years? And you didn't have the heart to tell me? "Bobo, put on makeup at dawn or you'll scare the horses? Or the clients? And they'll take their puny business to younger, more attractive seamstresses." *(Surveying himself in the white face)* Oh my—I look like a plowed field after a snowstorm.

SOPHIE: You're better as yourself.
        Beauty is a trap.

BOBO: That's what it's for, Sophie.

SOPHIE: The first person he wanted to marry—

BOBO: Who?

SOPHIE: Who? Who else? You know he's coming.
        Everyone's coming. Why else would you be in such
        a state?

(Bobo doesn't argue this time)

The first person he wanted to marry was Bellino, the castrato.

BOBO: What?

(Casanova is bent at the waist, hands on knees, in pain. He and Uta are out of the coach)

UTA: But what's a castrato?

BOBO *(To Sophie)*: Tell me.

CASANOVA *(Straightened up, better)*: All this is wasted on you. No one is going to understand my life. *(Exits, limping)*

SOPHIE: It's just gossip

UTA *(To the exited Casanova)*: I don't have to be here. I could get back in that coach and just go.

CASANOVA *(Offstage)*: Don't!

(Uta exits)

BOBO: *Tell* me.

(Bellino, a young castrato, and his teacher, Salembini, are meeting in a sanctuary with a Monsignor and Priest. Young Casanova is there—he's still a novitiate and is cleaning some altar candlesticks and a large wooden crucifix with a life-size Jesus on it. Salembini is above them at the organ)

SALEMBINI *(From the organ)*: Begin.

BELLINO *(Singing—some rococo piece that will show off the voice. The lyrics are from* Carmina Burana, 153): Tempus transit gelidum mundus renovatar verque redit floridum forma rebus datur *(Does a flourish of scales to show off his voice)*

SALEMBINI: He's perfect, isn't he, Monsignor?

PRIEST: Another perfect voice from an excommunicated boy.

SALEMBINI: So you agree, too, Father!

PRIEST: I'm here to listen to the singing. I want no part of it.

SALEMBINI: It was done against his will. He was six years old. His parents had no money so they sold him to a recruiter. Not I!! No, I got him from the school. In Pisa.

MONSIGNOR *(To Priest)*: You're from Pisa. Visited that school?

PRIEST: Other side of town.

MONSIGNOR: He does look a little effeminate.

BELLINO: What do you mean? I'm no girl!!

SALEMBINI *(A secret cue)*: I had to take a dagger from him this morning!

BELLINO: Yes, I have a dagger!

MONSIGNOR: He's fierce. With such a perfect voice.

(Salembini signals Bellino to sing another scale)

One wonders if it's worth it.

PRIEST: To lose your soul to everlasting hell?

MONSIGNOR: No—to lose your testicles.

PRIEST: Well, we don't use them anyway, do we, your Eminence? And one can become erect, if one is a eunuch—one just can never ejaculate. It's a sort of purgatory.

SALEMBINI: Or Paradise. Ha! Ha!

Monsignor, you know me. My Bellino is a true castrato, yet we've been hounded with accusations that he is a girl. If you could observe his sex and sign this document, we could perform in peace.

MONSIGNOR: Salembini, I shouldn't be involved—the Church's position—

(Salembini has pulled Bellino's pants out at the waist and is inviting the Monsignor to examine Bellino. Monsignor and Priest look down Bellino's pants. Monsignor puts his hand down Bellino's pants)

Everything seems to be in order—that is to say that everything that is supposed to be there is there and everything that

is supposed to have been removed is not there. This is a boy.
An excommunicated boy. But a boy, nevertheless.

SALEMBINI: Thank you. Thank you.

MONSIGNOR: Anyone else? *(Signs the document)*

SALEMBINI: Say thank you, Bellino

BELLINO *(Sings some more as a thank you)*:
>Tempus transit gelidum
>mundus renovatar—

MONSIGNOR: Can't he sing in Italian—I can't understand Latin
when it's sung.
>Who can? The accents are all off—it's impossible.

YOUNG CASANOVA *(Translating)*:
>Cold times are passing by,
>the world renews itself,
>spring with blossoms comes once more,
>beauty is given to every thing—

MONSIGNOR: Yes, yes, very nice. That's more than—

BELLINO *(Singing to Young Casanova, overlapping the following)*:
>Tendit modo retia
>puer pharetratus
>cui deorum curia

YOUNG CASANOVA *(Translating, simultaneously with the preceding)*:
>Now spreads out his nets
>the boy with the quiver
>whom the court of the Gods—

MONSIGNOR: That's absolutely enough Latin, thank you.

*(Bellino is quiet but Young Casanova keeps on—he knows the
rest of the song)*

YOUNG CASANOVA:
>—offer its services
>whose domination

spreads far and far.
By him was I
overpowered and injured.
I fought—

BELLINO *(Singing again, overlapping the following)*:
et fueram
in primis reluctatus
sed iterum
per pueram
sum Veneri prostratus

YOUNG CASANOVA *(Translating, simultaneously with the preceding)*:
and had
at first resisted,
but yet again
I am subject
to Venus.

MONSIGNOR: They're like two silly dolls! Can't you shut them up?

SALEMBINI: Bellino, what are you doing?

BELLINO *(Besotted, overlapping the following)*:
nec cinnamum
et balsamum—

YOUNG CASANOVA *(Turned on, simultaneously with the preceding)*:
cinnamon
liquid honey—

SALEMBINI: Bellino, we are going now.

(Salembini exits with Bellino)

MONSIGNOR *(To Young Casanova)*: Now, really, my son, you're taking your Latin much too seriously! *(Exits)*

PRIEST *(About Bellino)*: Strange—I didn't feel the attraction of that boy at all. I must be getting old.

(Priest exits. Young Casanova tries to return to polishing and cleaning. As he is wiping the crucifix, he sees the carved face of Jesus as that of a beautiful man. He caresses it, then runs his hand down Jesus's chest, ending at the groin, which he also caresses, in wonder)

CASANOVA: The Church and Eros—who could explain it? But it certainly kept happening to me.

BOBO *(To Sophie)*: Tell me there's more.

(Young Casanova and Bellino are alone in another space)

BELLINO: Why are you here?

YOUNG CASANOVA: I don't know. The night . . .

BELLINO: I'm a boy.

YOUNG CASANOVA: Yes, I know. *(Kisses Bellino)*

BELLINO *(Kissing him back)*: Don't. Don't.

(They progress and Young Casanova feels Bellino's chest, just as he had done to the Jesus statue)

YOUNG CASANOVA: Oh my God!

BELLINO: Go! Get out!
        Oh God!

YOUNG CASANOVA: A breast!

BELLINO: I'm just a curiosity to you, aren't I?

YOUNG CASANOVA: No!

BELLINO: I'm used to it. You'd be amazed at the number of men who try to buy me so they can have all of their favorite things—two breasts, and a penis.

YOUNG CASANOVA: No, no . . .

BELLINO: We grow breasts after we've been cut. And our arms and legs and our hands grow long! I'll be a completed monster soon! You want a freak!

YOUNG CASANOVA: You're wrong. I just want . . . you.

BELLINO: Well, you can't have me. I'm not to be had. I have to sing to make a living. I have brothers and sisters, a mother and a teacher to support. Now, get out!!

YOUNG CASANOVA: Alright. Do I really have to go?

BELLINO: YES!

YOUNG CASANOVA: Wait. I can't leave right now. I'm too excited. Let me breathe. *(Pause)* Come out with me. As long as I'm in trouble, I'm going to take the boat to Corfu or somewhere. Come on—we'll have a lost day or two—as men! What do you have to lose?

BELLINO: Everything.

YOUNG CASANOVA: They'll forgive you. Afraid a little masculine activity will lower your voice? I've been good. I've been devout. I'm sick of it. Listen, we'll be prodigal—we'll be the prodigal sons when we return.

BELLINO: You will have run off with a castrato.

YOUNG CASANOVA: So I've just fulfilled every cleric's dream!

BELLINO: You're being brave with your reputation. And mine.

YOUNG CASANOVA: Are you a boy or a man?

BELLINO: I'm coming.

YOUNG CASANOVA: We'll get some girls. We'll get drunk. I know two sisters.

(Young Casanova starts to pull Bellino offstage. Bellino looks at the audience in fear—they exit.

Two Young Women enter—they are onboard ship and not feeling well. They head for the railing to throw up. Bellino and Young Casanova, their dates, enter. They try not to look at each other)

Having a good time?

BELLINO: You bet.

BOBO: Skip this part.

(The couples exit. Dark. Young Casanova enters with a lit candle. He feels his way across the stage until he finds a bed. He undresses and climbs in)

YOUNG CASANOVA: Hello? Bellino? *(Lies back, discouraged. After a beat, he sits up again)* Hello? *(Young Casanova blows the candle out and sighs deeply. After a long beat, we hear the rustling of the bedclothes)* Bellino.

CASANOVA *(By himself, watching the scene)*: I am overcome to see him moving toward me. I ache to clasp him to me, and see that he is fired by the same transport of feeling which floods out in a deluge of kisses from both our mouths.

His arms are the first to slip down from my back to my loins. And I stretch my arms even lower—but the question that has been so important to me disappears in the revelation that I am happy, and I give myself, body and soul, to the joy which fills my entire being and which I see shared. And then—

BOBO: What?! What?! Sophie, darling, don't pause here.

(Young Casanova shouts in pleasure)

YOUNG CASANOVA: You are a woman! You are a woman!
BOBO *(As if hit with a blow)*: Uhn!
YOUNG CASANOVA: Where is it? Where is your—whatever the Monsignor felt and saw—where is it?

(Young Casanova lights a candle while Bellino gets a little box, hands it to Young Casanova, who opens it, looks inside)

BELLINO: I keep it in a box. I keep it with me.
YOUNG CASANOVA: How do you . . . keep it on?
BELLINO: Tragacanth gum, freely applied.
YOUNG CASANOVA: How do you pee?
BELLINO: I don't until I can take it off.

You knew I wasn't a boy all along, didn't you?
YOUNG CASANOVA *(Lying)*: Of course. I did.

(One of them blows out the candle and they continue their lovemaking)

CASANOVA: Bellino. I did love you. *(A twinge of guilt)* Let it pass. In love, men and women are complete equals—they dupe each other! *(Exits)*

SOPHIE: Bobo, I didn't think you cared who my father slept with.

BOBO: I don't. But find some better gossip. *(Exits)*

(Bellino and an Older Woman enter. The Older Woman is helping Bellino get dressed as a woman. Bellino reads a letter that she has written)

BELLINO: Dearest Giacomo,

I am writing to tell you that our problems are over. I received a wonderful offer from the manager of the San Samuel Theatre in Naples to be a permanent part of his company—as a soloist. You were right—in Naples, women can sing on the stage. So I've thrown away my box and bought women's clothing and am living my dream. I've enclosed a copy of my contract for you to peruse. I've even hired an older woman to pose as my mother so I will remain respectable until you can join me as my husband. I await your answer. *(Pause)* I await your answer. *(Silence. Not knowing what to do, Bellino exits, stopping one last time)* I'll be waiting.

(Young Casanova enters and sits in another space. Bellino enters her space and reads another letter)

My Dearest Giacomo,

I hope you are all right. I miss you terribly and do wonder why you haven't written. I've signed the contract and am in rehearsal for my first opera! I'm getting a wonderful salary and have sent money home. If you need any money, I will send it immediately. I long to hear from you. I am so worried.

(Filled with guilt, Young Casanova puts his head in his hands. Bellino, having a hard time closing her letter off:)

Your . . . Beloved Bellino.

(Young Casanova gets up and exits. Bellino, hoping that it's true:)

Did you lose your passport?

(No answer—she exits.
Sophie sighs and exits)

CASANOVA *(Entering)*: How could I be just someone's husband?
She wouldn't have understood that. No. They never under-
stand about that.
UTA *(Offstage)*: Where are you? *(Enters)* We can't keep stopping.
The coachman is getting angry.
CASANOVA: Get me to an inn. *(Gives her the small bottle)* No
more laudanum.

(They exit.
Lights up on Sophie and Bobo—in his room)

SOPHIE: If he wants to see me, he can ask. Does he know my
married name?
BOBO: You wrote to him both times you were married.
And the second time he sent you that necklace.
SOPHIE: Marco thought it was ugly so I stopped wearing it. Why
did I do that? And now I'm waiting for Victor—I made him
a shirt when I had so much work to do—paying work.
From now on, Bobo, I shall no longer be a victim of love.
I will fall in love with a man ONLY because he is handsome.
I will sleep with him, and then I will leave him, never looking back. And when he confronts me in the cafe or wherever, I will look at him with incredulity, make a joke with
my companion for the evening, and then leave the ex-lover
pining, a pathetic and ridiculous sight. I will be as hard and
shiny as silver and I shall always be on my way out the door.
BOBO: Well, that's a speech worthy of the Place de Concorde,
and about as empty, too.
SOPHIE: Empty?! What makes you think I can't be that way?
I can change! The entire world changed!

BOBO: Where is this change, Sophie? People went mad, tore everything up, left it in piles, peed on it, and replaced it with nothing! What's left? Tawdriness and blood! And a nation of hideously dressed people, speaking bad language, and wearing wigs that look like an enormous cat coughed them up! And Rousseau! Don't talk to me about Rousseau! He was a music copyist, and an ugly, little pretentious hypocrite who kept young girls, YOUNG girls, and his ideas DESTROYED MY WORLD.

SOPHIE: It was a world without equality, Bobo!

BOBO: Equality is useless to one who is superior! And speaking of superior—you are superior in every way to the dreadful Vincent or Victor and Marco and Julius! Why do you let them get inside you?!

SOPHIE: *JULIEN!* His name was *Julien!* And Vincent's name is *VICTOR!* And they all are men I love! Do you know what's wrong with you, Bobo? You've never been in love in your life!! It's easy to make fun of my feelings when you spend all day primping on a gown and working on a wig the size of a small child! And I've been meaning to ask you since I was eight years old—why do you wear gowns, anyway? YOU'RE A MAN!! *(Exits)*

BOBO: IF THE POPE CAN WEAR A GOWN, SO CAN I!!! *(To himself)* I've worn gowns all my life and dresses and fabulous underwear that I made myself. Missy. But it does attract . . .

(Bobo has a memory from his childhood. Boy Bobo enters, pursued by a Countess. He is in drag)

COUNTESS: Come here, my little Bobo! Come here, my darling! Come here, my little pear!

(He outruns her. She fakes a turned ankle and falls. He stops and goes to her)

BOY BOBO: Are you all right?

COUNTESS *(Grabbing him)*: The advantage of being a woman.
I know my way into the clothing—Aha! *(Has her hand in his
underwear—she kisses him)* Love drop.
Yum.

(French Fop enters)

FRENCH FOP: Alphonsina, really.
COUNTESS: Just having some fun.
FRENCH FOP: Leave the weird boy alone.

*(Countess exits with French Fop. Boy Bobo gets up,
straightens his clothing, checks his panties, feels that they
are wet with cum)*

BOY BOBO: I'm wet. My new silk—it's ruined.

(French Fop reenters)

FRENCH FOP: Did she get inside you?
BOY BOBO: She got inside my pants.
FRENCH FOP *(About Boy Bobo's genitals)*: No. That's not you—
that thing down there. *(Points to Boy Bobo's head and heart)*
That is you, and this is you. That thing there has a mind of
its own and a world of its own. It's separate—it's a toy.
Think of it that way and protect yourself in love.
BOY BOBO: But I'm wet.
FRENCH FOP: Then wash up. Someday you'll tell this story—no
names, please—and entertain a roomful of people, at least.
BOY BOBO: Am I a real man now?

*(Boy Bobo and French Fop exit. Lights down on his room as
Bobo is still.
Uta and Casanova are together, sitting on a bench at an inn.
He is eating enthusiastically. They have a platter between them
and a pitcher of wine)*

UTA: Where are we? I can't understand what anyone is saying.
And they're looking at me.

CASANOVA: That's because you're with me. Now do you believe that I am someone of importance?

UTA: Or maybe you're just strange.

CASANOVA: Hand me more of that paté.

UTA: What is this horrible mixture?

CASANOVA: Food. Food for mankind, not livestock. *(Takes a drink of wine—it is wonderful)* Ahh. This is as wonderful as returning to Venice after a long absence. Home is wine.

UTA: I want to go home.

CASANOVA: Uta, don't cry again. Everything will be alright.

UTA: You don't know anything! You can't tell a boy from a girl.

THERESE *(Entering with platter)*: More paté? It's good for the heart. *(Slaps a lot on his plate and exits)*

CASANOVA: Who was that?

(Young Casanova enters, still dressed as an abbé. He carries a uniform, chosen for the color only, and begins to change into it. An old servant, Paolo, enters)

YOUNG CASANOVA: I live here. I just got back home. I'm Señor Casanova.

PAOLO: He's dead.

YOUNG CASANOVA: No—no. That was my father. I am Giacomo.

PAOLO: He's a priest.

YOUNG CASANOVA: Not anymore.

(Paolo flicks Young Casanova on the nose. It begins to bleed immediately)

PAOLO: Welcome home, then, Sir! *(About the nosebleed)* Sorry, I had to be certain.

YOUNG CASANOVA *(Talking with nose full)*: Where'dz Baba?

PAOLO: Doing a play in Florence. The house is yours.

(Beat. Paolo watches Young Casanova finish getting into his uniform)

My sister brings me supper. Would you like some macaroni?

YOUNG CASANOVA: No, I'll be dining out.

(*Young Casanova exits. Paolo picks up the abbé garb that Young Casanova shed and exits.*
    Back to Casanova and Uta)

CASANOVA: I went to the Café Florien and ordered whatever I wanted. I walked the streets of Venice all night. I drank to excess when I felt like it. I went to the Riddoto and played faro. And no one tried to stop me. And that's when I discovered the Secret all the women in my life had been trying to keep from me—all the women and the Church—

YOUNG CASANOVA: —the world is mine. And it has been here all the time. All I had to do is take it!

(*Young Casanova reaches out his hand. Young Therese enters and takes his hand and pulls him along. They are teenagers*)

Therese, wait!

YOUNG THERESE: Hurry, hurry! It's over there!

YOUNG CASANOVA: What is that smell?

YOUNG THERESE: It's the beast. Come on!

VENETIAN FOP (*Emerging from having seen it*): I've seen an animal like that before. They're all over Sicily.

YOUNG THERESE (*Reading the sign*): Ree-no-kerras.

YOUNG CASANOVA: It's Latin. Rhinoceros.

VENETIAN FOP: It's a giant pig. With a horn. Please. (*To Young Casanova*) Waste of time. There's a line. (*Exits*)

YOUNG CASANOVA: Be careful, Therese. Whatever it is—it's wild.

YOUNG THERESE: You're always telling me to be careful.

YOUNG CASANOVA: You don't know what it is.

YOUNG THERESE: I didn't know what you were, either. And I went ahead and looked. (*Gets erotic with him*)

YOUNG CASANOVA: People will see.

YOUNG THERESE: Ri-no-serras is a beautiful beast. Like you, Giacomo.

YOUNG CASANOVA: What do you see? I'm not a beast.

YOUNG THERESE: Then why do you make me so wild?

> The smell excites me. *(Kisses him)* Come on—let's get closer. I must see all of it.
>
> I'm going to have a wonderful life, Giacomo. I can feel it! *(Exits to see the rhino)*

YOUNG CASANOVA: Therese! Wait. Therese! Don't talk to those men—you haven't been introduced! Therese—people will think you're a flirt! *(Exits after her)*

THERESE: That's it? That's our courtship? That's all you remember? And me in the worst outfit I ever owned? Where's me washing my breasts in the window? Our violin lessons? The conception of our daughter? That time . . . pressed . . . up against the wall . . . in my mothers' bedchamber . . . yes. *(Comes back from her erotic memory)* But nooooo. My virginity, my passion is forever a visit to a smelly beast from the dark part of the world. As dark as your heart, my dove? As smelly as MY ANGER? Oh my, listen to that. In the world a few breaths and I'm swept into the full disaster again! *(Exits)*

UTA: Every boy thinks he knows all about love. But none of them understand the heart of a girl. And then they become men, and they know even less. And Jakob is no different. And you're too old to even remember what being in love is.

CASANOVA: When I became a man, I fell deeply in love. I was a free citizen of Venice, but I was her prisoner. Her name was Caterina and she was fourteen years old.

(Caterina enters in another space. She is young and well-dressed)

She was young and I was a grown man. But it was love—it was the full disaster.

CATERINA: You rented this garden just for me?

(Young Casanova enters—he is dressed very well, a bit rakish now, with a stylish wig)

YOUNG CASANOVA: Yes.

CATERINA: It's just for me?

YOUNG CASANOVA: Yes.

CATERINA: No one will come?

YOUNG CASANOVA: No.

CATERINA: I can do anything I want?

YOUNG CASANOVA: Yes.

CATERINA: May I shout very loud?

YOUNG CASANOVA: Except that.

CATERINA: I don't know what to do.

YOUNG CASANOVA: Enjoy yourself.

CATERINA: I'm never by myself except in bed. *(Skips a bit, then laughs nervously)* Someone is always watching.

YOUNG CASANOVA: I won't watch, then. I'll leave for a little while. I won't go far—just outside.

(Young Casanova exits.

After a beat, Caterina realizes that she is alone, unsupervised, for the first time in her life. She begins to hyperventilate, gets hold of herself, then laughs and begins to run around and around, faster and faster—she stops and takes off her dress and her corset, then she really runs, whooping. Young Casanova reenters—she stops)

CATERINA *(Runs for her clothes)*: You came back so soon.

YOUNG CASANOVA *(About putting her dress on)*: Don't, don't. You don't have to.

CATERINA: I think I have to.

YOUNG CASANOVA: Who is watching? Only me.

CATERINA: God is watching.

YOUNG CASANOVA: God was watching before.

CATERINA: That's right.

YOUNG CASANOVA: Go on—do what you were doing before.

(Caterina begins to skip, then trot, then run until she no longer feels inhibited)

You're wild! Why are you so wild?!

CATERINA: It feels so good not to wear that.

YOUNG CASANOVA: This dress?

CATERINA: No, the corset.

YOUNG CASANOVA: Catch me!

CATERINA: Alright!

(Young Casanova takes off his jacket and starts to run—Caterina tries to catch him)

YOUNG CASANOVA: Wait. *(Takes off more clothing)* Now—go!

(He runs, Caterina pursues—he turns his ankle and falls, she catches him. He grabs her sweetly, laughing, then kisses her. She stands up, confused, he comes to her and kisses her again. He moves in with lots of petting, until she breaks away)

CATERINA: I'm dizzy—I'm—

CASANOVA: TAKE HER! TAKE HER!

(Young Casanova picks her up and kisses her hard, carries her off. Casanova picks up Caterina's clothes and smells them. He watches as two women enter.

A Woman Reading a Newspaper and a Happy Woman enter. The Happy Woman addresses the audience)

HAPPY WOMAN: We always wanted to get them, and now we've got them. We came close to getting them before, but we couldn't get them. Not really. But now—

WOMAN READING A NEWSPAPER *(Reading the headline)*: "Experts Confirm Semen Causes Pregnancy."

HAPPY WOMAN: We always wanted to get them and we've got them now.

(They exit. Casanova follows.

Bells ring. Young Casanova is on the island of Murano, at a convent, in the basement. A pile of dirty rags is on the floor near him. Idiot Woman enters, takes his coat and puts it on, exits)

YOUNG CASANOVA: Hey! Wait!

(Laura, a lower-class woman from Murano, enters with some good linen that is bloody and a small bundle in a sheet)

Oh my God! Is she all right?

LAURA *(About the bloody linen)*: Well, the worst is over. The culprit's in there. We'll know if she'll live by this evening.

YOUNG CASANOVA: What?

LAURA: Why are all men deaf?

YOUNG CASANOVA: The culprit?

LAURA: Don't open that sheet up. I'll just dump it in the canal and let the tide and the fishies take care of it.

YOUNG CASANOVA: I have to see her. How can I see her?

LAURA: You're in a convent. No men allowed. That's why her father put her here. He didn't know he was too late.

YOUNG CASANOVA: Did she get my note?

LAURA: I put it in her hand.

YOUNG CASANOVA: Dear God, Caterina.

LAURA: I'll bring you some supper while you wait.

YOUNG CASANOVA: I'm not hungry. Someone took my coat.

LAURA: You're helpless, aren't you.

(Laura exits. With great trepidation, Young Casanova looks in the bloody bundle, at the lump that would have been his child. He can't bear it and closes the sheet. He prays for Caterina and then lies down and falls asleep. The Idiot Woman enters, wearing his coat. She lies down on his stomach and sleeps, too. A nun, Marina Morosini, enters and sees Young Casanova. She exits.

Time change. Laura enters, carrying a covered bowl with food in it)

YOUNG CASANOVA *(Sits up immediately)*: Yes?

LAURA: Brought you supper.

(Idiot Woman starts to eat Young Casanova's supper)

YOUNG CASANOVA: Caterina?

LAURA: The bleeding's stopped. She'll live.

YOUNG CASANOVA: Oh! Oh! thankgodthankgodthankgod! I have to see her, PLEASE.

LAURA: Eat and then go home. And be careful no one sees you.

YOUNG CASANOVA: Tell her that I love her always. Tell her.

LAURA: Yes yes.

YOUNG CASANOVA *(About Idiot Woman)*: Can you make her give me my coat?

LAURA: Were you born this way? *(To Idiot Woman)* Give the nice man his coat, Violetta.

IDIOT WOMAN *(Not giving it up)*: COAAAAATTT!

LAURA: She likes that coat.

YOUNG CASANOVA: It doesn't matter

LAURA *(About the bundle)*: I'll take this. *(Gives him a note)* Oh, here's a note for you.

YOUNG CASANOVA: From Caterina?

LAURA: No. From someone who knows you haven't had a woman in months.

YOUNG CASANOVA: Who told them that?

LAURA *(About the note)*: Take it.

YOUNG CASANOVA: How can you suggest such a thing?

(Laura drops the note at his feet)

LAURA: I get my tip either way. *(About not picking up the note)* But you needn't be rude. *(Holds up the bundle)* Life goes on.

(She exits. Young Casanova can't help himself—he picks up the note and starts to read it to himself. As he does, a figure in a tricorn hat, bateau mask and cloak enters another space. This is Marina in disguise)

MARINA: You must meet with me. I desire you with all my heart. I'll wait by the quay under the lion. I'll be carrying a candle. One hour after sunset tonight. Please. Come in disguise, too. No one will ever know we met.

(Young Casanova checks his pocket watch—he starts to exit and the Idiot Woman tries to follow him, but he ditches her. She squats and puts her head in her hands.

Marina waits. Another masked figure enters, looks at her. She raises her candle—he approaches and produces a cigar, lights it from her candle. She touches his hand—he takes it and embraces her. She takes off her tricorn hat—her hair falls down. The other masked figure recoils)

BOBO: Pardon. Pardon. *(Exits quickly)*

SOPHIE *(In another space, to the screen, behind which Bobo is dressing)*: I never knew you smoked, Bobo.

(Young Casanova enters, sees Marina—she takes off her mask and crosses to him—they exit)

BOBO *(Emerging from behind the screen)*: I was there to study church architecture.

SOPHIE: Yes, there are so few really beautiful churches in Paris. I can understand how one would need to go to Venice.

BOBO: Fasten me here and be quiet.

SOPHIE *(Fastening the underwear)*: Do you know where Mamzell is?

BOBO: Oh my, oh my, oh my.

(He goes to the vanity, takes out an old package that is wrapped and unwraps it carefully, removing an ancient, beat-up doll. He hands it to Sophie)

SOPHIE: Just for a little while.

BOBO: Ah . . . the churches of Venice. I remember each one.

(Young Casanova and Marina are in a beautiful private room at the Riddoto)

YOUNG CASANOVA: I shouldn't be here.

MARINA: Why not? It's beautiful here.

YOUNG CASANOVA: A private room at the Riddoto.

MARINA: These rooms belong to an influential friend.

YOUNG CASANOVA: You're not married, are you?

MARINA: Yes.

YOUNG CASANOVA: Well, so am I. In the eyes of God, anyway.

MARINA: I, too, in more than the eyes.

(She takes off her cape—she is dressed in a nun's habit.
Young Casanova bows on his hands and knees before her
immediately)

YOUNG CASANOVA: Forgive me, Sister. I swear to you that
Caterina and I are married totally and completely and that
I would take her to the Church instantly, were I given the
opportunity.

(Marina moves forward, putting her skirt over Young Casanova's
head. He rises up—his head inside her dress)

MARINA: I saw you in the basement of the convent, and I knew
you were mine.

(Therese enters)

THERESE *(To audience)*: Do you believe in love at first sight?
Me neither.

YOUNG CASANOVA: I'm true to Caterina.

MARINA: Fidelity in a man is so erotic.

(Therese reveals an easel on which a chart is displayed of an
incomprehensible drawing of two naked human figures
interlocked)

THERESE: "Straight-tree"—just one of the thirty-two erotic
positions described by Pietro Aretino (1492–1556) in his
Sonetti drawings by Giulio Romano. *(Squints at the area*
where Young Casanova and Marina are in bed together) Well,
now they've moved on to something else—looks like Position
Number Eleven: "Unfolding the Cabana Chair." I guess I'll

just put this easel away IN THE CLOSET. Why, here's a CLOSET now.

(She opens the closet door and finds an older man watching Marina and Young Casanova. This is Abbé Bernis—François Joachim de Pierre de Bernis, ambassador to France. He looks at the audience and freezes. Therese laughs as she carries the easel off and exits. Bernis shuts the closet door)

MARINA: Why did you stop?

YOUNG CASANOVA: I thought I heard something—

MARINA: Shhhhhhh. It's nothing. My name is Marina. Say it, say it . . .

(In the coach again are Uta and Casanova)

UTA: I don't know about traveling with you anymore. I thought the food would make you better, but you drank all that wine and then I find you with an arm full of leaves, smelling them and mumbling.

CASANOVA: I'm in . . . pain.

UTA: What were you eating at the inn? That can't be good for you—it smelled terrible.

CASANOVA: Garlic. Garlic, Mademoiselle, is a civilizing herb without which there would be no art or music or painting or—beauty.

UTA: Smells like pig fart.

CASANOVA: Do you know what a barbarian is?

UTA: The people in France who killed the King.

CASANOVA: How do you know about that—you can't even read.

UTA: It doesn't have to be written down to have happened. *(Notices)* We're stopped.

CASANOVA: We're not turning back. We're going to Paris.

UTA: We're going all the way to Paris!? I've never been further than Schmattsburg!

CASANOVA: Robespierre is dead and there's a ball.

UTA: Jakob will never find me!

CASANOVA: I—must—go. Please get me there. Please. *(Big pain)* Uhhhhhn.

UTA: Coachman? We need to go on. I guess.

CASANOVA *(In pain)*: Please, Uta, my darling, please.

UTA: Coachman! Hurry.

THERESE AS COACHMAN *(Appearing)*: You talking to me? *(About Casanova)* Is he alive there?

CASANOVA: Uhhn.

UTA: Of course he is.

THERESE AS COACHMAN: Well, all these stops. They got me worried. Just between you and me, little lady, I don't think the old guy's gonna make it. And you and me are both gonna be stiffed, if you pardon the pun. So you'd better fork over the rest of the fare to beautiful Paree or all you will see is Schmattsburg. And it's not a pretty sight, believe me.

CASANOVA *(Not quite tuned in)*: Thank you, Sir, for your concern. I am quite fine, thank you very much. No need for you to worry. No need, no need, no need. Merci. Danke . . . something . . . very much.

UTA *(To Therese)*: You leave him alone! And get this coach rolling!

THERESE AS COACHMAN: You're the boss.

CASANOVA *(Out of it)*: Dear lady, your hospitality has been most appreciated. And your salon, quite superb, but I must be gone. I have other appointments. Luminaries await my . . . ahm . . .

UTA: He's gone. Put your head on my lap. Lie down. There.

(Casanova puts his head in her lap)

CASANOVA: Newfoundland cod—glutinous, rich.
    I never forgot from whence I came.

UTA: There, there.

THERESE AS COACHMAN: Women! Nice, nice, nicey nice. *(Exits, shouts offstage to the horses)* HEEYAW!!

(Casanova and Uta lurch as the coach starts again. The lurch gives Casanova pain.

In Marina's room at the Riddoto—a nun stands with her back to the audience. Young Casanova enters)

YOUNG CASANOVA: I couldn't stay away.
> What's wrong? Turn around.
> Why are you afraid to face me?

(The nun turns around—it's Caterina)

CATERINA: It's alright that you don't love me anymore.
> *(Embraces him)*
YOUNG CASANOVA: My God—Caterina.
> Are you feeling all right?
CATERINA: Oh, I'm fine. Just as I've said in my letters. Marina got me out for tonight.

(They sit in silence for a few beats. He takes off her hood and frees her hair)

YOUNG CASANOVA: Such nice hair.
> My little wife.
CATERINA: Still?

(She kisses him on the mouth. He is polite. She kisses him again—he is just sweet to her)

YOUNG CASANOVA: I'll go order you some supper. You must be starved.

(Marina enters, in a dress, not a habit)

Marina.
MARINA: I'm to meet my French friend here. I've missed you.
> I'll just go into the casino and wait.
YOUNG CASANOVA: Marina—
CATERINA: You want to be together and you should be.
MARINA: Yes, but I will only stay if you stay, Caterina.
> *(To Young Casanova)* I will stay only if Caterina stays.

YOUNG CASANOVA: Supper for three then.

MARINA: That's one way of looking at it. Since we would all be here together, feasting on each other, no one would then be untrue to anyone. Why haven't other love triangles thought of it! *(Kisses Caterina)*

YOUNG CASANOVA *(To Caterina)*: Surely you don't want to stay?

CATERINA: Do you want me to?

MARINA: She must.

YOUNG CASANOVA: Oh. Well—

CATERINA: Then come here.

YOUNG CASANOVA *(Stops)*: What about your influential friend?

MARINA: We'll know when he's here.

(All three begin kissing. Ecstatic rattling begins in the closet. Therese enters with a big sign that says "THE FRENCH AMBASSADOR"—she holds it next to the closet and points. She exits)

YOUNG CASANOVA: I hear something.

MARINA: Shhhh. It's nothing.

(Young Casanova goes to closet and stares inside holes in the door)

BERNIS *(From inside closet)*: Bonjour.

(Young Casanova opens the door, revealing Abbé Bernis)

MARINA: He's here! This is my friend, Abbé Joachim de Bernis, the French ambassador.

BERNIS: Bonjour. Bonjour. Continue.

(Marina shuts the closet door)

Merci.

MARINA: Never mind, my loves. We will let nothing disturb our trinity.

(She leads Young Casanova back to Caterina. She kisses them both—they stare at the closet. She gets them involved briefly, but they keep staring at the closet)

One person watching or one hundred and sixty-eight. What difference does it make?

YOUNG CASANOVA (*By himself in a neutral space*): I'm exhausted. I spent blood that last time—terrified them both.

My lovely, precious Caterina is debauched. And I am, at least partly, responsible. Oh, the looks that passed across her face—pleasure! passion! What it has unlocked in her! And to have to watch her in this state when she is with Marina and I am resting. What lover could stand it! What husband! And then when we took time in the casino just to get our minds on something else—she wins and wins at faro. I had just taught her the rules! "What will you do with all this money, Caterina?" "Buy my way out of the convent." She will, at that rate.

I can't marry her. She's my wife under the eyes of God, but I can't marry her. No man can have a debauched wife. No, she has appetite now—I see it in her eyes.

(*Caterina enters, looks at Young Casanova—he doesn't see her*)

Those eyes would look on my children. There's an injustice here, but I can't quite put my finger on it. In any case, I can't marry her.

Well, that's at least one disaster averted. I'm not married to anyone. No one is pregnant. Anymore. I'm a free agent in the most beautiful republic in the world.

(*Caterina exits. Sbirri #1 and Sbirri #2 approach Young Casanova*)

SBIRRI #1: Giacomo Casanova?

SBIRRI #2: We have orders from the Holy Inquisition to arrest and incarcerate you indefinitely for holding secret meetings with the French ambassador.

(*Manuzzi enters, carrying a bunch of books*)

YOUNG CASANOVA: Those are my books.

MANUZZI: Thank you. *(To the Sbirri)* Evidence identified. Take him away.

(Both Sbirri exit with Young Casanova and the books. Manuzzi notices a Woman Passing By walking alone)

Hey, little one. What are you doing out without a chaperone? Let me walk you home.

WOMAN PASSING BY: No, Sir.

(She starts to exit. Manuzzi laughs and runs to her, blocking her way—she dodges him, afraid. He chases her)

MANUZZI: Hey! What's wrong with me!

(The Woman Passing By is really afraid now and runs off-stage—he catches up with her offstage)

WOMAN PASSING BY *(Offstage)*: No no no nononononono.

(Lights up on Bobo and Sophie in their space)

BOBO *(At his vanity)*: Her hand went down my panties, as quick as a weasel, and I was suddenly wet with the lecherous Countess Alphonsina, in a hideous yellow gown, heaving passionately on top of my small boy body when her silly foppish escort rescued me. "Alphonsina? Leave the weird boy alone." He turned out to be my benefactor in every way. He willed to me my title—the Chevalier D'Eon. And gave me a way to protect myself in love.
Sophie?

(She's asleep on the couch, holding her doll)

My life bores you. Your father's life fascinates you. Oh, there is no such thing as literature. Or love. Only blood. Blood is all that matters.

(Bobo covers her with some frilly thing of his to keep her warm. He exits. Sophie wakes up)

SOPHIE: Victor? Victor? Is that you?

(*It's not—she's alone.*
In the coach, Casanova still has his head in Uta's lap)

UTA: I don't know why but I can't leave you. Even for an old man, you're not good looking, you know.

CASANOVA: Everyone says that.

(*Sound of the loud clank of a prison door shutting. Small light on Young Casanova, hunched on the floor. Therese Imer is close to him, skin to skin, looking at him. He can't see or feel her*)

YOUNG CASANOVA (*Incredulous*): I'm innocent.

(*Therese runs her tongue slowly up his cheek, licking him like a confection, closes her eyes in pleasure*)

THERESE: I'm lost.

ACT TWO

Casanova is wearing a cloak with a hood, so we can't see him that well. He is lying with his head in Uta's lap—his groin hurts.

CASANOVA *(In pain)*: Uhhhhhn. Uhhhhhhn.

UTA: All those bumps and holes on the way. France—no one works on the roads. No, they're too busy getting dressed up.

CASANOVA: I'll be all right.

UTA: Well, I got to piss this time.

CASANOVA: Don't be crass, please. I'm starved for gentility—for civilization.

UTA: What's your piss? Poetry? I've seen it—it's usually bloody—not gentle at all.

Just don't wander off and get lost.

(She exits. Suddenly, there's a lot of light and Casanova sees the garden Young Casanova rented for Caterina. Caterina, age fourteen and dressed well, enters. After a beat, Young Casanova enters. This time, Caterina speaks to Casanova)

CATERINA: You rented this garden just for me?

CASANOVA AND YOUNG CASANOVA: Yes.

CATERINA: No one will come?

CASANOVA AND YOUNG CASANOVA: No.

CATERINA: I don't know what to do.

CASANOVA AND YOUNG CASANOVA: Enjoy yourself.

YOUNG CASANOVA: I'll leave for a little while. I won't go far—just outside.

(Young Casanova exits. Casanova sits down to watch. Caterina begins to breathe—just as she did in the first memory; but, instead of running, she turns to Casanova and leaps on him, a succubus)

CATERINA *(Straddling him, until she's sitting on his groin)*: How big is it? Bigger than a sausage? And what size sausage? Is it big enough to sing to? Can I sing it a little song? Does it stick straight up? Is the foreskin purple or pink? Will it like me? Will its little eye like what it sees? Can I see it? Can I see its little helmet head? Its little doge hat? Will it come out for me? Will-ums get hard for little me? Come, come, let me have it. Rubba-rubba-rubba-rubba! COME, COME, COME, COME!

CASANOVA *(Fear)*: AHHHHHHHHHHH—

(Blackout. Casanova is still screaming when the lights come up. He is in the same position—lying there, but Caterina has been replaced with Therese, her wraith-self, demurely straddling him, working on some lace-making)

—AHHHHHHHHHH! Therese?

THERESE: Venetian 60-point. Very difficult to do.

CASANOVA: Get off me!!!

(She gets off and he feels the pain in his groin)

What are you doing? You look terrible.

THERESE: I'm dead.

CASANOVA: What? Utaaaaaaa!!
Go away, spirit! Begone!
Help! Jesus!
Gooooo!

THERESE: Love to.

   Can't.

   Destiny.

CASANOVA: I've had too much laudanum. *(Closes his eyes)*

THERESE: Perhaps.

   Perhaps not.

   Open.

(He opens his eyes—she's still there)

CASANOVA: No!

THERESE: Yes.

CASANOVA: Get away! My dreams are my own! My life is my own!

THERESE: Fine. Then, live it.

(Blackout. Sound of snoring—it fills the theatre. Dim lights up on Casanova lying on a prison floor, sleeping. He's the one who is snoring. Jailer enters)

JAILER: Who's there?

CASANOVA: What? Where am I?

JAILER: They must've locked you up over the weekend. Well, stand up.

CASANOVA: I feel surprisingly good all of a sudden. I feel wonderful.

JAILER: It'll pass. Come on.

(Jailer leads Casanova on a route to his sentencing. Therese enters and follows them, unnoticed, giving a tour of the Ducal Palace as she walks. Several tourists surround Casanova as he walks)

THERESE: Passing from the Piombi, prison, so-called for being situated under the lead—"piombo"—roof of the Ducal Palace, we pass quickly onto the Bridge of Sighs which traverses the Rio de Palazzo and decants the traveler into the Camera del Tormento—torture room—that leads to the

Quarantia Criminale, down the corridor and up the Staircase of the Censori, through the Hall of the Bussola with its wooden ceiling of simple design: "St. Mark in Glory Crowning the Three Theological Virtues" by Giulio Carlini, painted in 1553—a modern copy of the youthful work of Paolo Veronese. From there we pass directly into the Room of the State Inquisitors with its gilded leather walls and magnificent ceiling: "Four Virtues" and "The Return of the Prodigal Son" by Tintoretto. Please stay together and don't touch the paintings. *(To Casanova)* You look like Hell, my darling.

CASANOVA: Therese—what are you doing here? I dreamed you were dead.

(Therese exits with tourists. To Jailer:)

Wait—there's someone who can vouch for me.

JAILER: Stand here.

(Three Inquisitors appear)

CASANOVA: It's a dream—*in* a dream. I know—I'll fly out of here. *(Tries to fly)*

INQUISITOR #1: Are you Giacomo Girolamo Casanova?

CASANOVA: I'm usually naked at these moments.

JAILER: Stand still—insanity won't get you off.

INQUISITOR #2: Answer the question.

CASANOVA: Yes. Why not?

INQUISITOR #3: Stand before your accusers, Giacomo Girolamo Casanova.

CASANOVA: Only God is my accuser.

INQUISITOR #2: Oh, where do they get these answers?

INQUISITOR #1: It has been witnessed and sworn that you, Giacomo Girolamo Casanova, do not believe in God, do not observe Fridays and other days of abstinence, that you are known to be intimate with foreign ministers who pay you large sums of money for information you obtain from your patrician friends, that you play cards with Albanians, that you are a Freemason.

CASANOVA: What? Albanians?

INQUISITOR #3 *(Reading the titles)*: The *Clavicula of Solomon*, the *Zecor-ben*, something by Picatris, and an essay on "The Planetary Hours," a book of erotic drawings. These books were taken from your room.

CASANOVA: I read many things. I am also a philosopher. Consider, for example, the eternal presence of—

INQUISITOR #2: God? Too late for theology.

CASANOVA: No, I was going to say something about the eternal presence of the past, but I don't know why.

INQUISITOR #3: Here is a book we recommend that you read.

(An enormous tome is thrown onstage)

The Mystical City by Sister Mary of Jesus of Agrada. Don't worry, you'll find the time.

INQUISITOR #1: No other books, pens, paper, and you are expected to pay for your food and laundry. The Piombi is impenetrable—enjoy your stay.

(Inquisitors disappear)

CASANOVA: What?

(Jailer leads Casanova away)

JAILER: Now on this wall is "The Circumcision" by Francesco Da Ponte il Bassano—sixteenth century—and on our way out, be certain to notice the later "Rebellion Overcome by Justice and Sacrilege Thrown into the Abyss," another pointless and rather heavy painting by G.B. Ponchino. The red damask walls were originally . . .

(Casanova and Jailer have exited.
The Idiot Woman enters, still wearing Young Casanova's coat. She stands still and looks up, watching. After a beat, people begin

*(to fill the stage—characters from the play, actors in partial cos-
tume, stagehands—they all look up, also, wondering what the
Idiot Woman is seeing)*

PERSON: What are we looking for?
ANOTHER PERSON: I don't know.

*(Therese enters with a large calendar—she tears off some
months, flings them away and exits. All the people exit until the
Idiot Woman is standing alone. A beat later, Casanova lowers
himself from the flies, lands on the ground. He is quite beat up,
but tries to look festive. Idiot Woman makes a happy noise when
she see him)*

CASANOVA: That's my coat. I need it.

(He takes his coat from her—she puts up a fight)

Give it to me!

*(He exits. Idiot Woman bawls loudly. Jailer enters, carrying a
lunchbox)*

JAILER: What's wrong with you? Get away, get away! Go
home!! The party's over!

(He pushes her offstage—she exits)

Tourism is gonna kill this town.

*(He picks up the calendar pages and exits.
    Uta enters and finds Casanova's cloak on the bench where he
left it)*

UTA: Where is he? Herr Casanova? Come to Uta right now!
Where are you? You're scaring me!

(She exits, looking for him. Young Casanova enters the garden)

YOUNG CASANOVA: Caterina? Caterina! I'm back. Caterina!

(He exits, looking for her.

Bobo enters, dressed in his underdress—everything except the gown and wig)

BOBO: Sophie, can you sew up this bodice? *(Doesn't see her)* Sophie? Sophie! *(Can't find her. Checks the wardrobe for her cloak)* Her cloak is gone. *(Holds up short cloak)* No, MY cloak is gone. What can she be doing?

(He puts the cloak on and exits.
     Lady #2, Madame D'Urfe, Man are in the loge at the ballet. Therese passes through, selling items)

THERESE: Opera glasses, programs, pomanders. Opera glasses, programs, pomanders . . . *(Gone)*
LADY #2: We have seen at the Comedie Italienne on Rue Manconseil a Venetian named Casanova making a magnificent appearance. He was in the loge next to ours and came to greet us, attired resplendently, bedecked with lace, and wearing two large diamond rings. Within the hour, he had managed to flourish two different snuff boxes, too, both set in gold and of excellent taste. He also dabbles in the black arts and is supposed to have been a Freemason, and is living beyond his means.

(Casanova enters)

MAN: Monsieur Casanova? Join us!
CASANOVA: The Chevalier de Seingalt.
LADY #2: Where did you acquire this title, Monsieur Casanova?
CASANOVA: There are twenty-six letters in the alphabet, Mademoiselle. I arranged them as I wished.
LADY #2: But are you a Chevalier?
CASANOVA: Are you a Mademoiselle?
MAN: This dancer is wonderful, is she not?
CASANOVA: Ah.
LADY #2: Where are your rings, Chevalier?
CASANOVA *(Lying)*: I gave them away. To admirers.

LADY #2: And not the snuff boxes, too.

CASANOVA: Your interest in my accoutrements borders on the obsessive, Madam—moiselle.

(Man offers snuff from his own snuff box. Young Casanova enters the loge—no one notices him)

MAN *(About the dancer)*: She executes this arabesque with such grace and skill.

(They watch this move)

MADAME D'URFE: She's not wearing underpants. *(Beat)* I would give all I possess to become a man.

LADY #2: Oh, D'Urfe don't.

CASANOVA: Gender jealousy. The cosmos would not be pleased, Madame.

YOUNG CASANOVA: These people are all speaking French.
    (Exits)

MADAME D'URFE: I would—pay—someone—a—great deal, I mean, an extremely large amount of money if they—this someone, say he were a magician or a sorcerer or even a Freemason—if this someone could and would metamorphose me into a man. I believe you might be that one.

CASANOVA: I . . . what?

MAN: Madame D'Urfe—not here.

MADAME D'URFE: I want to be a man.
    Physically, spiritually, entirely.

MAN: I give up.

CASANOVA: It's not possible, Madame.
    Lead into gold, eternal youth, perhaps—

MADAME D'URFE: I want a penis.

LADY #2: Oh God.

CASANOVA: There are objects one can buy. I could, perhaps—

MADAME D'URFE: I want a man's soul.

MAN: There she goes.

CASANOVA: Perhaps remarriage is the answer.

Marry a weak man with a large member, enough for both of you, and dominate him.

LADY #2: Ah.

MADAME D'URFE: I want the spiritual release that only a man can have because true genii speak only to men, they appear only to men, because they have a more perfect nature—men.

CASANOVA: Who told you this?

MADAME D'URFE: The Catholic Church and the Man in the Moon.

LADY #2 *(To Man)*: I can't bear it. Let's find a coffee.

(They exit)

CASANOVA: How would this magician, whoever he might be, be paid?

MADAME D'URFE: In government bonds and jewels.

Of course, I could ask St. Germain.

He is three hundred years old and can melt diamonds.

CASANOVA: I'll think about it.

I admit to knowing some magic.

MADAME D'URFE: Hurry. I'm in pain.

CASANOVA: Oh?

MADAME D'URFE: Spiritual pain. Longing.

My Galtinardus.

CASANOVA: So you've read forbidden books, too. Semiramis.

MADAME D'URFE: I only ask that you try.

I am, after all, very old.

And I have discomfort in my female parts, anyway.

I REFUSE to pass on into the next world as a spiritual INVALID!

CASANOVA: For your—that is to say, my ceremony—we'd need a virgin.

MADAME D'URFE: Try anyway.

CASANOVA: Paralis will have to be consulted.

MADAME D'URFE: And the Man in the Moon.

The planets are my confidants.

I talk to Venus when I can see her.

I wear a magnet in the hope of attracting a lightning bolt which will carry me up to the sun.

Someday.

Patang! WHOOOOOSH!!

(Motions for Casanova to cross to her—he does. She pats him)

You're a nice man.

Hurry.

Oh— *(Taking off a large jeweled ring—she hands it to him. She gets up and walks away painfully)*

CASANOVA: No, no, no, no, no. No. No, no. *(Goes after her)* Madame.

(She stops)

The only way you can be regenerated into a man is if your soul is born into a man's body.

MADAME D'URFE: But wouldn't I be dead then?

CASANOVA: Exactly.

(She gives him another ring)

MADAME D'URFE: Now you have two rings again. You'll find a way.

(She exits. Therese enters with her opera glasses, programs and pomanders)

THERESE: Pomanders, programs, opera glasses, free appraisals—

(Therese takes the ring out of his hand and uses the opera glasses to look at the jewel, the way a jeweler does with diamonds. Casanova is distracted, thinking)

It's real. You'll do it.

CASANOVA: What?

(Therese exits.

Sophie is outside, on a street, standing in the shadows and star-ing up at a window. She has tried to cover herself in Bobo's cape because she's still in her nightgown. Bobo enters and sees her. He's wearing her too-short-for-him cape)

BOBO: Sophie? Is that you? *(No answer)* Is that you?

SOPHIE: No.

BOBO: What are you doing? It's not safe on the streets at night! You know that!!

SOPHIE: I needed to get out. You said I did.

BOBO: Oh, this is my idea. I see. I see. *(Pause)* Vincent lives here.

SOPHIE: *Victor! (To Bobo)* Shhh. Shhh. Shhh.

BOBO: Is he at home?

SOPHIE: There's a light.

BOBO: Come on. Come on. Don't do this.

SOPHIE: I feel more alive standing out here under his window than in all those days of nursing my "honor" by staying away.

BOBO: Twenty days without getting dressed is hardly "honor-able," Sophie. Come on. Come home. It's really not safe. Come on.

(Sophie starts to go with him)

SOPHIE: I'm starting to die again.

BOBO: Come on. You can't be here forever!! You can't live under his window!! They'll take you away.

SOPHIE: Why? I just look like a beggar. WHICH IS WHAT I AM!!

(Captain approaches—just some drunken guy pretending to be a captain)

CAPTAIN: Ladies. Don't fight. Come to the Captain. I'm a Captain.

BOBO *(To Sophie)*: See? *(To Captain)* Goodnight.

CAPTAIN: I must persist. I persist, my dears . . .

(Man grabs Sophie's cloak. Bobo floors him with a whack)

BOBO: I SAID "GOODNIGHT"!!!

(Bobo rushes Sophie offstage)

CAPTAIN *(Calling after them)*: CUNTS!!! YOU CUNTS!!! CUNNNNNNNTTTS! *(Feeling sorry for himself)* Mama, I'm lonely. And some bitch just hit me. Ow.

(Staggering off, he exits.
   Casanova is sitting, very irritated. Lady #2 enters, from a boudoir, undressed)

LADY #2: I—I—I—ah—darling—the—

(She exits back into the boudoir. Marcoline enters from the boudoir)

CASANOVA: Ah, the French, yes! The seat of culture! Well, I come from Venice, the greatest republic in the world, and believe me—

MARCOLINE: Those are beautiful trousers.

CASANOVA: Perhaps you should wear them!

MARCOLINE: You were shocked to find me making love to your latest mistress.

CASANOVA: No. No, I was entertained!

MARCOLINE: You loved all those things when I did them to you.

CASANOVA: What you did to me is completely different.

MARCOLINE: Oysters or sausage—it's all delicious to me.

(Lady #2 reenters, partially dressed, and exits)

I should never be jealous of your mistresses, if you let me sleep with them. Is that not a mark of a good disposition? Tell me.

CASANOVA: Your good disposition is not in doubt, Marcoline, but it could be just as good without this . . . dominant passion.

MARCOLINE: You mean my passion for persons of my own sex?

CASANOVA: Your dominant passion—yes.

MARCOLINE: It's not a passion. A passion exists on its own and looks for an object. Love always precedes desire with me.

CASANOVA: How much does it precede it? By a second? A glance?

MARCOLINE: I have desires only for those I love. And that is the difference between men and women.

CASANOVA *(About being deceived by her)*: The difference between men and women is that women are much less likely to fall into self-delusion. Women don't lie to themselves as men so often do.

MARCOLINE: Oh, but they do. Women. They tell themselves that they are loved. That they will be loved tomorrow. And the biggest lie of all—that they will be loved when their beauty fades. That is why I love women. Women love wrinkled babies out of the womb and old men. Women love cripples—doesn't the hunchback whatshisname have a devoted mistress?

CASANOVA: And it's that very thing that makes men question the sincerity of women's love. How can they love such ugliness? Of what value is a love that can be spent on a cripple!

MARCOLINE: You're not as cruel as you sound.

CASANOVA: Thank you.

MARCOLINE: You're welcome.

CASANOVA *(About Lady #2)*: You can't possibly have loved her.

MARCOLINE: But you make love to her.

CASANOVA: We're getting off the point. The point is: I caught you in bed with her.

MARCOLINE: If you don't love her, what difference does it make?

CASANOVA: Who gave you this taste is all I want to know.

MARCOLINE: Nature. I've always loved women.

CASANOVA: And you love me? But, surely, there is nothing feminine about me.

MARCOLINE: Your soul could be reborn into a woman. And then you'd find your other self—you'd recognize her. And so would I.

CASANOVA: But I'd be dead then.

(Therese enters with light-bulb sign. Beat)

Wait a minute. Do you believe in magic, Marcoline?

MARCOLINE: Yes.

CASANOVA: Good. That's good.

(They exit.
Madame D'Urfe is sitting naked in a bathtub full of water. She wears a necklace made of large jewels. There is a large cupboard upstage of her. Lighted candles are placed ceremoniously around the room. From behind a curtain, Casanova is heard singing an oriental-sounding tune)

I am come—
I am come—
I am come from the Rhone
To bathe you.
The hour of Oromasis hath begun.

(Casanova enters from behind the curtain, dressed in a bizarre robe and turban. He is reading from the book the Sorceress gave him when she cured his nosebleed)

MADAME D'URFE: And what exactly is this bath going to do? My Galtinardus?

CASANOVA: It . . . begins the process of regeneration.

MADAME D'URFE: I still have breasts.

CASANOVA: It takes time.

MADAME D'URFE: I have no time.

CASANOVA *(Intoning)*: O, Divine Being, touch the soul of Semiramis.

MADAME D'URFE *(Looking down at her body)*: I'm waiting. O, Divine Being.

CASANOVA: The only way you can be regenerated into a man—
the only way that can happen is if your soul is born into a
man's body.

MADAME D'URFE: But I'd be dead then.

(Pause)

CASANOVA: Not if the man is a baby inside you.

MADAME D'URFE: But that's brilliant!! Of course. I'll be reborn
as my son! *(Puts the necklace over his head)* I have found my
magician.

   And now I'll have a penis after all.

CASANOVA *(Getting into the bath with her, he looks down at his
groin, hoping for an erection)*: Very soon—I hope. *(Kisses
Madame D'Urfe, trying to get himself aroused. After a beat, he
intones)* O, divine being, be the witness of my union with
Semiramis, to the glory of the immortal Horomadis, King
of the Salamanders.

*(At that moment, the cupboard opens up, revealing Marcoline,
stark naked, holding her breasts. She licks her lips, erotically)*

Thank you, divine being. *(Penetrates Madame D'Urfe)*

MADAME D'URFE *(With pleasure)*: Ah!

(Lights down.
   *Lights up. Madame D'Urfe remains in her bathtub. Casanova
is getting dressed)*

You are now my husband and my father.

CASANOVA: Ah.

MADAME D'URFE: Did you give the offerings to the planets—
however you do that?

CASANOVA: Yes. I took them to Calais. I launched them onto the
sea, when the planets were aligned.

MADAME D'URFE: Did they accept all the offerings?

CASANOVA: Yes, all the jewels were accepted. I wish you could
have been there.

MADAME D'URFE: It's painful for me to travel.

CASANOVA: Yes.

MADAME D'URFE: But you cause me no pain. I never feel pain from you.

CASANOVA: Ah.

MADAME D'URFE: Ah. Now I say, "Ah." You taught me that. We are one person, my love. We are very much alike.

(Young Casanova appears in the cabinet where Marcoline was)

YOUNG CASANOVA: Caterina? Where am I? And who is that terrible man?

MADAME D'URFE: You seem depressed, my love.

CASANOVA: No. I'm just—the ceremony was taxing.

MADAME D'URFE: Casanova.

CASANOVA: Yes.

MADAME D'URFE: I love you.

CASANOVA: And I love you, Madame. *(Exits)*

MADAME D'URFE: Thank you, Venus, for letting ME get something out of this body which has done nothing but serve, serve, SERVE.

YOUNG CASANOVA: He has my name.

(Young Casanova gets out of the cupboard, pauses by Madame D'Urfe—she doesn't see him. He exits.
Lights up on Bobo and Sophie in Bobo's rooms)

BOBO: In a garden, at dusk, I watched him once.

It was a large function, and everyone had gone to hear the concert by the ornamental waters, but I had stayed behind to relieve myself. I was in a gown with some intricate under-pinning and the process of relieving myself promised to be somewhat complicated and potentially alarming to anyone who might observe it. So I approached a section of hedge that contained an enclave and a very tall topiary. And that's when I heard his voice—it was unmistakable, and his French had gotten much better. The demands of my bladder disappeared entirely from my consciousness as I positioned myself to observe, my mouth dry, quite certain that I was to see the most erotic vision.

There he was, your father, with a woman—a rather ordinary-looking woman, I thought. They were sitting on a stone bench, very close, but not touching. She was speaking now, telling of some incident, growing more and more animated in her speech, enjoying herself, and he was simply there, listening, his face mirroring her emotions, laughing, then intent, then serious. So strange—he did nothing and yet his simple attention seemed to have the most erotic effect on her—suddenly she took his face in her hands and kissed him, passionately, on the mouth. When she released him, his head fell back, and I could see the ecstatic expression of his face. He closed his eyes and reached for her breast, like a drowning man reaches for the shore. He must have been gentle in this grasp because she gave—all. I watched him swim through the satin that encased her, unbuttoning himself as he went. Not my taste, but, oh God, it was lovely.

They lasted through the rest of the Vivaldi and were into several measures of the Boccherini when she heard something—not me. I was transfixed. I was silent, still. I was topiary. Topiary of an exquisitely dressed, very tall woman with a rampant hard-on. She left him, she bolted, suddenly alarmed. And he collapsed, face down, like he'd been shot. I couldn't bear it. I crept, limped away.

A few heartbeats, I swear, a few steps, breaths, and he was right behind me. "Madam," he said, "Madam," in a voice clouded with lust. I stopped and he pressed himself up against my back. "Mademoiselle." And then he ran his tongue up the back of my neck.

I'd always thought my neck was ugly.

SOPHIE: What happened then!?

BOBO: Nothing. She came back. Inexplicably. "Forgive me," he said to me. "Find me," he whispered. "Later."

SOPHIE: Did you?

BOBO: He thought I was a woman.

SOPHIE: All these years I thought you hated him.

BOBO: No.

(*Casanova enters, in full regalia. He is at the height of his sexy powers—he looks fabulous and rich, having had access to D'Urfe's money. Therese enters with two whores. Casanova doesn't recognize her*)

THERESE: Fifteen. Ten if we stay in the doorway.

CASANOVA: Not interested tonight, darlings. Leave me.

THERESE: Can't do that. You're too fabulous. Heads up! Charpillon approaches, my dear.

(*A young girl, age twelve, Child Charpillon, moves across the stage—Casanova sees her and walks over toward her*)

CASANOVA (*To no one in particular, in amazement*): Who's that child?

(*Child Charpillon crosses to Casanova*)

CHILD CHARPILLON (*About the buckles on Casanova's shoes*): I want those buckles.

CASANOVA: And so you shall have them, my dear.

(*Casanova takes the buckles off his shoes and hands them to Child Charpillon*)

Aren't they a little large?

CHILD CHARPILLON: I'm not grown yet. (*Skips off*)

CASANOVA: What a wonderful child.

(*Charpillon's Mother enters*)

CHARPILLON'S MOTHER: I am Mademoiselle Charpillon's mother, Sir. She is anxious to see you again.

She remembers you, although I don't. Your reputation precedes you.

CASANOVA *(Pleased)*: Oh, what of mine have you read?
CHARPILLON'S MOTHER: What of your ... what?
CASANOVA: Poetry? Essays? Utopian literature?

(A blank stare from her)

You've heard of my ambassadorial escapades, no doubt.

(Still nothing from her)

I brought silk manufacturing to France, you know. The lottery—is my idea. Two million a year for the French government from my idea.

(Nope)

Well, I do have a reputation as quite a gamesman—
CHARPILLON'S MOTHER: We heard you were a good lay.
     Mademoiselle Charpillon wishes you to come to her— she's in the bath. But since she met you when she was a child, she feels quite at ease with you, Sir.

(Charpillon's Mother opens the curtains, revealing Mademoiselle Charpillon in a bathtub. She is about seventeen, naked and beautiful)

MADEMOISELLE CHARPILLON: Mister Casanova?
     Remember me?
CASANOVA: Not quite.
MADEMOISELLE CHARPILLON *(Moving erotically)*: I'm still wearing the buckles.
CHARPILLON'S MOTHER: She is most talented, Sir. And unpenetrated. It's a shame to waste her on one less capable. She will be introduced to society, Sir—we have offers from many gentlemen. But she wants you.
CASANOVA: Excuse me. *(Tries to walk but has a major erection— he tries to cover it with his coat)* Can you leave us alone?

(Charpillon's Mother pulls the curtains. After a beat, Casanova sticks his head out)

She won't leave the bath.

This is a new suit.

CHARPILLON'S MOTHER: Perhaps she requires some seduction.
When she's dry.

MADEMOISELLE CHARPILLON: Come back—when I'm dry.

(Mademoiselle Charpillon gets out of the bath, wraps a towel around her, opens the curtain and exits. Casanova is sitting on the side of the tub, holding another towel to his crotch)

CASANOVA *(To his penis)*: I know if you have her once, we'll be free of her. It's always worked before. My Hawk. *(Shouts to the absent Mademoiselle Charpillon)* I'll show myself out!! If you don't mind!! Thank you so very much!!

(Casanova leaves the bathtub and exits. Young Casanova rises out of the bath behind him and exits. Casanova reenters, carrying candy. To the audience:)

I have this terrible feeling. Why don't I just go to a nice, cozy whorehouse? She is the abyss—I am the pebble.

(Charpillon's Mother enters and takes the sweets and begins to eat them)

CHARPILLON'S MOTHER: Mmmm. Hmmmm. HMM!
MMMMMM.
Mmmmmm.
Ah.
What are these little—? *(Eats it)* Yummm.
That was particularly— *(About another candy)* Now
these— *(Eats one)* Good. Good. Not as wonderful as these
over here, still— *(Eats another)*

CASANOVA: Madame Charpillon.

CHARPILLON'S MOTHER: Hmmmm?

CASANOVA: Your daughter is driving me mad.

CHARPILLON'S MOTHER: She adores you. Take her.
  Take her, Sir. Don't hesitate.
  Bring more of these next time.

(Mademoiselle Charpillon enters, looking beautiful. Casanova escorts her offstage. Charpillon's Mother eats contentedly. After a beat, Casanova enters, limping with an erection)

CASANOVA: This is intolerable!
CHARPILLON'S MOTHER: The raspberry ones are my favorites!

*(They exit.
  Mademoiselle Charpillon enters and lies on the chaise. Casanova enters and goes to her immediately. She submits for a much longer time)*

MADEMOISELLE CHARPILLON: I just needed more time.
CASANOVA: You will be worth the wait—I can tell.
MADEMOISELLE CHARPILLON: You know I adore you.

(Charpillon's Mother enters—she is very fat now)

CHARPILLON'S MOTHER: Everything alright? Don't get up.
  Oh, here it is. *(Finds a last cake)* Don't want to waste any.
  I'm off to bed.
  Night, night. *(Exits)*
MADEMOISELLE CHARPILLON: You've taken good care of Mother.
CASANOVA: A few chocolates . . .
MADEMOISELLE CHARPILLON: It's appreciated.

(Casanova moves in for the kill, kissing her and then getting her in position for the deflowering)

CASANOVA: My darling, darling, darling—

(Mademoiselle Charpillon rolls up into a small, tight ball)

No, no, no, no— *(Tries to laugh it off)* Come on—it's not funny.

(She doesn't move)

You're NOT doing this to me again! *(Tries to unpry her—gets nowhere. Stops)* This is the last time I'll be made a fool of!!

(Gets up and starts to get dressed. Mademoiselle Charpillon unrolls herself and goes to him—she begins to caress him)

MADEMOISELLE CHARPILLON: Just a cramp. A momentary—
CASANOVA: Are you all right now?
MADEMOISELLE CHARPILLON: Yes.
CASANOVA: Why didn't you say so? That it was a cramp?
MADEMOISELLE CHARPILLON: I'm fine.
     Let me loosen my dress a bit.

(She loosens her dress. Casanova gets more and more excited, begins to caress her again, gets her into the position and she rolls into a ball again)

CASANOVA: NOT ANOTHER CRAMP!!!

(Mademoiselle Charpillon doesn't answer. Casanova gets up and exits. Mademoiselle Charpillon unrolls herself and sits up—she stares at the audience for a few beats. Casanova reenters. He crosses to her)

You are too beautiful.
MADEMOISELLE CHARPILLON: Too beautiful for what?
CASANOVA: To be this evil.
MADEMOISELLE CHARPILLON: Are you evil?
CASANOVA: I've done evil things.
MADEMOISELLE CHARPILLON: Perhaps that's why I'm attracted.
     To you.
CASANOVA: I'm attracted to you—that's certain.
     Why, I don't know.
MADEMOISELLE CHARPILLON: You don't know?
CASANOVA: Why won't you give yourself to me!
MADEMOISELLE CHARPILLON: Oh, but I have.

CASANOVA: Not completely and you know it.

MADEMOISELLE CHARPILLON: Once I give myself completely—you'll be gone.

CASANOVA: That's not true.

MADEMOISELLE CHARPILLON: Are you a virgin?

CASANOVA: Don't be absurd.

MADEMOISELLE CHARPILLON: Where is the first woman you slept with?

CASANOVA: Married to someone much older than she. Much, much older.

MADEMOISELLE CHARPILLON: And the second?

CASANOVA: I don't know.

MADEMOISELLE CHARPILLON: And the third?

CASANOVA: What?

MADEMOISELLE CHARPILLON: And the fourth and the fifth and the sixth. Where are any of the women you've slept with? You're not married, you're alone—did all these women leave YOU?

CASANOVA: Oh, please. You can play this game, too.

MADEMOISELLE CHARPILLON: And I plan to. The difference is—my commodity loses value in its use. Yours gains.

CASANOVA: Commodity? What happened to romance?

MADEMOISELLE CHARPILLON: Romance is a drug to keep me dazed and compliant. The note-writing, the intrigue, the waiting, the pining, the midnight visitations, the waiting, the pining, the waiting. Without romance, women would think clearly and do what I am doing.

CASANOVA: What? Torment men?

MADEMOISELLE CHARPILLON: Drive up the price.

CASANOVA: Like a whore?!!!
     Alright—how much do you want?

MADEMOISELLE CHARPILLON: I don't want money.

CASANOVA: What do you want?

MADEMOISELLE CHARPILLON: Your life.

CASANOVA: You're a demon!

MADEMOISELLE CHARPILLON: I'm beautiful.

(Casanova kisses her—she opens up, he gets very excited and then she rolls into a ball again. He loses it completely and begins to claw at her, forcing her open, then he rapes her quickly)

CASANOVA: Oh my GOD.

(He exits quickly. Charpillon's Mother enters)

CHARPILLON'S MOTHER: What happened?

MADEMOISELLE CHARPILLON: He took it.

CHARPILLON'S MOTHER: What do you mean?

MADEMOISELLE CHARPILLON: I turned him into a thief in the night! The great Casanova had to rape because he met someone he could not seduce.

(Charpillon's Mother slaps her)

CHARPILLON'S MOTHER: You let him rob you?!

MADEMOISELLE CHARPILLON: No, I conquered him, Mother! I won!

CHARPILLON'S MOTHER: My baby. Wash up. We're finished.

YOUNG CASANOVA *(Entering from somewhere)*: Are you all right? Are you all right?

(Backing out and running away—he's gone. Bobo is nearly dressed. Sophie enters)

BOBO: Is Alain coming 'round to help?

SOPHIE: I told him last week.

BOBO: How—?

SOPHIE: I knew you were going to go, no matter what.

BOBO: I wish you'd—

SOPHIE: No.

(Sound of the Young Girl breathing—from the beginning of the play)

Listen!

BOBO: What?

SOPHIE: Listen!

BOBO: I can't hear anything.

SOPHIE: Bobo, we're haunted!

BOBO: I'm not surprised.

SOPHIE: I mean it!

(Breathing stops)

It stopped. I'm fine.

I know he's here, Bobo. Somewhere in this city.

BOBO: Probably.

SOPHIE: I wish I knew for certain.

BOBO: He's here, darling. Alain said that he wrote for rooms a
month ago.

SOPHIE: So now I know.

I'm not going to seek him out. I'm done with all of that.
And this damned doll, too. I'm going to deliver this gown to
Madame Poquelin.

BOBO: Take Alain with you—it's getting dark.

(The breathing starts up again. Sophie covers her ears in alarm)

SOPHIE: BOBO!

*(Bobo rushes across to her, stepping on the chamber pot and
spilling it)*

BOBO: Virgin Mary's CUNT! *(Crosses himself quickly)* Damn,
damn, damn.

Here, hold onto me. Let me sit. No, I can't put my feet up.

SOPHIE: Why?

(The breathing stops)

BOBO: Because I just spilled the chamber pot and my feet are
wet.

SOPHIE: The breathing's stopped again. I'm sorry, Bobo. How
did I get to be so silly?

BOBO: It's this age, darling. You're hearing voices. I'm standing
in my own pee. It's just one humiliation after another.
SOPHIE: I'm going. And I'll get the money she owes us, too. *(Exits)*
BOBO: Thank God. She's back.

(Bobo cleans up the spilled pee and exits.
Therese enters and sees Mamzell)

THERESE: Look! It's Mamzell. I've been so absorbed, I forgot
about Sophie. Oh, she's not doing well at all. I wonder why.
I taught her everything I knew—well, everything I thought
was important. Let's see, what did I know back then? Color,
makeup, hair, turn of phrase, the fan, the eyes, wiles.
I should tell her something—I will tell her—

(Casanova enters with a piece of luggage. Therese stops talking
as soon as she sees him, stands up, dropping Mamzell on the
floor—Therese is completely absorbed with Casanova again)

Here he is in another sweet reverie, thinking he's strolling in
the Villa Lodovisie. *(As a concierge, to Casanova)* Let me get
someone to take those bags for you.

(Therese takes out a bellhop bell and rings it. Mariucci's Hus-
band enters and picks up the bag. Therese exits)

MARIUCCI'S HUSBAND: I'll introduce you to your daughter.
I've baptized her under the name of Jacomine.

(Casanova looks at him)

Oh, she's yours alright. You had my Mariucci four weeks
before we were engaged.
CASANOVA *(Denying it)*: You must be—
MARIUCCI'S HUSBAND: Oh, there's no doubt. You supplied her
dowry—don't you remember? She hadn't even been your
mistress—just "wham" one night.
I was a barber then, but now I'm a corn merchant. I'm
doing very well. I just do wigs to get by.

Jacomine is nine—in case you're counting.
Jacomine knows me as her father—.
But she looks like you. She looks like you, alright.

(Mariucci enters. Husband exits with Casanova's bag)

MARIUCCI: Casanova!

CASANOVA *(Formal, covering)*: Chevalier de Seingalt. Madame.

MARIUCCI *(Curtsies)*: Chevalier.

Imagine my surprise.

CASANOVA: This Jacomine—

MARIUCCI: Yes. And did my husband tell you? A niece of yours also lives nearby—she's a friend of Jacomine's. So you can meet two young relatives in one day.

CASANOVA: A niece?

MARIUCCI: Your brother knew a woman in town who now runs a school of drawing—Jacomine does very well there and her best friend is your niece Guillelmine, who's older—she's thirteen. But they're very close.

CASANOVA: Family reunion—ha, ha!

MARIUCCI'S HUSBAND *(Reentering)*: You're staying with us. I assume it's alright with Mariucci.

MARIUCCI: Oh. Fine.

(Casanova kisses her hand and crosses away. Mariucci exits and her Husband follows)

CASANOVA *(To the audience)*: No sooner had I heard this, than I was determined to love this niece— *(Stops, confused)* Why am I speaking in the past tense? Surely, I'm in the present— *(Notices a chamber pot, picks it up, then puts it down quickly)*

THERESE *(Entering)*: I'll be waiting. Bring your coat. We'll keep each other cold.

(Mariucci appears, letting him in)

MARIUCCI *(Embracing him)*: My husband's gone for the evening.

CASANOVA: I can't bear it—I must see my daughter. And her friend, my niece, is it?

MARIUCCI: They're asleep. Guillelmine stayed the night.

(Pause. Casanova waits)

We could go look at them, if you promise not to wake them.

(Mariucci picks up a lamp and they tiptoe to a white bed upon which two figures lie—much more visible to Casanova than to the audience)

CASANOVA: Oh!

MARIUCCI: All children are beautiful when they sleep. *(Pointing to each girl)* This is your daughter. And that is Guillelmine.

(Mariucci laughs softly, then slowly raises the coverlet to reveal the two naked children. Casanova stares, transfixed)

CASANOVA: Here lies my daughter and Guillelmine. The coverlet leaves bare their young breasts. My daughter's are unfurnished; but the other's are like the swellings one sees on the head of a calf on the eve of growing its horns. What a vision! What fascination!

(Mariucci laughs and lifts more of the coverlet—Casanova stares)

MARIUCCI: Each has been pleasing herself. I did that, too, when I was a girl. It helped me sleep.

(Casanova replaces the coverlet and starts to exit. Mariucci follows. A few feet away, he stops and she touches him—he turns and embraces her passionately. She drops the lamp. Young Casanova enters, picks up the lamp)

YOUNG CASANOVA *(Desperate)*: Caterina—help me. Find me!

(He exits.
Lights up on Casanova in his bed. Jacomine and Guillelmine enter demurely, holding their pictures from art school)

GUILLELMINE: Sir?

CASANOVA: Come in.

GUILLELMINE: You said at supper last night that we were to bring you our pictures from school.

CASANOVA: Yes, I want to see them. Come on.

(They approach the bed)

Come on! Sit—one on each side.

(They join him on the bed)

Well, these are very good. Is this a pear, Jacomine?

JACOMINE: It's an apple.

CASANOVA: It's a very good apple. And Guillelmine, who is this?

GUILLELMINE: Aphrodite.

CASANOVA: Are you drawing from imagination? Free drawing?

GUILLELMINE: No, Sir. Aphrodite is Mother's housekeeper.

CASANOVA: Yes, I can see that this Aphrodite is quite substantial.

GUILLELMINE: The real Aphrodite may have been also. We don't really know.

JACOMINE *(Pointing to his breakfast)*: Is that jam?

CASANOVA: Why yes it is. Have some.

JACOMINE: You, too, Guillelmine.

(Guillelmine leans over him to reach a pastry)

GUILLELMINE: Thank you.

JACOMINE *(Mouth full)*: Thank you.

CASANOVA: This is an excellent picture of Aphrodite. May I put it up in my room? And your apple, too, Jacomine.

(Girls kiss him on the cheek and exit. He wipes the stickiness off his face)

Family life. Perhaps I should have married . . . sometime.

(He lies back down. Time change.
Lights up and his bedboard is covered with many drawings

from the girls. Casanova is standing in front of a water bowl and is washing his face. As the scene progresses he finishes dressing and takes his traveling bag from someplace, checks it, closes it.

In another space, Mariucci is sitting and embroidering. Guillelmine enters really tarted up. She sits beside Mariucci)

MARIUCCI: Guillelmine! What's all this? Look at yourself!

GUILLELMINE: I'm a woman now.

MARIUCCI: What is this? Dress-up? You're a little old for that.

GUILLELMINE: I'm thirteen. And it's not dress-up.

MARIUCCI: Well, Jacomine isn't here right now.

GUILLELMINE: I'm not waiting for Jacomine.

MARIUCCI: Clean your face. Your mother will have a fit.

(Casanova enters the scene, dressed for traveling. Guillelmine looks only at him)

CASANOVA *(To Mariucci)*: Well, I'm ready, dear. I've ordered a coach. I said goodbye to your husband late last night.

MARIUCCI: I wish you wouldn't go.

GUILLELMINE: You're going?!

CASANOVA: Yes, Sweet. Here's a pomander I bought in Paris. *(Gives it to her)* Don't tell Jacomine. I've nothing for her.

GUILLELMINE: No! *(Bursts into tears)* Nononononononono.

CASANOVA: I've grown fond of you, too. *(To Mariucci)* Thank you for your hospitality.

GUILLELMINE *(Sobbing now)*: But I LOVE you!! I love you!!

CASANOVA: And I love you, too. *(To Mariucci)* Kiss Jacomine again for me, will you?

GUILLELMINE *(Holding him around the waist, sobbing)*: No don't no don't no DON'T!

CASANOVA *(Removing her arms)*: Now, REALLY, darling. I MUST go!

(Casanova hands her to Mariucci. Young Casanova enters with the lantern he picked up off the floor after Mariucci dropped it. He witnesses the following scene, but no one notices him)

MARIUCCI: Come to me, Guelly. Come on— *(To Casanova)*
     What have you done?

CASANOVA: Better me than some local boy.

MARIUCCI: She's only thirteen.

CASANOVA: Thirteen, fourteen, fifteen. Sixteen, married,
     pregnant—never having known true passion. Never having
     known the joy and abandon of pure sensuality. What is so
     wrong about it? She's only as God made her. I am as God
     made me. Why not me rather than a furtive poke in a barn
     with some other . . . child? Tell me the truth, Mariucci, if she
     were a boy—if you had a boy in your arms and I were the
     older woman who initiated him, what would be happening?
     Would the child be crying or crowing? And would you
     be berating me or thanking me? Why shouldn't girls be
     initiated as boys are?

GUILLELMINE: I—want—to—die.
     Stay.

MARIUCCI *(To Casanova)*: You entered her. You entered a child!

CASANOVA: You showed her to me!

YOUNG CASANOVA: Who are you? WHO ARE YOU?!!

*(Young Casanova crosses to Casanova and, unnoticed, looks
closely at him. Young Casanova then crosses down toward the
audience, looks out and withdraws slowly and exits.*
     *Mariucci exits with Guillelmine. Jacomine enters with a large
picture)*

JACOMINE: Papa? I wanted to know why you couldn't do to me
     what you did to her in the mornings. I have a bagina, too.

(Casanova exits.
     Sound of the overture to Don Giovanni *played by a small
orchestra. Casanova is at the opera house in Prague. He and Da
Ponte are sitting in the loge and Casanova is reading to Da Ponte
from a notebook. Below is a conductor directing an orchestra we
don't see.*

In another space, Guillelmine appears, still thirteen years old—with her sketchbook. She sits and gets ready to draw)

CASANOVA: She brought out my tenderest feelings, and my most erotic—erotic, not bestial. I relived, again and again, the surprise in her eyes when I first entered her. At that moment, I was a God, what I brought was so powerful. And from her, there was no knowing look because there had been no knowledge. There was no acting because the experience was entirely new. It was the sex act at its purest. She was Eve on that first time, and so, I was able to become Adam.

DA PONTE: Ah. Adam. Very good.

(Guillelmine starts to sketch)

CASANOVA: And the days that followed—desire, like a drug, began to course through her veins. Her cheeks would flush when she saw me—her eyes would flash when I walked into the room—her small body would seem to jump slightly. Yes—"ardent need"—I had awakened it in her and now she was living the life of a woman, she need never doubt what her place was, she knew what she was meant for. And she began to live—for me.

DA PONTE: Wonderful, Giacomo. What a writer you've become.

CASANOVA: That means so much coming from you, Lorenzo.

(Guillelmine holds up the drawing for Casanova to see. It is a tiny, black stick-figure drawing of a girl, dominated by a huge expanse of unfilled space around her)

GUILLELMINE *(Pointing to the stick figure)*: This is me.

(She smiles at Casanova. He turns away. She exits)

DA PONTE: What are you looking at? Is something wrong with the scenery?

CASANOVA: No, I—. The great Rousseau bought a twelve-year-old girl in London—they sell their young girls instead of finding them decent husbands. What a dreadful country. Dinner never begins or ends—there's no soup! I always wondered what happened to her?

DA PONTE: Who?

CASANOVA: Rousseau's girl.

DA PONTE: Nice?

(We hear the sound of the Young Woman in labor from the top of Act One)

CASANOVA: I don't remember—surely, yes.

(The conductor hits his baton on his music stand. It is Therese posing as Mozart. The orchestra stops)

THERESE AS MOZART: Who is talking! Someone is talking! Ah! Abbé Da Ponte. I'm glad you're here. *(To orchestra)* Our librettist, boys and girls.

(Da Ponte stands, then pulls Casanova up)

DA PONTE: Maestro Mozart, my fellow Venetian, Giacomo Casanova, Chevalier . . . something—advised me on Leporello's—

THERESE AS MOZART: May I see you for a moment, Abbé? I had a question about a couplet or two. The tenor has been talking to me. Come?

DA PONTE: I'll be back. *(Exits)*

THERESE AS MOZART: No, you won't.

CASANOVA: I beg your pardon, Maestro?

THERESE *(Taking off her Mozart wig, revealing herself)*: It's not really an apology, but, for myself, I accept. As for others— *(Shakes her head "no")* There's someone here to see you.

(Uta enters)

UTA: There he is!

(Casanova doubles over in pain, back to his seventy-plus-year-old self again)

Aha! Herr Casanova, don't run! Uta has tracked you down! Don't move!

CASANOVA (*In pain*): I can't.

(*Uta goes to him*)

UTA: See how he leans on me? He needs me. (*To Casanova*) Come on, old man.

(*Therese crosses to him*)

THERESE: We're very close, my darling. It's very near.

(*They take him away.*
Young Casanova enters and looks around for the entrance to the garden)

YOUNG CASANOVA: Caterina? Caterina?

OLD WHORE (*Appearing suddenly*): Fifteen. Ten if we stay in the doorway.

YOUNG CASANOVA: You're not Caterina!!

OLD WHORE: I can be. I can be anything you want.
Tell me what you want! Tell me what you want!
(*Sees someone else*) Hello. (*Exits to get this new client*)

YOUNG CASANOVA: Caterina. Save me, please!

(*He exits.*
Sound of dogs barking. Uta and Casanova are in his rooms in Paris. He is getting ready for the ball)

UTA: I will never see Jakob again.

CASANOVA: Help me with this makeup? My hand is cramped.

(*Uta starts to put white face on Casanova*)

It's nice to be touched. It's been years.
I wish those dogs would stop barking. I don't remember this many dogs in Paris before. What can it mean?

UTA: There's a bitch in heat somewhere locked up.

CASANOVA: Why don't they let her out?

UTA: She's probably too young. They'll tear her apart.

CASANOVA: Nature is cruel. Come to me.

UTA: What is it?

CASANOVA: Pain.

(She goes to him and comforts him)

Bad one.

UTA: Where's the pot?

CASANOVA: I don't need it.

(Uta finds the pot and looks in it)

UTA: It's full of blood again.

CASANOVA: I know.

UTA *(Finds some food)*: What have you been eating?
I've never seen food like this!

CASANOVA: I've been starved for years—all my life, in fact.

UTA: Well, I'm going to empty the pot. *(Exits)*

CASANOVA: Don't go too far with that! *(Puts on his glasses and uses a mirror to place his beauty spot and put on his wig)* I look good for my age.

(Sophie enters the room, carrying a gown)

Hide the dinner over there. My woman won't let me eat.

(Sophie doesn't move)

I have no money, if you're selling that wardrobe. *(Thinks he's figured it out)* Ah! Listen, my darling. I would be very interested, but my parts are long since unresponsive. Even to manipulation. You can shout at it, it still won't—

SOPHIE: Papa—

CASANOVA: Jacomine?

SOPHIE: No—Sophie. Look at me, Papa.

CASANOVA: Who?

SOPHIE: Sophie.

CASANOVA (*Trying to remember*): It's possible.
How old are you?

SOPHIE: Forty-two.

CASANOVA: You don't resemble your mother.

SOPHIE: No. I look like you.

CASANOVA: Ah. Your mother was very beautiful.

SOPHIE: Yes.

CASANOVA: Are you married?

SOPHIE: I was.

CASANOVA: Children?

SOPHIE: None that lived.

CASANOVA: I can't help you financially. I have some jewelry.

SOPHIE: No, no. I just wanted to . . . find you.

CASANOVA: Then everyone knows I'm here. See, Uta? (*Can't find Uta*) She's gone. Well, you appreciate that I am an elder statesman of the world.

SOPHIE: Yes.

CASANOVA: Yes, I thought your mother was ruining you. I wanted to take you with me.

SOPHIE: You did?

CASANOVA: Yes, I knew of an excellent convent in Paris. But she would not give you up. She was selfish—your mother.

SOPHIE: I see.

CASANOVA: And now you have to work to support yourself. (*Worried that she might be a prostitute*) What—what do you do to support yourself?
Ah—you're a seamstress.

SOPHIE: No. I'm a clairvoyant. I see into the future.

(*Uta enters*)

UTA: What's this, then?

CASANOVA: My daughter. Her mother thought she looked like me.

UTA: She does. But it doesn't look right on her. When you're a girl, looks is all.

SOPHIE: I must go.

CASANOVA: Write to me. Tell me what you see—in the future.

SOPHIE: Why would you want to know that, Papa?

CASANOVA: Will I be remembered?

SOPHIE: Yes.

CASANOVA: With love?

SOPHIE: Yes.

CASANOVA: And admiration?

(No answer from Sophie)

Will I be admired?

(Silence)

You're not really clairvoyant! Why did you come?! What do you want from me?!

SOPHIE: I just wanted to see you.

CASANOVA: Well, you've seen me!

How do I know you're Sophie? I don't even recognize you!

SOPHIE: Goodbye, Papa. *(Exits)*

CASANOVA: Adieu. *(To Uta)* What did she want? How can she be anyone's daughter? She's an old woman!

(Lights down.
  On the street, Alain waits with a lantern. Sophie joins him. Young Casanova enters, sees her)

YOUNG CASANOVA: Scusaté.

SOPHIE: What?

YOUNG CASANOVA: Scusaté . . . me.

(Sophie crosses over toward him—he tries to make her understand what he's asking)

Campo San Pietro?

(She shakes her head "no")

Campo San Tomá?

(She doesn't recognize this name either)

Rialto? Giudecca? VENEZIA?

SOPHIE: You—are—in—Paris. PARR-ISS.

(She smiles at him, sorry she can't be more help. He stares at her)

YOUNG CASANOVA *(Suddenly embarrassed)*: Mi dispiace.
Pardon—ay.
　　You—are—bellisima. *(Exits)*

SOPHIE: What a sweet young man.

*(She exits.
　　Back in their rooms)*

BOBO *(Offstage)*: A little more to the left. Alain! Don't let it tip
don't let it tip don't let it—! Oh, that could've been
disastrous!

(Sophie enters from the street)

SOPHIE: Bobo, are you going to eat the rest of this stew?

BOBO: And get into this gown? I don't think so. Alain!

*(Alain enters, pissed off, and looks at Sophie. She smiles
knowingly and Alain exits)*

SOPHIE: Bobo, Alain has stepped out temporarily. May I help
you?

BOBO: I am beyond help. I am a fat, old elfin thing that shouldn't
be allowed— *(Suddenly pleased)* —oh, that's not too bad.

SOPHIE: I can't wait to see you.

*(Bobo enters in full eighteenth-century female drag, with a large
wig, et alia)*

BOBO: Fuck Rousseau.

SOPHIE: Bobo! You are magnificent!

BOBO: I am, aren't I?
　　There's pudding.

SOPHIE: Thank you.

BOBO: Will you tell your Bobo the truth? This wig's not too high, is it? Oh, never mind, I don't want to know—I wouldn't change it anyway. Fix the bodice here, please? Alain is terrible with a needle and thread.

(Sophie does this as they talk)

You are suddenly so energetic.

SOPHIE: They know now that babies are made from—you know.

BOBO: I have a vague memory of the act—yes.

(She accidentally pricks him with the needle)

OW!

SOPHIE: Sorry. I meant that scientist proved that babies come from something that comes from . . . cum.

BOBO: Is this a game?

SOPHIE: No, Bobo. Cum.

BOBO: Where?

SOPHIE: There is something in the semen of men that is necessary for the creation of babies.

BOBO: See? That's the problem with the New Thought. You take something like love, examine it too closely, and what are you left with? Science. Where's the mystery? Where's the magic? Where's the romance? Where's my brooch? *(Finds it)* Oh.

(Hands it to Sophie who puts it on for him)

I do dread this new century we're about to enter. I have a very bad feeling about it.

SOPHIE: It's the future, Bobo. The future is always better.

BOBO: I'm probably going to be the only one at this ball with a wig this high. But I don't care. This is who I am! And this is who your father is, too. With pants, of course, and a less elaborate bodice, and different sleeves. And— *(Looks at himself in the mirror)* Will they laugh at us, Sophie?

SOPHIE: I expect many will be dressed as elaborately as you are.

BOBO: No, I didn't mean at the ball.

    I'm so glad you're dressed and feeling better. This brown thing is lovely. But, Sophie, we may not be able to afford live-in servants, but we have the wardrobe for you to dress beautifully. Why don't you put on something colorful and gay?

SOPHIE: Because it always causes me pain, eventually. When I'm old and ugly, I shall dress brightly and beautifully because no one can break my heart then.

BOBO: Your mother dressed beautifully. She was such a devotee of amore. She was so good at it.

SOPHIE: What good did it do her? And when the first baby came everything changed.

BOBO *(Suddenly alarmed)*: Why all this talk about babies?

SOPHIE: Oh no—not me.

    I was just talking about my father.

    That's all he was, Bobo—spermatozoa.

BOBO: Oh—what a dreadful word! What does it mean!

SOPHIE: Cum.

BOBO: Where?

    Stop. I remember now. *(Beat)* My darling, it's simple— when two dogs meet each other, one lays down and offers the other its throat. That is how one keeps from being attacked. That's how one stays alive. It has nothing to do with one's genitals.

SOPHIE: It has everything to do with one's genitals.

BOBO: I want to stop talking about genitals. Is that alright?

    Thank you. Good Lord. *(Shouting)* Alain!! *(To Sophie)* If you change your mind—it's lasting all night.

SOPHIE: You look wonderful.

BOBO: You could go as my page.

SOPHIE: No.

BOBO: It'll be the last time, you know. Unless you go to visit him in that foreign place. *(No answer from her)* Any message I could—?

SOPHIE: No.

BOBO: You only get one father, Sweetness. Only one.

SOPHIE: You're my father, Bobo.

BOBO *(A beat—this amazes him)*: Thank you. *(Reaches down to kiss her—his wig begins to tip)* Never mind. Alain!

(Alain enters, picks up the extra gowns. He and Bobo exit.
Ball music. Casanova enters, dressed very well. He is walking with a bit of difficulty, but has a cane. A Footman comes up to him and stands. Casanova hands him his invitation. The Footman looks at it, then at Casanova, then at the invitation again)

FOOTMAN: It's . . . possible. *(Announces)* The Chevalier de Seingalt, Giacomo Casanova!

(Casanova bows deeply and manages to get back up, although it costs him. Under his breath:)

Are you all right?

CASANOVA: Yes. Thank you.

(Footman exits. Casanova crosses away and tries to look as regal as possible)

A VOICE: Is this a masquerade?

ANOTHER VOICE: A decrepit Don Giovanni!

(Casanova exits as Footman reenters with another invitation in his hand)

FOOTMAN: The Chevalier D'Eon!

(Bobo enters in full regalia. Footman looks for Bobo's escort, the "Chevalier D'Eon")

BOBO: I am the Chevalier.

A VOICE: Chevalier! I see you saved your wardrobe, too!

BOBO *(Waving at someone he knows)*: Madame Scott! *(Someone else)* Madame Poquelin! Lovely! *(To another person, about his attire)* For days—weeks! Thank you. *(In answer to an*

unheard question—can you make me something that
wonderful?) Of course. For you.

(Applause for Bobo. Music change—new dance. Casanova
reenters)

CASANOVA: May I have . . . *(Looks Bobo up and down)* We have
    met, you and I.
BOBO: Yes.
CASANOVA: Versailles.
BOBO: Yes.
CASANOVA: Madame— *(Wants Bobo to supply the name)*
BOBO: I was your daughter's tutor.
CASANOVA: Ah.
BOBO: That's right.
    I was slated for an ambassadorial post . . .
CASANOVA: Yes?
BOBO: Nothing.

(Casanova seems a little weak)

    Are you . . . well?
CASANOVA: May I have this dance . . . Sir?
BOBO: Of course.

(They dance. Lots of whispering is heard.
    In Sophie's space, Victor enters)

VICTOR: Sophie!
SOPHIE: No!
VICTOR: I love the shirt. Forgive me?

(Sophie considers for a second and then runs to him, and they
embrace passionately)

SOPHIE: Will you promise to never, never leave me again?
VICTOR: Yes.
SOPHIE: Will you love only me?
VICTOR: Yes.

SOPHIE: Will you love me forever?

VICTOR: Yes.

SOPHIE: And ever and ever and ever . . .

VICTOR: Yes yes yes . . .

Trust me.

SOPHIE: Yes yes yes.

(They begin to make love. Their lovemaking sounds mingle with the sound of the Young Girl in labor. She begins to scream with pain. Lights up on her. The baby is born and is still connected by the umbilical cord)

YOUNG WOMAN *(Trying to clear the baby's mouth)*: Here. Here. Breathe.

BREATHE!

Why won't you cry?

My daughter. Breathe. PLEASE. *(A post-labor pain comes)* Mother! Mother! *(After a beat, picks the baby up, holding it out)* Rousseau?! Here is your daughter!!

(Lights down on the Young Woman.
Casanova and Bobo are sitting)

CASANOVA: I have to tell you something. Listen.

One night, as a child, I lay weak, suffering from a hemorrhage of the nose—I had been to a sorceress that day and she had prophesied that a visitation would occur, and that I was never to reveal it, or the blessing I was to receive would be forfeit. So I'm telling you now, my darling, because I no longer believe in the power of magic or the power of God or even the power of monarchs. I've seen the sky crack and darkness pour in like streams of the Last Deluge—we are all soaked to the skin with Night!

BOBO: I think we have to leave, my dear.

CASANOVA: No. There's a garden just outside. We'll walk.

(Young Casanova enters)

YOUNG CASANOVA: Caterina? Please . . .

BOBO *(To Casanova)*: You're bleeding.

(Casanova quickly reaches for his nose to check for a nosebleed)

CASANOVA: No . . . *(Feels something wet in his crotch, looks down, sees the blood. He whispers to Bobo)* Get me out of here.

BOBO: Lean on Bobo—hush, hush, hush.

(Victor and Sophie have finished making love and he is buttoning himself up again)

SOPHIE: Victor? Victor? Look at me.

(Casanova is lying down—Bobo covers him with a cape)

CASANOVA: Am I dying?

BOBO *(To Young Casanova)*: Stay with him. *(Crosses to exit)* Sophie. SOPHIE!! *(Exits)*

CASANOVA: Madame, it's been so lovely . . .
    Mademoiselle, you . . .
    My dears, where are you?

(Suddenly, they are there: Jacomine, Caterina, Mademoiselle Charpillon. They administer to him as they speak)

JACOMINE: You come inside of me—that's why it means so much. I can't even reach some of those places with my finger. What are your genitals to you? An appendage on your body, like breasts? Is that why you can't understand?

MADEMOISELLE CHARPILLON: Does taking me against my will seem just rude to you? You ram your prick inside me and it hurts because I'm dry because I don't want you. And my two most erotic places are never touched—my clitoris and my consent. And as you tower over me, completely absorbed in your own passion, I see what I am to you—a toilet.

CATERINA: Spent, you withdraw—neat. I lie full of your fluids. You are dressed, out of the door, thinking of something else—things explode inside my body—a machine of life begins to churn and I am made its servant. I become life's handmaiden, a servant to my own body, everything I am, all my individuality, secondary to this ancient function.

MADAME CHARPILLON: And what is my payment—pain, even death in childbirth, and if I survive it, servitude, invisibility, loneliness, celibacy, poverty, violence, and even rape again.

JACOMINE: This is my understanding of the world now.

(The woman wearing hoops appears, but this time she is fantastic and radiant—we see the perfect vision he saw as a little boy. But the woman is Therese)

CASANOVA: Can you forgive me?

THERESE: No.

CASANOVA: Is that why you've been in Hell?

THERESE: Yes.

CASANOVA: Then we're both doomed.

THERESE: That's alright, darling. As long as we're together.

(Therese opens her arms to him.
Victor gives Sophie a peck on the cheek, shrugs and exits)

SOPHIE: Don't leave me. Don't leave me. Don't LEEEAVE MEEE!

CASANOVA *(To Therese)*: Take me inside of you.

YOUNG CASANOVA *(Distraught)*: I'm lost. I'm lost.

(Lights down on everyone except the Young Girl and her baby. She is blowing breath into the baby's mouth)

YOUNG GIRL: Breathe. *(Blows)* Breathe. *(Blows)* Breathe. *(Blows)* Breathe.

(Slow fade on this action)

LOSING FATHER'S BODY

LOSING FATHER'S BODY was first presented as a workshop at the Gathering at Bigfork, Bigfork, Montana, in May 1992, under the direction of Greg Leaming, and subsequently at Circle Repertory Company, New York City, in April 1993, under the direction of Ray Cochran. It premiered at Portland Stage Company, April 17–May 14, 1994. The cast and creative contributors were as follows:

KIM ANDERSON	Christina Rouner
SCOTT ANDERSON, JR.	T. Scott Cunningham
PAULINE ANDERSON	Jeannine Moore
DR. RYAN	Don LaBranche
GEORGE BOYLE	Peter Boyden
JERRI	Catherine Lloyd Burns
DOROTHEA CROFT	Alison Edwards
TODD	Paul Drinan
MICHELLE	Maura O'Brien
ALICE BEAR	Jan Leslie Harding
CLARENCE BEAR	Chad Henry
CECIL ANDERSON	Benjamin Stewart
FELICIA	Catherine Lloyd Burns
DIRECTOR	Greg Leaming
SETS	Rob Odorisio
COSTUMES	Tom Broecker
LIGHTS	Christopher Akerlind
SOUND	Jim van Bergen

LOSING FATHER'S BODY was a recipient of a grant award for New American Plays from the W. Alton Jones Foundation.

CHARACTERS

KIM ANDERSON, early thirties

SCOTT ANDERSON, JR., early thirties, a year or two younger than
     Kim, his sister

PAULINE ANDERSON, 55, their mother

DR. RYAN, middle-aged, the family internist (could be doubled
     with Cecil)

GEORGE BOYLE, forties, the company lawyer

JERRI, 25 or so, a beautician

DOROTHEA CROFT, 60, their neighbor

TODD and MICHELLE, brother and sister, contemporaries of Scott
     and Kim

ALICE and CLARENCE BEAR, Canadian Indians on their way to
     New York (can be doubled with Todd and Michelle or Todd
     and Jerri)

CECIL ANDERSON, 50 or so, "Father's" brother and business
     partner

FELICIA, a chauffeur (doubles with Michelle or Jerri)

TIME

The present. Early fall.

The action of the play takes place on the patio, lawn and in the
two rooms that can be seen from the backyard of an immaculately
kept, raised ranch house in an upper-middle-class suburb somewhere in the northeastern part of the United States. The decor is a
little fussy, like powder-blue Ethan Allen in the living room, but
everything looks as new as the day it was bought, largely because
the inhabitants rarely live in the living room. There is a console
television in the living room, a couch, coffee table, end tables and
appropriate lamps, and large sliding glass doors separate the living
room from the patio. Scott's old room, a bathroom and a study
are offstage left, connected by a hallway to the living room. The
garage is offstage right of the kitchen and a door, closed, connects
them. The kitchen, with refrigerator, sink and some upstage cupboards can also be seen—someone standing at the sink, looking
out the window, would be looking over the backyard at the audience. A dining room, largely unseen, exists upstage right and is
only important to the action of the play in that it allows people to
enter the house from the front door without going into the living
room. Upstairs, unseen, is Kim's old room, her parents' bedroom,
two bathrooms. The staircase to the upstairs faces the front door
of the house, which is upstage right of center. A picture window
is on the upstage living-room wall. One of the living-room walls
contains a closet.

There are also a few scenes in the woods in New York State.

ACT ONE

Scene One

*It is midnight. The kitchen lights are on and a blue glow
emanates from the television, which is also on. Another small red
light can be seen on the patio. It is the lit cigarette of Kim. She is
sitting on a wooden folding chair, holding her cigarette and an
ashtray, being careful about the ashes. She is in her nightgown
and slippers and is wearing a down jacket.*

*The sound of a car driving up. Kim seems slightly confused
at what she's hearing, but doesn't act on it. Engine off, car door
slams, and the garage to the kitchen door opens and Scott enters,
carrying a garment bag and a shoulder tote. He's wearing a
trench coat over a suit and tie. He crosses directly to the telephone and dials.*

SCOTT: This is Scott Anderson, Jr. Messages.
    Uh-huh.
    Uh-huh.
    Got that one.
    Dump that one.
    Number again? *(Writes)* 9-1-0-4. Go on.
    Uh-huh.
    Uh-huh.

No.

Huh? That must be for my father. Wait. I'd better take it— *(Listens)* Got it.

That it?

What?

Oh. Oh—no problem. No, I should get his messages . . . now. No, don't apologize. We appreciate . . . your . . . ah . . . condolences, thanks. *(Hangs up, puts appointment book away, looks at watch, looks up and notices his sister on the patio, gets up and opens the sliding glass door slightly)* Hi.

(Kim turns matter-of-factly to him)

My room alright?

(Kim nods and Scott carries his stuff down the hall. After a beat, he returns, still wearing his trench coat, goes to the closet, takes out a folding chair, brings it out onto the patio and sets it up near his sister)

KIM: Still smoke?

SCOTT *(Sitting down)*: Oh yeah. *(Lighting up his own cigarette)* How's mother?

KIM: Okay. Doctor gave her a sedative.

SCOTT: Right.

KIM: Couldn't meet you.

SCOTT: No problem. Got your message. Rented a car.

KIM: The Seville's out there.

SCOTT: I'll need my own. Could get some work done at the main office. Should.

KIM: Deductible—the car.

SCOTT: Oh, right. How ya been?

KIM: Okay. Busy.

SCOTT: Me, too. Trip okay?

KIM: Fine.

SCOTT: Cab from the airport?

KIM: No, Mrs. Croft. Next door? Picked me up.

SCOTT: Circular driveway?

KIM: Dorothea—Dorothy.

SCOTT: Yeahyeahyeah. You look good.

KIM: So do you.

SCOTT: Didn't get to jog today. Gotta do it. *(Sets watch alarm)*
Pretty night.

KIM: Little nippy.

SCOTT: How's Mother?

KIM: Upstairs.

SCOTT: What?

KIM: Sedated.

SCOTT: Oh yeah. I forgot. How's the job?

KIM: Great. Really. Up for tenure. Peer review.

SCOTT: When?

KIM: Right now.

SCOTT: Oh God, wouldn't you know it. Worst time for me, too.

KIM: Yeah.

SCOTT: So, how are things progressing? Lots of details?

KIM: Everything's set. Prearranged. By him.

SCOTT: Of course.

George all set, then? Do we need to go downtown
tomorrow?

Haven't had time to call.

KIM: No. Nothing to sign, as far as I know.

SCOTT: Good. Talk to Cecil?

KIM: Uncle Cecil had to rent a small plane for the transportation
of the—ah—ahm—

SCOTT: Oh. Of course.

It'll save time, too.

KIM: And then he's driving all their gear back here in the station
wagon.

SCOTT: Who's picking up the tab for the plane?
The estate?

KIM: No. The company.

SCOTT: And Cecil okayed it?

KIM: Had to. No choice.

SCOTT: Who's meeting the plane?

KIM: Besemer's. We don't need to do anything in that
    department. Everything's arranged there, too.

SCOTT: So when are the go dates?

KIM: Viewing—day after tomorrow. Ten a.m. Funeral at four.

SCOTT: Viewing?

KIM: Visitation. Not viewing. They know that.

SCOTT: So, nothing tomorrow.

KIM: A free day.

SCOTT: I'll work on the phone. . . . I've got a car. . . . No problem.

KIM: I brought my laptop.
        So I'm set.

SCOTT: So we're set then.

KIM: Looks like it.

SCOTT: Great.

*(They put out their cigarettes carefully, get up and fold up their
chairs, return chairs to the closet, hang up their coats)*

I am gonna jog. I get a little down when I miss a day.

KIM: Well, I'm gonna take a shower and then I've got an article
    I'm working on, so I'd better use what time I've got.

SCOTT: So I'll see you in the morning.

(They share a perfunctory kiss)

You take care of the ashtray?

KIM: No problem.

*(Scott exits to his room to change for jogging. Kim gets the
ashtray, dumps its contents carefully in the trash in the kitchen,
washes the ashtray out, dries it, then washes her hands and dries
them, polishes the sink fixtures with the towel, hangs the towel
inside the sink cupboard door, turns out the kitchen lights and
exits upstairs.*

Scott enters from his bedroom, dressed for jogging. He does some stretching exercises, remembers he's wearing his watch, takes it off and puts it on the coffee table, and exits out the front door.

A beat. Their mother, Pauline, appears, having just come downstairs—a frail bird, hair sticking up, wearing only a night-gown. She crosses quickly downstage, out the glass doors and exits across the lawn. We hear a large splash.

Kim comes downstairs in her robe, goes directly to the television, turns it off, exits back upstairs. From the living room, we hear Scott's watch alarm going off—the sound grows larger)

Scene Two

The next morning. Dr. Ryan comes into the kitchen from upstairs, carrying a breakfast tray, puts it on the sink. Kim enters from the patio where she has been having her morning cigarette—she's carrying an ashtray. She sees Dr. Ryan and hides the ashtray, then crosses to his coat on the couch, picks it up and straightens the pillow underneath, as if the weight of the coat might have marred the appearance of the couch.

DR. RYAN: Hi, Kimmy.

KIM: Oh.

DR. RYAN: Scotty let me in. Still smoking, huh? *(Takes coat)* Gotta run. Your mother didn't eat any of her breakfast. I think she may have caught a bit of a chill last night. How long was she in the pool?

KIM: They heard the splash and got her right out.

DR. RYAN: It wasn't your pool?

KIM: We don't have a pool.

DR. RYAN: Oh yeah. Tear out a beautiful lawn and put in a pool—music outdoors, kids. Terrible. *(Writing out a prescription)* Now here's a very good sleeping pill. *(Hands Kim the prescription, puts on his coat, then fishes in both coat pockets,*

pulls out some more medicines, samples from drug companies)
And give her two of these twice a day. And—ah— *(Looking
at a sample)* one of these, you know, for ah . . . *(Makes a vague
gesture)* I trust you—read the cartons.

KIM: Okay. *(Takes all the bottles)*

DR. RYAN: You should probably keep these in your room—
control the dosage.

KIM: Oh?

DR. RYAN: No problem or anything. You know, your mom's just
confused right now, and she might mix up, you know,
confuse the dosage.

KIM: Oh, right. How is she?

DR. RYAN: Sleeping. I gave her a shot. Start her on those when
she wakes up.

KIM: Okay. No problem.

DR. RYAN: That's my girl. *(At door)* Oh—Kimmy. You might
call whatever beauty salon your mother uses and ask if
they'll make a house call—just this once. It might do her a
world of good. Bye now.

*(Dr. Ryan exits out the front door. Kim crosses to the refrigerator
and puts the medicine away, puts the prescription on the refrigerator door, with a magnet. Doorbell rings—she crosses to open the
front door. Dr. Ryan doesn't come in, just hands her a golf club)*

Your dad's putter. I was borrowing it—meant to return it
last week.

*(She takes it. He closes the door and is gone. Kim looks at the
putter for a beat, then goes to the closet to put it away with the
rest of the clubs, but they aren't there. She exits down the hall
to put it away, comes back, still not having found the golf clubs.
Sound of a car, the garage door opening, closing, engine being
turned off. Meanwhile, Kim finds herself strangely annoyed and
upset by not being able to put the putter away. Scott enters from
the garage, with cigarettes and a brown bag)*

SCOTT: Hi. Ran out of cigarettes. And got some papaya tablets. Stomach's been funny since yesterday—don't know why. Where'd this tray come from? Got us some decent coffee, too.

(Kim crosses quickly to clean up the tray, doesn't know what to do with the putter, hands it to Scott)

KIM: Mother didn't eat.

SCOTT *(About the putter)*: What's this?

KIM: Father's. Dr. Ryan returned it.

SCOTT *(Plugging in the electric teakettle)*: How's Mother? Knocked on her door this morning. No answer.

KIM: She's asleep.

SCOTT: Doctor give her another sedative?

KIM: He was up there this morning. Yes, he said he did.

SCOTT: Ran into Todd and Michelle. *(Getting out a two-cup Melitta and a filter he's bought)* They said sorry of course. You want a cup?

KIM: Yeah. Great.

SCOTT *(Fixing the coffee)*: Want to know if we can meet them for doubles.

KIM: When?

SCOTT: Cocktail time.

KIM: Today? Mmmmm—I don't know.

SCOTT: Yeah.

KIM: It'll be getting dark by then.

SCOTT: It's indoor courts, Kim.

KIM: No, I meant Mother. I don't want to leave her when it's getting, you know, dark.

SCOTT: Maybe someone could come and stay. The circular driveway—

KIM: Dorothy whatshername.

SCOTT: Right.

KIM: What about dinner?

SCOTT: We could eat at the club. *(Pours hot water into the Melitta)*

KIM: I meant the—ah—tray. Mother's tray.

SCOTT: Oh. Anytime. I'll do it. Half 'n' half or milk?

KIM: Milk.

(They fix their cups at the sink. Lots of sugar and milk. Quiet stirring)

I tried to find the clubs.

SCOTT: Maybe he took them.

KIM: A fishing trip?

SCOTT: Sometimes.

KIM: Canada?

SCOTT: Guess you're right. *(About the clubs)* Somewhere. Garage?

KIM: Of course.

(Scott picks up the putter, heads for the door to the garage. He holds the putter throughout the rest of the scene)

SCOTT *(Stopping at the door)*: It was quick, wasn't it?

KIM: Heart attack. Must have . . . been.

SCOTT: Todd and Michelle wanted to know.

(Scott exits into the garage. Doorbell rings, Kim crosses to answer it)

KIM *(At door)*: Oh! Glenn!

GEORGE *(Correcting her)*: George. *(Greets her)* Kimberly. *(Comes into living room carrying an attaché case, looks around)* Lovely place.

KIM: You've never been here before?

GEORGE: Your parents always entertained at the club.

KIM: I thought you were here last Christmas.

GEORGE: No, that was the Marriott.

(Scott enters from garage, still carrying the putter, sees George, crosses to greet him)

SCOTT: George! How are you? Everything okay?

GEORGE: Great. How is Pauline?

KIM: She's sleeping.

GEORGE: Ah—good. That's good. Best thing.

KIM: Can I take your coat, George?

GEORGE: No—can't stay.

SCOTT: Coffee?

GEORGE: No. No. Thank you, though. Thank you.

You kids are looking great, you really are. *(About Scott)* 'Course I see this guy all the time. *(About the putter Scott is holding)* Been practicing?

SCOTT: Father's.

GEORGE: Let's sit down.

(George sits heavily on the couch or chair, reaches for his cigarettes and lights up. Scott and Kim are frozen with the violation)

Got an ashtray?

(Kim runs to get the ashtray, finds it where she stashed it when Dr. Ryan was in the kitchen. Offering one to Scott:)

I know you hate menthol.

SCOTT *(Refusing the cigarette and crossing to the sliding doors)*: No, thanks. *(Opens one of the glass doors quietly)*

KIM *(Putting the ashtray next to George)*: I'm trying to quit.

(George takes a long drag, then leaves the cigarette in his mouth as he fools with his briefcase)

GEORGE: Why don't you kids sit down?

(Kim and Scott sit gingerly on the edge of the furniture)

SCOTT: What is it, George?

GEORGE: Well. Scott. Kimberly. Fact is, we've hit kind of a snag. It's no big thing, really big thing, anyway. I mean, everything is legally going forward. It's a personal, more of a personal— *(Blows out some breath, starts over)* Basically, it's this: your

Uncle Cecil feels very strongly that the chartered plane costs too much and has decided to drive your father back in the station wagon. Himself. From Canada. He's stored him— your father—under the canoe, on the roof, carefully wrapped, and has been advised by some Mountie up there— some guy who knows what he's talking about—that game is transported at this time of year with no problems in—ah— you know, preservation. So. Now, I know this may seem a little bit—I mean—ah—a little, ah, a little, ah, a bit uncomfortable. But Canadian law on the transport of, you know, remains is incredible. Incredible. I mean, the red tape— *(More than George can express)* Now, I know what you may be—what's running through—what you may be thinking— I mean, it's, it's NOT, by any stretch of the imagination, ideal. I realize that, and so does your Uncle Cecil. But he is—you know how he is. He and your father built this company from a very modest—well, you know the story, of course. All of this from these principles of frugality and practicality, which I admire so much—have always admired in them both, and in you, and in Pauline. And determination. It's incredible, really, Cecil's determination is incredible, really. I wish you could hear him on this subject. I mean, the immediate subject at hand . . . that we're discussing here. So, what do you think? Before you say anything, though, here are some things to consider. It's not a long drive, and he is driving straight through, so our basic timetable would be the same. The other thing is, well, this is really the thing, he's on the road, you see, already. He called me from a place called— *(Takes out his notepad, opens it and shows them where he's written down the place)* —Chee-bow-gam-mow. I looked it up on a map—it's near, well, it's really not near anything. A place called— *(Reading from his notepad)* Waswanipi— another place called Boo—French— *(Hands his notepad to Kim)*

KIM *(Reads and pronounces the place correctly)*: Bourlamaque.

GEORGE *(Trying to duplicate the sound)*: Bourlamaque?

KIM: Bourlamaque.

SCOTT: What is it?

(Kim rises and takes the notepad to him. Trying to pronounce it:)

Bourlamaque.

KIM: Bourlamaque.

SCOTT: Bourlamaque.

KIM: Right.

GEORGE: Well, kids. I've got to get going here. Ah—if you need anything— *(Quickly)* I don't think Pauline need know anything about any of this.

KIM: No.

SCOTT: No.

GEORGE: No. *(Gets up, crosses to front door)* So. I'll call you as soon as Cecil arrives. He'll go straight to Besemer's. They're on hold. Medical examiner is an old client of your dad's, so no problem there. So—no problem. Everything's gonna be just fine. Give my best to Pauline.

(George exits.

Kim and Scott rise. Scott opens sliding glass doors fully and then the front door to move the smoke of George's cigarette out as Kim straightens the couch and chairs. Scott gets a spray can out of the kitchen cupboard, sprays the living room, puts can away, as Kim gets folding chairs out of the closet)

KIM: Want one?

SCOTT: Uh-huh.

(Kim carries chairs outside and sets them up. She returns and gets her cigarettes and then takes the ashtray from Scott who has been standing in the living room. He comes to and shuts the front door. Kim sits in a folding chair)

KIM: Scotty?

SCOTT: Coming.

(Scott joins her outside and sits on his folding chair. They light up and smoke a bit in silence. Scott is now gripping the putter)

KIM: Couldn't find the clubs, huh?
SCOTT *(Surprised at finding the club still in his hands)*: No.

Scene Three

Noon of the same day. Sound of "Mantovani plays Mancini," or some such music found on Muzak-like FM stations, emanates from an elaborate, showy radio/cassette player held by Jerri, a 25-year-old beautician dressed in a pants-suit uniform with a fussy sweater over the top. Jerri is standing on the patio, also clutching a blow dryer and one of those plastic coverall bibs old salons still use. She is waiting. The barbecue grill has a platter on it containing a can of spray net, brushes, scissors, comb, a box of Kleenex, etc., and a folding chair has been set up next to the grill. A beach bag, used to carry all this stuff, is neatly placed nearby. Scott enters from the hall of the house, trailing an extension cord made from several short extension cords. He crosses to Jerri on the patio and plugs her blow dryer into the extension cord. She clicks it on—nothing.

SCOTT: Is it on?
JERRI: No.
SCOTT: Turn it on.
JERRI: I did.
SCOTT: But I don't hear anything.
JERRI: I know.

(Beat)

SCOTT: Oh. Oh, I see. It must be the—something must've come unplugged. Why don't you put your radio . . . thing down, and we'll work on getting the hair dryer to work.

JERRI: There is nothing wrong with this hair dryer— *(Corrects herself)* —blow dryer.

SCOTT: No, I know that. I meant, you look like you're holding a lot of things. I just thought—

JERRI: I'm alright.
Thank you.

SCOTT: Make yourself comfortable. I'll check the cords—I'm sure it's one of ours.

(Scott, checking the cords as he goes, disappears into the garage. After a beat, Jerri sits down in the folding chair, gripping her blow dryer and radio to her. She feels exposed, uncomfortable. She checks over her shoulder to see if her customer is coming— sees nothing. She begins to hum along with one of the songs on the radio, vainly trying to comfort herself. The blow dryer comes on suddenly—she jumps from the chair in a sudden panic, holding the blow dryer, not knowing what to do with it, afraid to let go of it. Scott enters from the garage)

That do it?

(Jerri turns the dryer off)

Great. We're set then.

(Pauline enters the living room, her head wrapped in a towel. Kim follows. They have just come downstairs and cross quickly onto the patio)

PAULINE: I don't want to drip on the rug. I'm not dripping on the rug, am I?

(Embarrassed to see his mother in less than perfect order, Scott crosses into the house and exits into the garage)

KIM: No, Mother. It's fine.

JERRI: Is she all right?
She looks alright.

PAULINE: I don't have my glasses.

KIM: Shall I get them?

PAULINE: NO! No. *(Sits in the chair)* Stay here.

KIM *(To Jerri)*: Are you warm enough? Is there anything I can get you?

JERRI: I have my sweater. *(Hands Kim the plastic coverall)* Would you put that around your mother? *(Shouting, as if to a deaf person)* WE'RE PUTTING THE COVERALL ON, MRS. ANDERSON.

(Kim puts the coverall around her mother. Kim is inept at touching people, especially her mother)

I'll adjust it.

(Jerri seems reluctant to let go of the radio or cross to Pauline. Pauline adjusts her coverall)

PAULINE *(To Kim)*: No one can see us?

JERRI: It's nice out here. You can hear birds.

KIM: No, Mother. No one can see us.

PAULINE *(Whispers to Kim)*: The radio. The radio. Neighbors.

JERRI: What?

KIM *(To Jerri)*: Would you mind turning off the radio?

JERRI: I always work with music.

KIM: We'll—er—we could turn it very, very low.

(Jerri tries to reach the volume, but is still holding the blow dryer. Kim tries to help)

JERRI *(Suddenly panicky)*: Don't change the station! Don't change the station! *(Puts the radio down and adjusts the volume)* There.
    Now you can really hear that bird. Peep—peep—peep—peep.

KIM: I think that's beeping from— *(Points to a house in the area)*— their security system. It lets them know it's on. It's stopped now.

JERRI: I guess that's good—security. *(To Pauline, getting herself ready to begin)* WELL, MRS. ANDERSON, THIS IS

CRAZY ISN'T IT? BUT YOU HAVE TO BE A LITTLE CRAZY TO BE A BEAUTICIAN. *(To Kim)* It's a crazy business. Green hair . . . what next? Yeah, I'm a nut.

KIM: So you're all set then.

PAULINE *(Meaning "don't leave")*: No—

JERRI: You're not leaving are you?

KIM: Well, I do have some things—

JERRI: Patricia told me to give her a facial.

KIM: Alright.

JERRI: We could skip it.

KIM: Maybe it would be good.

JERRI: Would you like to give it?
Just a peel-off mask—very simple.

KIM: No. You go ahead.

JERRI: Okay, then. *(To Pauline)* WE'RE GOING TO DO YOUR FACIAL NOW, MRS. ANDERSON. *(Reaches into her bag and takes out a jar. She tries to overcome her dread of touching Pauline but finally plunges in and applies the facial mask. Working a bit too fast)* Here we go. *(Finishes and wipes her hands on a lot of Kleenex, dropping them around her on the patio)* There. Now that should dry very quickly. Can I wash up—this stuff is sooo sticky.

KIM: There's a bathroom right down the hall. First door on the left.

JERRI: Thanks very much. That wasn't hard, was it?

(Jerri crosses into the house and exits down the hall to the bathroom. Kim stands awkwardly near Pauline, not knowing what to do or say)

KIM: That looks . . . good.

(Kim picks up the dirty Kleenexes that Jerri has left. She'd like to go throw them away, but it seems strange to leave her mother out here alone. Finally, the messy Kleenexes are too much to stand and she crosses away and into the kitchen with them. Immediately,

panic hits Pauline. She looks around, slightly inhibited by the towel on her head and the coverall, and can't see Kim)

PAULINE *(Unable to speak well because of the now-stiffening facial mask)*: Kin?

(Kim doesn't hear her—she's too busy cleaning up at the kitchen sink. Kim exits upstairs)

Ki?
Ki?

(Pauline gives up and looks straight ahead. She begins to cry.
   Jerri enters the patio, talking as she goes, with the euphoria of someone who has conquered a fear)

JERRI: There. All better. All clean. *(Straightens Pauline's coverall efficiently, then takes the towel off Pauline's head, rubbing her hair a bit with it)* Now, what do we need to do today? I just gave you a nice trim last week, or was that Vanessa that did you? Anyway, why don't we just give you a nice styling with the blow dry? And some teasing on top? Something nice and soft around the face, you know? *(Notices that Pauline is crying)* Uh-oh. Oh, Mrs. Anderson— *(Looks around frantically for Kim)* Mrs. Anderson, PLEASE. I'm just a hairdresser. *(To herself)* I knew it. I knew it. *(To Pauline)* Look, I'll just— I'll just—why don't I— *(Realizing that she has too much stuff to make a quick exit, she grabs her radio and holds it up to Pauline's ear)* Listen to the nice music. *(Turns the volume up. It doesn't work. Puts the radio down)* And look at your facial!

(In desperation, picks up the blow dryer, turns it on and tries to dry Pauline's tears with it.
   Kim comes downstairs and crosses out onto the patio.
   To Kim:)

Thank god you're here!!
KIM: What's wrong! What's wrong!

JERRI (*Exasperated, almost indignant*): Your mother is CRYING!

(*Jerri starts stuffing her things into the beach bag. Kim stands
next to Pauline, looking at her in helpless amazement. Jerri has
all her things and crosses with them into the living room, blow
dryer still plugged in. She runs into Scott, entering from the hall*)

She is not ready for people yet!

(*Pauline is sobbing openly now.
   At front door:*)

Will you unplug me!!!??

(*Scott grabs the nearest extension cord section and unplugs it.
Jerri exits out the front door, cord disappearing after her. Scott
watches it go and shuts the front door.
   Pauline gets a grip on herself. She stands with some dignity,
blots her eyes on the towel that was on her head—some of the
facial comes off on it*)

KIM (*Taking the towel*): I'll—I'll—

(*Pauline turns and starts her exit into the house, sees Scott*)

PAULINE: Scott! I didn't see you. Welcome home. (*To Kim*)
Kimberly, make sure he gets clean towels. (*Starts for the
house again, turns, remembering something. Speaks to Scott*)
And you want to air out your closet. It's already been damp
this fall.

(*Pauline crosses into the living room and exits upstairs. Kim and
Scott don't move as they watch her. After she's gone, they start to
clean up. They are silent and embarrassed at their mother's show
of emotion and don't look at each other. Finally, Scott and Kim
run into each other in the kitchen—she is preparing some more
medicine for her mother and Scott is putting the extension cords
away. Speaking is unavoidable*)

KIM: She's just tired.

scott: Yes, I know.

(Kim exits upstairs with the medicine. Scott takes two papaya tablets from his stash in the refrigerator and rubs his stomach. It's hurting again. He crosses to the patio and looks at the lawn, as if that will tell him something)

Scene Four

Cocktail time. Kim is in her tennis togs. She is putting finishing touches on Pauline's dinner tray. Dorothea Croft, a middle-aged woman, enters from the edge of the lawn, carrying a large chocolate cake, crosses to living-room sliding glass doors. Kim sees her, lets her in.

dorothea: I'm not late.

kim: No. Not at all. Come in.

dorothea: I bought this cake at the bakery when I was shopping.

Thought it might come in handy. Lots of guests at a time like this. *(Hands it to Kim who tries to find a place for it)* Nobody doesn't like chocolate cake. *(Cracks herself up with this one)* I should write those commercials.

kim: Thank you.

dorothea: Don't put it in the fridge. That frosting'll seize right up—you won't be able to get a knife in it.

(Scott enters from his bedroom. He's also in tennis togs)

scott: Hello.

kim: You remember my brother.

scott: We really appreciate this.

dorothea: No problem. You kids need to get out. Tough couple of days. *(To Kim)* Show him the cake.

scott: Yum.

KIM: Mother's sleeping. Upstairs.

SCOTT: We'll be back by nine or so.

KIM: Her tray's ready. She's sleeping now.

SCOTT: Nine-thirty at the latest.

DOROTHEA: Take your time.

SCOTT *(To Kim)*: Everything's in the car.

KIM *(To Dorothea)*: Bye.

SCOTT *(To Dorothea)*: Thanks again.

(Kim and Scott exit out the garage/kitchen door)

DOROTHEA: Bye. *(Looks at the tray. She then goes through a couple of cupboards, finds the liquor cabinet, pours herself a double, walks to the foot of the stairs)* Pauline!? Pauline!? *(Crosses to the living room, turns on the television, finds whatever is on at five o'clock—a quiz show, whatever—lies down on the couch, pillows propping up her head, watches, and drinks entire drink in two or three gulps. Phone rings and she answers it)* Andersons.

No.

They just left.

No.

Sure. *(Writes some information down as she talks)* Uh-huh. Uh-huh.

Uh-huh. *(Beat as she listens)* Uh-huh.

Uh-huh.

Uh-huh. *(Beat)* Uh-huh. *(Beat)* Oh no. *(Beat)* Dorothea. Close friend of the family.

Yes, I've got it.

Thanks. Bye.

(She hangs up, crosses to fix herself another drink, does so, drinks half of it and lies down to watch TV, falls asleep. Light change: dusk goes to dark and the television is showing the ten o'clock news.

Pauline comes downstairs. She is dressed and wearing a wig, but she has it on backwards)

PAULINE: Kimberly?

   Kim?

   Scott?

(She notices the sleeping Dorothea, crosses immediately to the kitchen, where she gets a placemat. She crosses to the couch and puts the placemat under Dorothea's feet. Pauline then notices the glass of Scotch and that it has left a ring. She carries the glass back to the kitchen and returns with a kitchen chemical of some kind and a rag. She works on the spot on the furniture. Sound of garage door opening, car turning off, car doors. The door to the kitchen from the garage opens and Kim and Scott enter, back from tennis. Scott goes to the front door and lets in Todd and Michelle, also in tennis togs. Kim gets out drinks stuff, moving Pauline's tray aside. Pauline stands in the living room, readying herself for the introductions, but no one notices her. Todd and Michelle have entered the kitchen from the front door through the dining room)

TODD: Not intruding?

SCOTT: No way.

KIM: Scotch and soda?

MICHELLE: You bet.

   Todd, scotch?

TODD: Yes, thanks.

   Good game.

SCOTT: *Great* game!

KIM: Todd's serve—

MICHELLE: Been practicing.

KIM *(Reminding him)*: Scott—Dorothea.

SCOTT: Oh yeah.

KIM: Our neighbor.

SCOTT *(Noticing the tray)*: Mother's tray.

TODD: Oh. Quiet?

KIM: Not necessary.

MICHELLE: Under medication?

KIM: Mother. Yes.

TODD: Best thing.

(Scott has put the tray in the refrigerator and crosses to the living room to get Dorothea up, sees Pauline)

SCOTT: Kim! Mother!

KIM: What? *(Seeing her)* Mother! *(Recovering)* Todd. Michelle.

PAULINE *(Trying hard)*: Oh yes. How-are-both—

TODD: Fine. Thanks.

MICHELLE: Very sorry—

TODD: Yes, sorry.

PAULINE: About what?

Oh—oh.

Thank you, I appre—

SCOTT: Mother? Drink?

PAULINE: Well, I don't think so. You know, I've—

KIM *(To Pauline, but for Todd and Michelle's benefit)*: Should eat.

PAULINE: How are your parents? I never—

TODD: Dad's great.

MICHELLE: Mother, too.

SCOTT *(Raising his drink)*: Cheers.

TODD, MICHELLE and KIM: Cheers.

(Silence)

TODD: Well, nice.

MICHELLE: Very nice.

TODD *(Looks at watch)*: Oops! Time.

MICHELLE: Wooo. Late.

TODD: Must go.

MICHELLE: Really must.

(They carry their glasses to the kitchen counter, put them down)

KIM: Not really.

SCOTT: Don't rush.

PAULINE: Please. Please don't go on my account. In fact, stay on my account. It's nice. It's so nice—

MICHELLE *(Moving toward door)*: Thank you so—

TODD *(To Pauline—condolences)*: Again. Sorry

MICHELLE *(To Pauline)*: Do anything?

TODD *(To Pauline)*: Just call.

SCOTT: Great game.

MICHELLE: Again soon?

TODD: Real soon.

MICHELLE: Bye now.

(Todd and Michelle exit out the front door. Kim and Scott stand still for a beat, somewhat at a loss)

SCOTT *(Back into gear)*: I have to take a shower. *(Exiting down the hall with no intention of helping with the sleeping woman on the couch)* Should we wake up Dorothea?

KIM *(Halfheartedly)*: Dorothea?

(Dorothea doesn't move)

I've got some typing to do. And I need a shower, too. That won't keep you awake, will it, Mother?

PAULINE: Oh, I thought you were talking to Dorothea.

KIM: She's really asleep.

PAULINE: Well, I'm not sleepy at all. Really. I won't sleep for hours. I feel—

KIM: Maybe you should take another pill. You should sleep. There's some in the fridge. And eat a little dinner. Your hair looks nice. You'll see about Dorothea, won't you, Mother? *(Exits upstairs)*

PAULINE: It's a wig. *(Stands over Dorothea)* Dorothea?!

(No answer. Pauline leans down to check if Dorothea is breathing—the alcohol breath repels her—walks disconsolately to the television, turns it off, crosses back to the kitchen, picking up her kitchen chemical and rag on the way. She prepares to clean, but

loses heart, opens fridge and finds what looks like her medicine.
She looks out at the patio and takes a pill, using the remainders
of the drinks in the glasses to wash it down. She takes another
pill, and another, and another—until she has emptied the bottle.
She notices the putter that Scott hasn't been able to put away.
She picks it up, walks to the kitchen cupboard that contains
the china, opens the door and whacks the contents of the cup-
board thoroughly and efficiently with the putter, closes the
cupboard door. She goes to the next cupboard and does the same.
Dorothea awakens with a start this time. Pauline goes to the
broom closet and gets out the broom and dustpan and sweeps up
the shards that have fallen from the destruction, even though she
was careful about closing the cupboard doors each time)

DOROTHEA: Wha—what? Clyde? *(Reaches for a light, turns it on,*
heads for the kitchen, sees Pauline) Pauline? Pauline? What's
wrong?

PAULINE: Nothing. Just cleaning up a bit.

DOROTHEA: Ooo. I got up too quick.

PAULINE: Are you alright?

DOROTHEA: Yeah . . .

PAULINE: So am I. *(Replaces the broom, dustpan and putter, shuts*
the broom closet door, collapses)

DOROTHEA: Oh my god! Oh my god! Pauline. Pauline!! *(Tries to*
revive her and finally drags her into the living room, as if that
will help. Gets to the telephone, dials a number) Clyde? Clyde?
Oh my god get over here! Something's happened to
Pauline again. *(Hangs up, crosses back to the kitchen sink,*
gets water in a glass, crosses back and sprinkles it on Pauline's
face)

PAULINE: Stop that.

DOROTHEA: What?

PAULINE: I'm all right.

DOROTHEA: Pauline, I don't think you're all right.

PAULINE: I'm all right.

(Pauline gets up and heads down the hallway. We hear her pounding on the bathroom door. After a beat, Scott enters from the hallway, having been ousted from the bathroom by his mother. He is wet, wearing a towel and holding his mother's wig)

SCOTT: What? What's going on?!!!

(Sound of retching in the bathroom)

DOROTHEA *(To Scott)*: Thank god you're here. I thought you were still playing tennis!

SCOTT: We got home.

DOROTHEA: Well, why in the hell didn't you wake me up?

SCOTT: Mother was supposed to.

DOROTHEA: She did.
    Look, Clyde's on his way over here, and I want to head him off. *(Exits out the sliding glass doors and offstage)*

SCOTT: Kim!!!

(Kim enters from upstairs)

KIM: What's wrong?

SCOTT: I was taking a shower and Mother made me leave. She's in there now. I think she's sick.

KIM: What did she have for dinner?

SCOTT: She didn't eat it.

(Kim crosses down the hall to the bathroom door. We hear off-stage knocking on the door. She returns after a beat or two)

KIM: She won't let me in.

SCOTT: I'm going to finish my shower upstairs.

KIM: I don't know what to do.

SCOTT: What?

KIM: I don't know what to do.

SCOTT: About what?

KIM: She won't let me in.

SCOTT: Why do you want to go in?

KIM: To see if she's all right.

SCOTT: Did you ask her?

KIM: I tried to, but she was . . . you know . . . throwing up.

SCOTT: I'll make you some coffee. (*Goes to kitchen, uncomfortable, but doing the best he can with the towel. He puts the wig on the counter, looks back at the living room*) I dripped on the rug.

KIM: I'll get it.

(*Kim gets the dishtowel and begins to blot up the rug. Scott has opened the fridge to get out the coffee, notices something odd*)

SCOTT: That's funny.

KIM: What?

SCOTT: My papaya tablets are gone—completely. You didn't take them, did you?

KIM: No. I'm going to check on Mother.

(*Kim exits down the hall. Scott plugs in the electric teakettle. Kim returns with a bigger towel. She bends down and blots some more*)

She says she's all right.

SCOTT: Good.

(*As he says this, he opens one of the cupboards. Broken crockery pours out*)

Scene Five

A little later. Kim and Scott are in their pajamas, slippers and jackets. They are sitting on folding chairs on the patio, smoking. Pauline enters the hallway, holding a towel—she's finally out of the bathroom. She sits on the couch in the living room. The phone rings and she jumps a bit—the sound is painful. Scott and Kim get up to get the phone, Pauline waves and smiles at them, picks up phone and answers it. Kim and Scott sit back down.

PAULINE *(Into phone)*: Hello.

No, I'm fine.

It was sweet of you to call.

No, I didn't. *(Looks for telephone message on end table, finds it)* Oh, here it is.

Got it. Thanks again, Dorothea.

No, I'm fine. Really.

Bye. *(Reads message)* Oh dear. *(Dials a number. Shouts to Scott and Kim)* Another problem, kids. *(Her call goes through)* George? This is Pauline.

No, I'm fine.

Yes.

Cecil called.

Yes.

Got a pencil?

Howard Johnson's.

I know Andy hated them, too. But what can you do when you're on the road?

New—burgh.

New York—state.

No, I never heard of it.

518—594-3111.

That is correct.

No, wait, George—that's not the message dear.

No, there's something else. Now, don't be upset because I certainly am not. I'm not going to even tell the children. And it's insured.

I'm coming to it, George, dear.

"Stopped for coffee at HoJo's—" see, he wasn't going to stay there. "Station wagon with all its contents"—all is underlined here—"stolen." *(Beat)* George? Did you hear that? George?

So, he went in to get a cup of coffee and bang, somebody got away with the station wagon. Isn't that terrible? But I know Andy wouldn't want us to worry about it now. It's only a car. So just write it off or whatever you do. I wish I could tell Cecil not to worry, but I know he wouldn't listen to me. Will you talk to him, George?

(Scott and Kim have turned around in their chairs and are looking at their mother)

Good. You have the number. *(Sees them and waves them away with a pleasant gesture)* No, the kids are in bed—I wouldn't dream of bothering them. No, no, no—I insist. And you should go back to bed, too. Let me talk to Helen—she'll make you do what's best for you.

Alright, then. That's better.

Night, night. *(Hangs up the phone, talks to Kim and Scott)* I'm going to bed now, children! I'm not going to take one of Dr. Ryan's pills. I don't think I need it tonight. Don't stay up too late.

(She exits upstairs. Kim and Scott look at one another)

KIM: We have a problem.
SCOTT: Yeah.

(Phone rings)

PAULINE'S VOICE: Don't answer that!!

(The phone keeps ringing and Kim and Scott stare at it)

ACT TWO

Scene One

Sound of birds singing. The woods at predawn. Alice Bear is standing addressing an imaginary TV audience. She is an Indian woman, dressed like a cowboy, and is drunk.

ALICE: So I really want to tell ya— *(To the imaginary talk-show host)* Give me a minute, Johnny—I gotta do this. I gotta tell 'em— *(Back to the audience)* You're a great crowd. You folks are GREAT!! *(Motioning to the "band")* Isn't that band great? I mean, GREAT!! *(Trying to get applause out of the audience for the band)* Let me hear it! *(Pause when no applause comes)* Well, that's alright. Everybody has an off night.

But I really want to tell you—

How many—how many—fat, white guys does it take to screw in a light bulb?

Give up?

Three.

One to stick his dick in the socket.

Another to pull the chain.

And a third to yell, "Don't you LOVE IT, baby!"

And that's how many FAT, WHITE guys it takes— *(Interrupted by "Johnny")* SHUT THE FUCK UP, JOHN-

NY! I got the GODDAM floor for ONCE!!
ALRIGHT?!!!

(Clarence, her brother, enters. He is younger, and is also dressed like a cowboy)

CLARENCE: Alice! I told you! No stand-up in the act on account of you are too angry and not funny.

ALICE: I'm funny.

CLARENCE *(Noticing her drinking)*: Alice! Alice! What the hell you doin', man?

ALICE: I am no man. I am a woman, Clarence. And don't you ever forget it.

CLARENCE *(Takes the bottle from her)*: You been drinking this stuff?!!

ALICE: What stuff?

CLARENCE: Are you CRAZY?? Are you NUTS???

ALICE: What are you doing with alcohol, Clarence. You know what it does to me.

CLARENCE: This stuff KILL you!!
You on ANTABUSE!!

ALICE: No.

CLARENCE: YES!! You gonna have convulsions!!!
Why aren't you throwing up?

ALICE: I haven't took my antabuse for days now.

CLARENCE: WHY?? You know what happens. THIS!!!

ALICE: Yeah.

CLARENCE: This is the last, Alice. This is the last time. No more. I take care of you no more. You puke your guts out, Alice. You be puking alone.

ALICE: I'm not gonna puke. I'm fine.

CLARENCE: You're an alcoholic, Alice.

ALICE: So big deal. I'm an alcoholic who's drinking. Big news.

CLARENCE: There's no more booze.

ALICE: There's a bottle of Drambuie!

CLARENCE: Come on and help me.

ALICE: I'm on the *Tonight Show* here. They love me. They love Alice. She's funnier than Joan Rivers.

CLARENCE: I could shoot you dead, I'm so mad at you!!!

ALICE: You stole the car, little brother. You the thief, little bro. Hell, I'm just drunk.

(Clarence exits)

Why couldn't we have just eaten at HoJo's, Clarence? Huh? That's what the damn place is for. I didn't take my antabuse because I felt good. I was high on life and all that crap.

(Clarence reenters carrying some camping equipment, dumps it, exits)

CLARENCE *(Offstage)*: Come on and help me with this stuff.

ALICE: Why we unloading the car? Why don't we just go?

(We hear the sound of pounding on metal)

Clarence! Jesus! What you doing?!

(She exits and reenters carrying a hammer, with Clarence following)

CLARENCE: Alice! Give me the hammer!!

ALICE: Clarence! That station wagon is the first nice car I ever owned!

CLARENCE: Listen. Listen to me, Alice. Okay. You're a Mountie and you see us two Indians drive by in a nice station wagon with no dents: What you think first off?

ALICE: If I was a Mountie? Let me think. I don't know, Clarence—being a Mountie has depressed me so much on account of I'm suddenly so damn stupid but being just smart enough to realize it, that I can't think of nothin'. Besides, there are no Mounties down here—they have regular police.

CLARENCE: Well, I'm sure regular police don't like us any better. And we be in just the same amount of trouble.

ALICE: Clarence, why did you do it??! What are you—some poor white-trash boy? White poor—trash . . .? You got that look in your eye—you forget how to be Indin. You not Indin enough.

CLARENCE: How come you always say that when you don't like what I'm doing. Listen, Alice. Stand still. Now, what chance, Alice, do the two of us—what chance do two Indins with guitars, amps and rhinestone costumes have of getting a ride on the New York Thruway? Huh?

ALICE: We have the truck.

CLARENCE: Truck's no good, Alice.

ALICE: Yeah, well, I hate the fucking truck, too, but it's ours.

CLARENCE: The truck wasn't gonna get us there.

ALICE: Why not?

CLARENCE: Remember that smell around Albany?

ALICE: Yeah.

CLARENCE: Yeah.

ALICE: I thought Albany smelled like that.

CLARENCE: It was the truck.

ALICE: It was the truck?

CLARENCE: It was the fucking truck, Alice.

ALICE: I noticed you got real quiet.

CLARENCE: Now, will you help me? We're gonna make a cache of the camping equipment. I switched the license plates. Come on! *(Exits)*

ALICE: You should've told me, Clarence.

CLARENCE *(Offstage)*: Alice, goddamnit!!! Give me a hand with this, will you?!

(Alice exits. After a beat, Clarence and Alice enter, dragging the canoe)

Boy, this is heavy.
    Just like the white man—improve the canoe—make it weigh a ton.

ALICE: Nice canoe, Clarence.

CLARENCE: I'm going to cache this good, and we can pick it up on our way back from New York City.

ALICE: I still think we should go Nashville. Go for it, man. New York don't like country music. *(Exits)*

CLARENCE: Listen, we're not gonna do nothing until you are sober. Maybe there's some coffee in this stuff.

(Alice reenters with a box and dumps the contents in front of him)

What are you doin', Alice?

ALICE: Where's the Drambuie?

CLARENCE: I threw it away.

ALICE: No!! NO!! You DIDN'T!!

CLARENCE: Yes, I did!! For your own good, Alice!

(Alice goes through the contents of the box, madly—doesn't find the bottle of Drambuie. She stands and looks around hopelessly, then runs to the canoe and rips the cover off. She freezes)

Hey, it's a tent!!!
Or something.

(Clarence opens the blanket covering Father's Body carefully, revealing more of the body. Alice exits. After a beat, we hear her retching offstage)

Whoa.
Alice?

ALICE *(Offstage)*: Clarence?

CLARENCE: Alice?

ALICE *(Offstage)*: Yeah?

CLARENCE: I don't think we should panic.

ALICE *(Offstage)*: Why not?

CLARENCE: I mean—this is, maybe, a good thing here.

ALICE *(Offstage)*: Why—is he asleep?

CLARENCE: No! That would be a BAD thing.

ALICE *(Reenters)*: Oh god oh god oh god, sweet jesus, jesus, jesus.

CLARENCE: Whoever was driving that station wagon was illegal as hell, Alice. They ain't gonna want that car back, ever! It's ours, free and clear!

ALICE: Illegal—what do you mean, Clarence?

CLARENCE: How do you think he got dead?

ALICE: You mean murderers??
Oh god oh god oh god.

CLARENCE: Even murderers have to stop for a cup of coffee. Help me.

ALICE: Help you what?

CLARENCE: Help me dump him.

ALICE: Clarence, I've been thinking, honey. Let's just load our stuff back into our truck, take our chances, and get out of here. Okay? Tuck the old guy in. And clear out. Come on, Little Bro. I got a new harmony on "Islands in the Stream." We can have it down by the time we hit the George Washington Bridge.

CLARENCE: That goes to New Jersey.

ALICE: Whatever. Look, I'm sober. He's dead. We're outta here. Come on.

CLARENCE: I'm not leaving my station wagon!!

ALICE: It's not your station wagon—it's his—or the guys who did him in. I want no part of it.

CLARENCE: We can sleep in the back an' lie down! There's a carpet. You won't have to hold the guitars when we drive. Our costumes won't get wrinkled. The tires will make it to New York and we won't smell like gas. No radiator problems. Smooth ride. It's got a tape deck with Dolby stereo. We can stop at a truck stop—get some new tapes. Suzy Bogguss. Garth Brooks. Wynonna.

ALICE: What the hell. It's no good to him, anyway.

CLARENCE: We'll put him under a tree.

ALICE: Leave him the canoe, Clarence.

CLARENCE: Can he use it?

ALICE: Maybe it's ceremonial.

CLARENCE: White people don't go to that kind of heaven.

(They lift him out, carry him upstage)

ALICE: He won't bend, Clarence.

CLARENCE: Just enough to sort of set him up.

(They place Father's Body behind a tree. Alice tucks the blanket around him)

We'll hide our truck in one spot and the canoe in another, so they can't be connected. The truck's not registered, so we can be thankful of that—for once. *(Finds something in the jacket)* Hey? Here's somebody's checkbook.

ALICE: Don't touch it!

CLARENCE: It was in the thing I'm wearing.

ALICE *(Grabbing the checkbook)*: Give me that.

CLARENCE: Now how is he gonna use it? White guys buying up heaven, too?

ALICE: We done enough. *(Puts the checkbook into a pocket on Father's Body)*

CLARENCE: What is it with you and him?

ALICE: Oh man, the bears'll get him . . . or worse.

CLARENCE: Better to be part of the earth than sealed up forever in some thick metal box. *(This thought gives him the willies)* Ooooooo.

ALICE: Bye, old guy. I wonder who you was.

CLARENCE: Help me with this canoe.

ALICE: Maybe somebody will find him.

CLARENCE: Listen, what white man's gonna ever be this deep in the woods?

(They exit with the canoe. Offstage:)

No problem.

(A couple of beats.
Sound of Scout Leader and Girls singing "White Coral Bells,"
the sound getting closer and closer)

SCOUT LEADER: Alright, campers! Stay in line and watch for low branches!

GIRL SCOUTS:
White coral bells
Upon a slender stalk
Lilies of the valley deck my garden walk.
Oh, don't you wish
That you might hear them ring,
That will happen only when the fairies—

(The song breaks off suddenly. Then the sound of the Girls doing one long scream. When the screaming stops, we hear the phone ring in the Anderson home)

Scene Two

Back at the house. The chairs are still on the lawn. The phone is ringing and Scott picks it up. It's dawn.

SCOTT: Hello?
Yes?
Can't—having trouble hearing you.

(The connection is lost. He hangs up and goes back to the kitchen, where he's been quietly cleaning the broken crockery out of the cupboards. Kim comes downstairs in her nightgown—she sees the chairs out on the lawn)

KIM: Did the phone ring?
SCOTT: Wrong number or something.
KIM: What are you doing?
SCOTT: Couldn't sleep. Cleaning.
KIM: You didn't even try to sleep. You're still dressed. Anything new from George?

(Scott shakes his head "no")

Uncle Cecil? The police? Mr. Besemer?

(Scott shakes his head "no" to each of these. Kim picks up the phone and clicks the hang-up buttons frantically)

SCOTT: Kim, you just heard the phone ring. So it's working.

KIM: Oh. *(Sees the chairs on the lawn)* Left the chairs out.

SCOTT: I'll get them.

KIM: Hope they don't warp in the—ah—whatdoyoucallit.

SCOTT: Dew. I think.

KIM: Whatever it is that warps the wood on lawn chairs.

SCOTT: I'll get them.

(He crosses out to the lawn and gets the chairs—all the time hoping Kim doesn't see the broken crockery)

KIM: You're cleaning the cupboards?

SCOTT: Stay out!! There might be broken glass—

KIM: I've got my slippers on—I haven't fallen apart completely.

SCOTT: No one said you were falling apart! No one said anyone was falling apart! Who's been talking about falling apart, anyway?

KIM: What's in these bags, Scotty?

SCOTT: I'm buying new glasses today.

KIM: So you broke all the old ones??!! *(Looking in the bags)* And the dishes, too??!!! What's wrong with you?? What's wrong with you?? Haven't we got enough to worry about without you going on some cleaning—throwing away— JAG??!!

SCOTT *(About the outburst)*: What are we doing?

KIM: I don't know.

　　I'm sorry.

SCOTT: So am I.

KIM: But this is weird.

SCOTT: I found it that way.

　　In the cupboards.

KIM: Maybe it was an earthquake.

SCOTT: Maybe.

(They finish cleaning up the glass, etc. in silence—Kim holding the door for Scott as he carries the bags of broken stuff into the garage. Pauline comes downstairs during this, goes to the refrigerator and begins to eat a large piece of chocolate cake, holding it in her hand)

PAULINE *(Seeing Kim and Scott looking at her)*: I'm so hungry children.

(Phone rings)

SCOTT and KIM: I'll get it.

(They go for it, but Pauline answers it and waves them away)

PAULINE: Hello?
    Yes.

(Kim approaches the phone. Pauline waves her away)

    Yes.
        Yes.
        Yes. *(Beat)* Yes.
        Yes.
        Yes. *(Beat)* No, thank you. *(Hangs up the phone)*
KIM: Who was it?
PAULINE: I couldn't understand what they wanted.
SCOTT: Who? Who?
PAULINE: Were you expecting a call?
KIM: What was the call about, Mother?
PAULINE: Well, it's rather garbled—
    Oh, I'm sticky.
    Anyway, people just do not speak clearly anymore.
    Look at the time!
    And rude, too. People.
SCOTT: Mother, may I get you a plate?
KIM: What was the call about, Mom?

PAULINE: Girl Scouts. *(Beat)* It's so good to have both of you home, did I say that? All we need is a Christmas tree . . . right over . . . there.

KIM: What was the call about, Mom? Was the call from George?

PAULINE: Why would George be calling at this hour? I told you—the Girl Scouts.

KIM: Girl Scouts?

PAULINE: Something about the Girl Scouts going on a hike.

KIM: Mother, maybe you should go back to bed.

PAULINE: I buy cookies every year. Although they are inedible, I think. I give them to the cleaning woman.

I am sleepy. I can't keep track of things anymore today. *(Exits upstairs)*

SCOTT: Two calls.

KIM: Should we call George?

SCOTT: Again. And at this hour? *(Beat)* Oh god, call.

KIM *(She dials, gets him)*: Hello, George? Sorry. I know it's early. Mother got a strange call.

No, another strange call.

Wasn't you? *(To Scott)* This phone is sticky—can you get me a dishcloth?

(Back to phone, as Scott crosses to the kitchen and returns with dishcloth)

Excuse me— *(Wipes off the phone, then talks to George on the receiver)* No, everything's fine. Just taking care of something—

SCOTT *(Takes the phone from Kim)*: Sorry, George.

Heard anything?

No, I have no idea what you would have heard—it's just—

Yes, well it is . . . confusing.

No, I wouldn't call it that. It's an unusual problem.

No, we're both still fine.

I have no idea—something about Girl Scouts—Mother is so confused. But the phone did ring—we were right here.

So the visitation is at ten a.m.—that's in four hours.

Yes, I know you know that, George.

(Kim is making gestures to Scott)

Kim asked me about the caterer.

What limo company.

But we didn't want—

Of course, it's a nice gesture, but— *(Longer beat)* Well, PARK THEM SOMEWHERE, George!!!

I DON'T KNOW WHERE!!

Sorry. Hold a minute. *(Takes the receiver away from his ear and takes a beat)* George, we appreciate everything you're doing in this somewhat . . . complicated . . . series of . . . events, and we shall all try to—what? *(Listens to George on the phone for a couple of beats)* George, it's important to remember that sometimes you can't get your ducks in a row no matter how hard you try.

Yes, I know he used to say that—I thought it would make you feel better, but I see that—

Bye. *(Hangs up the phone)* George is upset.

(They both cross to the sink and wash their hands. Then Kim comes back and cleans the phone with Windex, etc., as they talk)

It was probably Uncle Cecil on his way.

KIM: The call?

SCOTT: And Mother just didn't understand it.

KIM: Right.

SCOTT: It's six a.m.

KIM: Visitation is scheduled for ten a.m.—four hours from now . . . and then a funeral with lots of people . . .

What if it doesn't . . . I mean, what if, Scotty, let's just say the police don't—I mean, it's rather, as you yourself said, complicated, and our chances of . . .

SCOTT: We'll meet with the funeral director at the earliest. I've got a message on his machine to clear the morning for me.

KIM *(Overlapping the following)*: What are we going to do, Scotty? I don't know.

SCOTT *(Simultaneously with the preceding)*: What are we going to do, Kimmy?
I don't know.

(They sink on the couch and sit catatonic for a long beat. They hear Pauline coming downstairs. They both jump up and straighten the couch)

PAULINE: Why isn't Cecil here yet?

KIM: He's on his way.

PAULINE: I'm worried. No Cecil—it's not right. And I'm sticky.

SCOTT *(Wiping her hands for her with the rag)*: It will be fine, Mother.

PAULINE: What?

SCOTT: Everything will be fine.

(She caresses his cheek)

PAULINE: My boy.

SCOTT: It'll be fine. Really.

PAULINE: Why does that make me so sad?

(Pauline wanders off, Kim follows, helping her upstairs. Scott touches the place on his cheek where she caressed him, and a sudden burst of emotion starts to well up. He wants to sit down, but can't find a place, leans against the wall, then exits to his bedroom)

Scene Three

An older man, wearing bifocals and dressed in hunting clothes is leaning back on the couch, his feet up on the coffee table. This is Cecil. He is snoring loudly. Next to him is George, his pajamas

sticking out under a pair of trousers. George is smoking heavily.
The TV is on—it's dawn. Scott comes jogging in from the back,
does some cooling-down on the lawn, sees George and enters the
living room from the patio.

SCOTT: I didn't see you.

GEORGE: You've been jogging?

At this hour?

With no sleep?!

SCOTT *(Leaning near Cecil to look at him)*: How is he?

CECIL *(Awakens, immediately in gear)*: Sonny!

Great—came in—you were out.

Jogging? Good. Good. *(Pats Scott's chest)* Heart attack.
Listen, been to the goddam funeral home.

That Besemer is a fruit—always has been—always will.
It's in the makeup they use on the damn cadavers—read
about it—does something to the hormones. I'm serious—it
does, it's a fact. Estrogen in the makeup. I read about it.
Anyway, he's being a complete jackass about the whole
thing. Got him to cancel this visitation nonsense—always
thought it was a damn stupid custom, anyway—but that little negotiation cost us an arm and a leg. AND . . . had to pay
him off to shut him up—don't know what we're gonna do.
Well that's a lie. I know what we've got to do—we gotta
have the damn funeral without your dad. It's a damn closed
casket—we'll pay Besemer off some more. I mean, it's not
like, it's not as if there won't be a funeral because there will
be. We'll have two—one without your dad for the company
and friends and relatives and the whole goddam mess. And
another for just us when we find the damn remains. Haven't
told Kim about this yet—George seems to think the women
will hate this idea, but—I've got a call into Besemer right
now. If he won't do it, we'll just go elsewhere—and for the
rest of the funerals for the family, the company—that
includes mine. And we'll badmouth him, too. So he'll lose

his damn shirt if he doesn't comply. And we'll get him a damn medical certificate, too—it's the least that shyster doctor of yours can do for us after letting Andy go on a goddam fishing trip in the GODDAM wilderness with a ticker like that and no nitroglycerin or any goddam thing—out in the middle of nowhere—like THAT— *(Snaps his fingers)* —like THAT— *(Snaps his fingers)* —He's talking to me. He's standing there talking to me and WHAM, he falls. Good-night, Nurse. *(Sits suddenly)* I have to sit down. Give me a minute—

GEORGE *(To Scott)*: He's right—

CECIL: Of course I'm right. I'm just worn out.

GEORGE *(To Scott)*: We do have this problem with Besemer—

CECIL: I have every right to be a little worn out.

GEORGE *(To Scott)*: The Besemer problem—

CECIL: I just need to sit here.

GEORGE: We do have this problem with Besemer. There are some legal problems here—

SCOTT: Legal problems?

GEORGE: Simply put, Besemer's Funeral Home has some real concerns about his . . . ah . . . their, ah . . . I hate to use this word—it's so loaded—but, their complicity.

SCOTT: Complicity, George?

GEORGE: I know, I know—but, fact is, a funeral without the remains is a sort of, well, grey area, legally at least, but Cecil's really—

CECIL: It's a mafia—a mafia of morticians. They're supposed to serve—SERVE—but nobody knows the meaning of the word anymore.

(Kim enters from upstairs and Cecil notices what's on TV)

Look at this!! Look at this!! Look at the crapola on the television! I mean, is this programming for adults? No wonder a man can't get a cup of coffee without his damn car being stolen!!

(Kim crosses to the television and changes the channel, then crosses to the phone and dials from a number in her hand— checks her watch. Her conversation is heard during Cecil's diatribe)

KIM: Pronto. Mario. This—is—Kimberly Anderson—please cancel the food for the Scott Anderson . . . function. Thank you.

SCOTT: George, should she be doing that?

KIM: I'm sorry Scott, but someone has to do something. *(To George)* George, as soon as it's office hours, I'd like some secretary to take over most of this. I'll call close friends to keep them from calling us, but everyone else—

CECIL *(To the TV)*: The news! The news! That'll be fine! That'll be just hunky-dory!

GEORGE: What are we doing, Scott?

CECIL: Rapes, murders, pillaging!! Lies! Criminals running around and no one is doing anything! Look at that! Now what do those earrings she's wearing have to do with the news, the serious news? Central America—who can understand it? It's worse than the Middle East. What do these people want? What do they want? A handout! From us! Why are all the brown people in the world upset and what the HELL are we supposed to—the Japanese—look at them. How can people that small make cars for us—they can't!

KIM: I'm calling people.

CECIL: They can't even begin to—!

SCOTT: George, you're the family lawyer—talk to her.

CECIL: These tiny little cars—well, that one isn't that small—but people are lining up to buy the damn things. And it's all a plot to crunch the American male body into a shape that will destroy his back and, god forbid, if he's in an accident, put the top of his head right through the top of the— Sigourney Weaver—now where did she get a name like that? What happened to the good ol' American names like Clark Gable

and Grable and Garland and Rooney and Gregory Peck—
there is a man. Henry Fonda. Those are men. Men's names.
Names for men. Look at these diapers. Look at these diaper
ads. What happened to washing diapers?

KIM: That's your list. It's all constructed from the address book.
Now these are just your friends—ones that aren't mine, too.
I did it all on the laptop, so there's no duplication.

SCOTT: George, I really think you're the one—

GEORGE: That little Toshiba does all this?

KIM: It's just a variation of the list and merge commands.

CECIL: Where are all these nasty, filled diapers going? They
have to go goddam somewhere. Where's the goddam EPA
on this one, huh? That's fine, ma'am, put the diapers right
into the river—we don't really mind—the stock market is
run by children, that's the damn problem—the floor of the
stock exchange looks like a . . . high school . . . pep rally or
some . . . damn . . . hamburger stand . . . gone . . . crazy—
have to . . . sit.

    Boy. Boy— *(Passes out into a deep sleep, begins snoring again)*

GEORGE: Is this that portable printer?

KIM: Yes, it's nice, isn't it?

SCOTT: George, for crying out loud! Tell her!

GEORGE: Actually, Kimberly, we have a sort of contingency plan
developing here, so this telephoning may not be—Scott?
Perhaps you could explain Cecil's—

SCOTT: Would you like some coffee, George?

GEORGE: Actually, no.

(Cecil snores)

KIM: I hope you understand my request, George. Scott. About
the secretarial help? I need it now—or at least in a couple of
hours.

GEORGE: Scott, we need to proceed in some direction, Scott—

KIM: Alright. Excuse my being so pushy, everyone, but I am a
little concerned about the time. We have seventy-five people

arriving at one place where there's not going to be a function and then proceeding to another place where there's not going to be a function, either.

(Scott opens the cupboard, remembers that all the crockery has been broken)

SCOTT: We don't have any cups, George.

GEORGE: So Scotty, what are we doing here? Is my question.

SCOTT: I've got to take a shower.

GEORGE: Not now.

KIM: How can we have a funeral without—without—you know—Father?
     It's absurd.

SCOTT: I really can't think when I'm physically uncomfortable.

KIM: It's impossible.

SCOTT *(Exiting down the hall)*: I'll be quick.

KIM *(To George)*: Isn't it? *(To exiting Scott)* Scott, you know how task-oriented I am. Now, we have our lists—are we going to call them or not? Or is everyone just going to get into the limos that George didn't cancel and just DRIVE AROUND! Sorry sorry sorry. Sorry.

(Scott has exited to bathroom—sound of shower. Kim to George, by way of an apology)

He's taking a shower.

GEORGE: Kim, I'm in a kind of a spot here. You know? This is not my territory, really.

KIM: A shower will make him feel better.

GEORGE: I mean, please understand, I'm not pulling out or anything of the kind, but I feel a little out of my—a little . . . uncomfortable in this particular—and Cecil is my—well, this whole company is my . . . livelihood, Kim. You know what I mean? So, I want to do—I want us to do what's best here. And soon.

KIM: Well, so do I, George. But what would that be?

GEORGE: Well, it's a—he meant—Cecil, WILL YOU STOP THAT DAMN SNORING??!!! HOW CAN YOU SNORE THAT LOUD AND STILL LIVE?!!!!!

(Cecil snorts himself awake)

CECIL: Are we there yet? Oh.
Oh.
KIM: Would you like to lie down, Uncle Cecil?
CECIL: My glasses are dirty.
GEORGE: Come on, Cecil. *(Helping him up and toward the hall)*
KIM: Yes—put him in Scotty's room.

(George exits down the hall with Cecil)

Take his boots off! Thanks!

*(Kim straightens the couch where Cecil was sitting.
Pauline enters from upstairs. She is dressed in mourning.
She crosses to a chair and sits in it)*

PAULINE: Well, let's get this over with.
KIM: Mother—
PAULINE: I'd like a cup of coffee, please.
I don't know why you did what you did. Having visitation so early, and without the wife, is very, very strange.
Who was there, Kim?
You didn't go dressed like that, did you?
What time is it anyway?
KIM: We seem to be out of cups, Mother.
PAULINE: They're all dirty?
Hasn't anyone done the dishes?! Henriette doesn't come until Monday, you know!
KIM: I'll find something.
PAULINE: This is not a hotel.
KIM: Mother, I was wrong, I'm sure. I meant that Scotty had washed all the cups, and they're wet.

PAULINE: We have a dishwasher. It's more sanitary. Scotty
    knows that. I don't know what he's doing washing cups.
    (Beat) Excuse me, Kimberly. I'm a little tense this morning.
        Sorry.
KIM: Would you like a pill?
PAULINE: A pill? What pill? I don't take pills.
KIM: Dr. Ryan left some . . . pills.
PAULINE: What kind of pills?
KIM: Pills for tenseness.
PAULINE: Tenseness?
KIM: Tense—ness. Is that a word?
PAULINE: I don't think it's a word.
KIM: Well, how do you say that, then?
PAULINE: Say what?
KIM: The state of being tense.
PAULINE *(Suddenly remembering)*: Tension!!
KIM: That's it! Tension!! Tension.
PAULINE: We remembered.
KIM: I don't know why I couldn't remember that word.
PAULINE: You're so good with words, usually. *(Long pause)*
    Use a glass for the coffee, then.
        Like the Greeks.

(George enters from the hallway)

GEORGE: Pauline—you're up!
PAULINE: Sorry about that call last night, George. I hope you
    took my advice and decided to just let the company deal
    with it. Just let the company deal with all of those sorts of
    things.
GEORGE: Cecil arrived, Pauline.
KIM: I had George put him in Scotty's room.
PAULINE: Where will Scotty sleep?
KIM: I meant just for today—he's so tired.
GEORGE: He's resting.
PAULINE: Did he bring a suit?

KIM: A suit? A suit . . .

GEORGE: No, he's just in his fishing clothes.

PAULINE: We have to get him a suit. And shirt and tie. And shoes—no one thinks about the shoes, but shoes, we need them.

KIM: George? George? What are we doing? I mean, my list or Uncle Cecil's suit—do I call people or do I drive to Wilton and pick up clothes? Because, correct me if I'm wrong, George, but today might not be the day.

PAULINE: We have to get Cecil ready. Cecil must be ready.

(Scott enters, clean and dressed)

SCOTT: I feel better now.

KIM: I knew you would. I told George you would.

PAULINE: Today might not be what day?

(Beat)

KIM: What day? No day.

PAULINE: Someone said today might not be the day. What does that mean "today might not be the day"? What day? Today? This day might not be the day? How can it not be the day? Today is the day. What does it mean "today might not be the day"? *(Long beat)* Yes?

GEORGE: Scott?

KIM: George?

SCOTT: Kim?

PAULINE: Kim, it was you. You said "today might not be the day." What did that mean?

KIM: Scott?

(Cecil enters from the hallway)

CECIL *(To Pauline)*: Polly.
    I was telling the kids here.
    It was like that— *(Snaps his fingers)*

PAULINE: What about your suit, Cecil?

CECIL: Oh Jeez, I forgot!

Scott, can you drive me? No, you'd better stay and
arrange . . . things—more things to arrange, you know, son?
George will drive me—no, George, you'd better stay and see
what you can do with Besemer. Kim—

KIM: What?

CECIL *(On his way to the garage)*: Come on.

KIM *(To Scott and George)*: What's happening?

SCOTT: The funeral is at four.

KIM: But—

SCOTT: The casket will be closed.

GEORGE: Yes, the casket will be closed, Kim.

KIM: The casket will be closed?

PAULINE: OF COURSE IT WILL! WE'RE NOT
BARBARIANS!!

KIM *(Understands the plan)*: Right.
Call Mario. Reschedule the food.

CECIL: Come on, honey, we gotta hit the road here! *(Stops in
front of Pauline)* It wasn't the money, Pauline. I want you to
know that. One thousand dollars for a container with stiff
sides, he said—this Mountie I talked to.

GEORGE: Cecil!

CECIL: Shush! And then I can't transport it—no, no, no—no,
I have to hire someone to transport it in a licensed hearse or
an airplane.

SCOTT: Cecil!

CECIL: We're up to fifteen hundred—two thousand dollars
already! You see? You see? They think that because you're
heartbroken, you won't add the figures up. Grief is no reason
to let yourself be taken!

GEORGE: Cecil—

CECIL: I'm hurrying for Chrissake!

(Cecil exits with Kim)

PAULINE: What in the world was Cecil talking about, George?

GEORGE: Nothing, Pauline—he's distraught.

PAULINE: Distraught? He didn't look distraught. And what is "distraught," anyway? For heaven's sake, we're not one of those families on the news where the furnace has blown up and everyone's dead! I'm sure he's tired and upset and—

SCOTT: Heartbroken? He said "heartbroken," Mother.

PAULINE: Oh, that.
    The heart's a muscle, dear.

GEORGE: Scott—we have to get going. We have a lot to arrange.

SCOTT: Oh. Oh, right. *(Everything hits him for a moment)*
    Ohmygod.

GEORGE: What?

PAULINE: Don't worry about me. I still have my hair to do.

(Scott looks from George to his mother)

GEORGE: Don't forget your checkbook.

*(Scott and George exit.
    Pauline takes off her wig and speaks to it)*

PAULINE: We never got our coffee, did we? *(Fluffs wig and puts it back on. Waits. After a beat, the phone rings and she answers it)* Hello.
    Yes, it is.
    Mrs. Anderson. *(Long beat as she listens)* Now really, aren't you a little old to be in the Girl Scouts? And why do you keep bothering me? And what you say is ridiculous—my husband has never been "lost." My husband is dead!
    (Slams down the phone) Some people are heartless.

Scene Four

Clarence and Alice are in the station wagon—Clarence is driving—and they're listening to the Judds do "Working in a Coal Mine" on the cassette player. Clarence is singing along. Alice is wearing the jacket Clarence took from the camping stuff.

ALICE: It's not right, Clarence.

CLARENCE: It's just a little high, Alice. I can pitch it down.

ALICE: That's not what I mean. *(Turns the cassette off)* It's not right.

CLARENCE: What's not right.

ALICE: You know what I'm talking about.

CLARENCE: I love this car, Alice.

ALICE: Keep the car. I'm talking about him.

(Clarence sighs)

Don't pretend. You know it's not right what we did back there.

CLARENCE: We didn't kill him!

ALICE: You took his jacket! We left him all alone!

CLARENCE: You're maudlin drunk now.

ALICE: He belonged to someone, Clarence. He wasn't no gangster.

CLARENCE: Maybe he was a spy. A spy that got assassinated.

ALICE: There are no spies anymore. Soviet Union's gone. You never watch the news.

CLARENCE: You never watch the news, Alice. They found a spy last week. And Johnny Carson's gone. In case you didn't know, Alice.

ALICE: I'm feeling kind of cold and everything.

CLARENCE: We'll stop and get you a cup of coffee.

ALICE: Oh man, look at this. Look. It's his fucking billfold in this jacket.

CLARENCE: Any money?

ALICE: No. *(Finds stuff in billfold)* No pictures—just credit cards. Wow. Gold cards, every one.
Look at this one here—the eagle flies.

CLARENCE: That's a hologram. *(Reads name on card)* Scott A. Anderson.

ALICE: That's no gangster, man.

CLARENCE: We could use these and buy all sorts of stuff.

ALICE: Clarence—

CLARENCE: I just had to say it.

ALICE: We got to do the right thing, Clarence.

CLARENCE: We'll send his billfold back to his family—whatever. We'll send it back, anonymously.

ALICE: Fuck the billfold. We have to—

CLARENCE: Noooo.

ALICE: We have to—

CLARENCE: No way, Alice—

ALICE: We have to, Clarence.

CLARENCE: No WAY am I doing that!!
I mean NO WAY!!! ForGET IT!!!
Forget it!!!

(They look at each other)

Scene Five

An hour later. Pauline is polishing the sliding glass doors with Windex. She is still dressed in mourning. Dorothea enters from the backyard.

DOROTHEA *(Approaching)*: Pauline?
Pauline?
Pauline, what are you doing?

PAULINE: This door was all smeary. *(Looking through the glass)* That lawn needs mowing.

DOROTHEA: Honey, shouldn't you be at the funeral home?

PAULINE: Today's not the day.

DOROTHEA: Yes, it is.

PAULINE: No, it's not.
Mr. Besemer won't let it be the day.

DOROTHEA: Honey—

(Scott and George enter carrying huge sprays of flowers)

GEORGE: There's no more room in the garage, Pauline.

(Pauline can't decide)

PAULINE: Uh—
    Uh—
    Uh—

SCOTT: George—come on. We'll put them in the backyard.

(They cross through the doors and put the flowers in the yard)

PAULINE: And I wondered how this door got so smeary.

DOROTHEA: Pauline, honey, what's going on?

PAULINE: Today's not the day.

DOROTHEA: But why, Pauline?

PAULINE: Can we sit down?

DOROTHEA: This is your house.

PAULINE: I don't know. I just got this couch straightened.

GEORGE *(Seeing her confusion on one of his trips with the funeral flowers)*: Everything's gonna be just fine, Pauline.

PAULINE *(To Dorothea)*: You know, everyone keeps saying that. Isn't that funny?

DOROTHEA: Where's the Scotch? Never mind. Why pretend?
(Goes to the cupboard, gets the bottle, opens another cupboard to look for a glass)

PAULINE: I broke all the glasses.

DOROTHEA: Fine. *(Takes a swig from the bottle)* Now, just tell me.

PAULINE: The—ah—
    The—ah—
    The—

DOROTHEA: Funeral.

PAULINE: Yes. It's been changed.

DOROTHEA: To what? A lawn party??! *(To George)* What's going on?

(Scott and George see possible trouble)

GEORGE: Hello. I'm George Boyle. I've been the Anderson family's lawyer for—I don't know how long. How long has it been, Pauline?

PAULINE: I don't—

GEORGE: Scott, how long have I been your family's lawyer?

SCOTT: Gosh, I don't know, George. At least fifteen years— maybe longer. Mother, how old was I when George came on board?

PAULINE (*It takes her back, quite literally, to his childhood—a memory coming into focus*): You were twelve. Your daddy loved you so much. You were twelve. You were twelve years old and you said to me, "When is Dad"—you called him "Dad" then—you had made yourself stop calling him "Daddy." "Dad." "When is Dad coming home?" And I said, "Soon." I said, "Soon." "Soon." (*Long beat. She tunes in to the present*) Is that what you wanted to know?

SCOTT: Yes.

Thank you, Mother.

GEORGE: Pauline, you look a little tired. (*To Dorothea*) But it's been very nice meeting you.

DOROTHEA (*To Pauline*): Pauline, you call me. You call me if you need anything. (*Hands George the Scotch and calls as she exits*) Call me!

PAULINE: Yes, dear! (*To George*) She's a dear old soul. But that circular driveway is god-ugly.

(*Cecil enters in a suit*)

CECIL: What's the goddam casket doing in the garage??!!! (*About the flowers*) AND WHAT THE HELL IS THIS?!!!! LOOK AT THIS SHIT!!! Besemer has CAN-CELLED us! That scared little twit—I'm gonna sue his tight little ass. He'll be crapping out his ears by the time—

SCOTT: Uncle Cecil—

PAULINE: Why is a casket in the garage?

SCOTT: Mother—

PAULINE: Why is a casket in the garage?
　　　　The garage is for automobiles and lawn furniture.
　　　　I WILL NOT have a CASKET in the garage!
GEORGE: Pauline—
PAULINE: Cecil!! BRING THAT CASKET INTO THE
　　　　HOUSE RIGHT NOW!! DO YOU HEAR ME?!!
SCOTT: Are you sure, Mother?
PAULINE: Cecil!!
CECIL: Yes, ma'am. *(To Scott and George)* Boys—

(They exit into the garage as Kim enters from there)

KIM: Mother, what—
PAULINE: Get the coffee table, Kim!!

*(Kim gets the other end of the coffee table and they move it
behind the sofa)*

KIM: What are we doing, Mom? *(Sees the men entering with the
casket)* Oh, jeez.

(Pauline watches silently as they put the casket in front of the sofa)

PAULINE: Oh my god, children.
CECIL *(Under his breath)*: ... kill that little fruit, I'm telling you.

(Pauline crosses slowly to the casket and then strokes it)

PAULINE: Andy... *(A beat and then Pauline opens the casket and
looks. Long pause)* Cecil?
CECIL: Yes, Pauline?
PAULINE: Get the children out of here.
SCOTT: Mother, we know.
PAULINE *(Trying to protect them by shutting the casket)*: Know what?
KIM: We know the casket's empty, Mother.
PAULINE: I don't understand. George, do something. Can't you
　　　　do something? You're a lawyer. Fix it!!
GEORGE: Pauline, believe me, I would if—

PAULINE: Where's Andy? Cecil? George?

    Kids? Where's your father?

CECIL *(Overlapping the following)*: We don't know.

KIM and SCOTT *(Overlapping the following)*: We don't know, Mother.

GEORGE *(Simultaneously with the preceding)*: We have no idea.

PAULINE: Oh. *(Sits. Stands up)* Oh. *(Sits)* Oh.

SCOTT: Can I get you something, Mother?

(Long pause as Pauline looks at Scott)

PAULINE: Y-yes.

    I would like your father's body returned, please.

SCOTT: Isn't there something else you'd like?

PAULINE: This-is-why today is not the day. It couldn't be the day. I see that now.

CECIL: Well, it was gonna be the goddam day except we couldn't get any cooperation from a certain Tweety-Bird gravedigger I'll never—

KIM: UNCLE Cecil, PLEASE!!!

GEORGE: Pauline, you see, Cecil decided to drive Andy— Mr. Anderson Senior, back—

CECIL: Hell, Pauline, it was just through New York State, and those small planes are pieces of shit, and—

PAULINE: New York State?

    Wait, I—

    I know something about New York State.

    The Girl Scouts were there.

KIM: Oh, Scotty—

(They flank their mother, sure she's lost her mind)

PAULINE *(To her suddenly affectionate children)*: Yes, you remember my phone call . . .

    Actually there were two—or three—

    There have been so many phone calls here lately. That

phone has been ringing and ringing—they really are intrusive, you know—

Wait a minute. *(Concentrates)* Oh, that Dr. Ryan and his pills—I could just kick him in the behind.

CECIL: New York State, Pauline?

PAULINE: The Girl Scouts were on a hike. And they found—*(Stops. It hits her)* Daddy's in Katonah, kids!

(She starts to cry and pats her children for comfort. Kim and Scott cling to her)

He's in Katonah.

(Kim and Scott cry with their mother)

CECIL: Well, we've got some dinky rental that Scott is driving and a Seville full of egg-salad sandwiches, and your—what the hell is that piece of Japanese tin you're driving?

GEORGE: A Mazda Miata.

CECIL: Well, I'm not spending another cent on transportation. Give me the keys, George. And you call the police and tell them I'm coming up there. And a funeral home—I bet some hick will be glad for our business.

GEORGE: No, Cecil.

CECIL: What?

GEORGE: Listen, you can torture me with no sleep for days, make my wife mad at me and make my life a LIVING HELL with all your indecision and inefficiency and your goddam cheapness— *(To all the Andersons)* —and the laptop and the lists and TAKING SHOWERS when EVERYTHING IS FALLING APART, but you CAN'T have MY MIATA!

CECIL: Well, hell, George.

GEORGE: I may be a lawyer—I ADMIT IT—but I have STANDARDS!!! *(Opens the front door to leave, speaks to someone outside)* If you ever want to go to sleep again, don't go in there! *(Exits out the front door)*

SCOTT: We've worn George out.

CECIL: Who the hell was he talking to out there?

(Doorbell rings. They are all frozen)

PAULINE: This is a bad time for company.

(Kim answers the door. A female chauffeur, Felicia, enters)

FELICIA: Hello. Limo service. I'm here to pick up the Anderson family for— *(Sees casket)* Wait—now this is a mistake. I only do the bereaved. I don't do— *(About the casket)* —those.

SCOTT: Have you ever been to Katonah— *(Reads her name tag)* — Felicia?

FELICIA: If you would just let me use the phone—

SCOTT *(To Felicia)*: Would you like to earn— *(Scott empties his billfold)* A hundred and forty-two dollars?

CECIL: Scotty! Good god!

SCOTT: Shut up, Cecil!

FELICIA: I just need the phone . . .

(Pauline goes to the kitchen and begins rummaging in the utensil drawers)

CECIL: Boy, this family has sure turned on me.

KIM: Do you take credit cards? Name your price.

CECIL: Kim!!!

(Pauline has found what she's been looking for and crosses into the living room)

FELICIA: Will someone listen to me? I'm a limo, not a hearse! I need the phone! Give me the phone! Give me the phone!

(Pauline raises meat cleaver—everyone screams. She chops the phone cord with it)

PAULINE: NO MORE CALLS! That phone has been the source of too much pain and confusion. Pain and confusion for days and days or however long it's been. *(To Felicia)* Young woman, we need your limousine.

(Felicia hands Pauline the limo keys)

Thank you.

FELICIA: It's an automatic.

(Felicia exits quickly. Pauline hands keys to Scott)

PAULINE: Cecil, put the casket in the limousine.

CECIL: It won't fit, Pauline.

(She gives him a look)

I'll figure something out. *(To Scott)* Get that cleaver away from your mother.

KIM *(Looking at the damage)*: Mother, the counter!

PAULINE *(Looking at the damage, too)*: This cleaver did that?

SCOTT *(Looking at the damage)*: Good lord! *(Puts the cleaver down with care)*

CECIL *(About the casket)*: I can't carry this by myself!

(Scott helps with the casket)

We'll strap it to the top of the limo.

(They exit out the front door with the casket. Kim and Pauline watch as the guys get it on top of the limo)

KIM: Oh, Mother. We look like the Joad family!

PAULINE: Well, I don't know who they are. But I have a lot of sympathy for them.

(Pauline and Kim exit out the front door)

Scene Six

That night, back in the woods in New York State. Two flashlights are seen—they are held by Clarence and Alice. They are looking for Father's Body.

ALICE: Fuck.

Fuck.

CLARENCE: Alice? This is nuts.

ALICE: Where is he?

(At that moment, police lights come from all over)

POLICEMAN'S VOICE: DROP YOUR WEAPONS!!! PUT YOUR HANDS IN THE AIR!!! YOU ARE UNDER ARREST!!!

(Clarence and Alice drop their flashlights)

CLARENCE: FUCK YOU, Alice!! FUCK YOU FUCK YOU FUCK YOU!! FUCK YOU AND YOUR WHOLE FUCKING FAMILY!!!

ALICE: You're my brother, Clarence.

CLARENCE: Fuck. I know.

Fuck.

POLICEMAN'S VOICE: Just proceed toward the light, keeping your hands above your heads!!!

ALICE: Tell me, do you guys write everything down before you say it?

CLARENCE: Don't make it worse.

ALICE: I heard if you're funny sometimes they go easy on you.

Hey, I got a great joke. . . . How many fat—

CLARENCE: We surrender!

Scene Seven

In the blackout, we hear the sound of the limo on a highway and Kim, Pauline and Scott singing.

KIM, PAULINE and SCOTT:

Seventy-three bottles of beer on the wall,

Seventy-three bottles of beer,

Take one down and pass it around,
Seventy-two bottles of beer on the wall.
Seventy-two bottles of beer on the wall,
Seventy-two bottles of beer. . .

KIM and PAULINE *(Singing, overlapping the following)*:
Take one down and pass it around— *(Etc.)*

SCOTT *(Simultaneously with the preceding)*: Cecil, isn't this the
turnoff?

CECIL: Who can drive with that goddam singing?

SCOTT: Watch this curve coming up!

CECIL: I was driving before you were born!!!

Scene Eight

*Lights up on Pauline and Alice, sitting on a log in the woods in
New York State. Alice is wearing Father's jacket. Pauline is still
in her funeral clothes. They are both relaxed. Long beat.*

PAULINE: It's so quiet here. After all that yelling at the police
station, it's nice.

ALICE: There was a lot of yelling.

PAULINE: I don't know why the police were so upset. It's none of
their business, anyway. I'd think they would have thanked us
for taking everything off their hands. *(Beat)* It's so beautiful
and secluded here. I'm surprised your brother could find it.

ALICE: Well, we have kinda been here before.

PAULINE: Oh, this is where you were looking for Andy.

ALICE: Yeah.

PAULINE: I just have one question.

ALICE: Yeah?

PAULINE: Are the police always that rude?

ALICE: We have Mounties.
   This is our first time with police. I think they're nice in
   Nashville.

What is that "Jaws of Life" thing everyone kept talking about?

PAULINE: As I understand, it breaks through metal so that people can escape when there's been a train wreck or some other . . . disaster.

ALICE: That would be a good thing.

To have.

PAULINE: Well, it's what the Katonah Police Department most wanted, so Cecil wrote them a check.

(Cecil enters and lies down on the ground)

Are you feeling better, Cecil?

(Cecil just lies there. Pauline talks to Alice, trying to explain Cecil's mood)

The casket marked up the top of the limousine and then it got sort of completely destroyed, the casket, when it fell off on the Parkway—you know that bad curve at— *(To Cecil)* What's the name of that place, starts with an "A"? *(To Alice)* He's really very tired.

ALICE *(Crossing to Cecil, says loudly)*: We're really sorry, sir! About everything!

CECIL *(Not moving)*: Shuddup.

PAULINE *(Shocked at his rudeness)*: Cecil! *(Nicer)* Did you throw up? I threw up yesterday and it really helped.

(Clarence enters, dragging some old camping equipment)

CLARENCE: This is the last of everything. There's no more.

CECIL *(Sitting up slightly to look at it, lying back down)*: Great. That'll save the store.

CLARENCE *(Looking down at Cecil)*: I just want to say, sir. We're real sorry, Alice and me. And we must have been nuts or something. We never done anything like this before.

CECIL *(Sitting up)*: You mean you never stole anyone's brother's body before? Well, I'm AMAZED! I am GODDAM— *(It*

hits him—Andy's dead) Andy. Shit. *(Starts to cry and reaches
for Pauline)* Polly—Andy's gone. He's really gone!

(Pauline goes to him and comforts him)

CLARENCE *(Really remorseful)*: Oh man.
ALICE: Clarence. See what you did?
PAULINE *(About blaming Clarence)*: What do you mean? Andy
    died of a heart attack. We lost him. You found him. No-
    body's to blame, and that's what I told that very rude police
    officer, and that's what Cecil explained to them when I was
    out of the room. Although I still don't understand why
    Andy wasn't brought back on the plane the way—
CECIL: Well, it's all over now. And—
PAULINE *(To Clarence and Alice)*: I don't care what the police say
    they think happened. All I know is that you were looking
    for him in those woods because you were worried about him.
    And you being total strangers.
       Thank you.
CLARENCE: She's thanking us again, Alice.
ALICE: I know.

*(Scott and Kim enter, covered with soot. They are holding large
pine bows)*

SCOTT *(To Clarence)*: Are these the right size?
KIM: Mine is too thin, I think.
CLARENCE: Size don't matter.
KIM: Oh. Oh. Of course! *(To Scott)* It's the—ah—the—
SCOTT: Spirit.
CLARENCE: Okay.
SCOTT: Thank you.
KIM: Thank you.

(Clarence is really uncomfortable with being thanked again)

PAULINE: It makes such a pretty light from here.
ALICE: It's reflecting off the lake.

PAULINE: Your brother is very smart. It's a good idea.

ALICE: It's a tradition.

CLARENCE: Especially in emergencies.

SCOTT *(Giving pine bows around)*: We brought some for you, too.
Mother.

KIM *(Giving Cecil a pine bow)*: Uncle Cecil.
It's about ready to sink.

SCOTT: Hurry! It's gotten hot enough to burn through the canoe.

PAULINE: Give me a hand up. Let's hurry!

CECIL: Wait for an old man! *(To Clarence, about the pine bow)*
What do I do with this?

CLARENCE: Just hold onto it. You can wave it if you want.

CECIL: Hold the fort, son. We'll be back.
And thanks for that ceremony earlier, and, well—

(Cecil shakes Clarence's hand and joins Kim, Scott and Pauline, who are watching the canoe)

CLARENCE: Did he say hold the fort?

ALICE: Uh-huh. Old guy's part of the lake now. Nice ceremony
Clarence. Where did you get it?

CLARENCE: Viking movie.
They couldn't tell I made it up.

ALICE: No. They're at peace now.

(Cecil, Pauline, Kim and Scott stare at the burning canoe. In the flickering light, we see their faces, tear-streaked and happy. Clarence and Alice watch them)

CLARENCE: Alice?

ALICE: Uh-huh?

CLARENCE: White people are strange.

ALICE: Heap strange, Dude.